# Marianne Moore
## The Art of a Modernist

# Marianne Moore
## The Art of a Modernist

Edited by
Joseph Parisi

With a Foreword by
Maxine Kumin

 Research
Press

Ann Arbor / London

Publication of this volume is made possible by a grant from the National Endowment for the Humanities

Produced and distributed by
UMI Research Press
an imprint of
University Microfilms Inc.
Ann Arbor, Michigan 48106


Library of Congress Cataloging in Publication Data

Marianne Moore : the art of a modernist / edited by Joseph Parisi.
    p. cm.—(Studies in modern literature ; no. 109)
    Includes bibliographical references and index.
    ISBN 0-8357-2031-4 (alk. paper)
    1. Moore, Marianne, 1887-1972—Criticism and interpretation.
    2. Modernism (Literature)—United States. I. Parisi, Joseph, 1944-
II. Series.
PS3525.05616Z6937    1990
811'.52—dc20                                                        89-20476
                                                                          CIP

British Library CIP data is available.


The paper used in this publication meets the minimum requirements of
American National Standard for Information Sciences—Permanence of Paper for Printed
Library Materials, ANSI Z39.48-1984. ⊗ ™

# Contents

# Foreword

"Miss Moore's work is frankly puzzling," wrote Louis Untermeyer in the 1942 edition of *Modern American Poetry/Modern British Poetry*, the bible of my undergraduate days at Radcliffe. Puzzling "not only to the disinterested reader [who may that be?] but to the student of modern poetry." His ambivalence about anthologizing her was palpable: "It has been asserted, and the editor shares this opinion, that Miss Moore's highly intellectualized dissertations are actually part of the domain of criticism rather than of poetry." She was then accorded a scant three and one-third pages as compared with thirteen allotted Elinor Wylie and eighteen to Conrad Aiken, both born in the same decade as she.

It is sometimes bracing and always instructive to see what the passage of fifty years does to a literary reputation. Certainly the publication of these essays as a final harvest of the Moore centenary attests to the distance traversed.

Marianne Moore's entry into the canon did not take place hastily. She is absent from Sanders and Nelson's *Chief Modern Poets of England and America* (Third Edition, Macmillan, 1943), which contains a solid batch of Millay, Wylie, Aiken, and Ransom, to cite a few of her contemporaries. This text was the cornerstone of the Survey of Modern Poetry course at Harvard in the forties, then Robert Hillyer's domain. The year I was in attendance I believe we began with Bridges and Hopkins and ended on Kenneth Fearing. Moore would have made a handsome addition to that syllabus.

Half a century ago the quirky appearance of her poems on the page, interlarded with quotation marks, presented more difficulty to the reader than we can now almost imagine—we whom the Beat poets have accustomed to lines that may run beyond the right-hand margin, our eye further trained by the Black Mountain school to accept highly individualized spacings and indentations.

Moore's fame was hardly posthumous, however. She was vividly lionized in the late fifties and captured virtually all of the top awards, to say nothing of the attention paid to her by *Life* and *The New Yorker* magazines, and by her beloved baseball team, the Brooklyn Dodgers. And when, in 1953, Robert Lowell praised her as "the best woman poet in English," Langston Hughes was quick to offer his rejoinder: "I consider her the most famous Negro woman poet in America."

Still, it must be confessed that she was little read—lamentably, all of her books went out of print during her lifetime. The renascence of interest in her work and in defining her stance as the eccentric, profoundly innocent and learned spinster in tricorne and cape has occurred quite recently. It seems that with the flowering of feminist literary history the figure of Marianne Moore has garnered new respect and attention. The picture that is now emerging is one of a rather more complicated woman, no less authentic than the proper Victorian but far more explicitly armored against the world than had been suspected. As Alicia Ostriker puts it, "Everyone is so fond of the Marianne Moore who is a sort of household pet that it is somehow criminal to point out that she bites."

But for a long time no one, it seemed, dared to examine the teeth of the poet. The same small poems turned up again and again in the teaching anthologies and elicited the same responses about precision, encyclopedic detail, and syllabic count. We encounter "No Swan So Fine," "To a Snail," and "Silence" over and over. Nowhere in these texts (which date from my hard days as a part-time English instructor at Tufts University in the late fifties) do I find, for example, "Marriage," which holds a patriarchal society up to the light and coolly disprizes the institution that underpins it. Instead, we are counseled to study Moore's method of syllabic patterning, which, says R. P. Blackmur, "Like a strange code of manners, you have to get used to . . . before you can understand it or feel it at work." Of "England," Hugh Kenner in his eminently useful *The Art of Poetry* (Rinehart, 1959) remarks, "We are kept on the move; each phrase disrupts an illusion of knowing all we need to, which is apt to be fostered by the neatness of the previous phrase." Although this statement has a dauntless ring to it, it did not in any way assist me in addressing for students the discursive and enigmatic path the poem takes, nor did it shed any light upon the intended relation between the title and body of the poem.

Looking back, then, I am flummoxed. How little we understood! How unwilling we were to tote up the contradictions: to find a suffragette inside the self-effacing maiden, an assaulter of militarism and male authority lurking behind the ladylike, shy public face; to reconcile an innovator in prosody and themes with an original who denied her role, claiming she had been lumped with the poets merely because there was no other place to put her.

What nourishes public interest in her work is at least in part admiration for the figure Marianne Moore cut. She cultivated this mystique as studiously as Frost strove to foster his identity as homespun New England rustic or Georgia O'Keeffe, hers as a desert primitive. Such half-truths in no way detract from their stature.

I had the good fortune to hear Marianne Moore once, at Wellesley College, where if memory serves me Anne Sexton and I sat in the balcony and could barely see the delicate face of the poet, so modestly did she incline her head over the page. Even amplified she was extremely hard to hear. We sat on the edge of our academic seats and strained for every word, following along in her books wherever we could do so. Afterward, we were too shy to join the group clustered around her. It was enough to know we had been in the presence of a poetic genius, even—or especially?—one who read badly.

Georgia O'Keeffe was born in the same year as Moore. Their lives ran on very different rails but a wonderful similarity exists in the totally unromantic way they viewed their chosen professions. This statement by O'Keeffe might have been made (elliptically, oxymoronically, but made nonetheless) by Moore: "One works I suppose because it is the most interesting thing one knows to do. . . . I have no theories to offer. The painting [the poetry] is like a thread that runs through all the reasons for all the other things that make one's life."

MAXINE KUMIN

# Preface

Among the many strong individualists who have been grouped for convenience as Modernists, Marianne Moore continues to stand out as an independent artist. Despite the major achievements in her innovative poetry and her extensive contributions as a prose stylist, she also retains curious and unhappy distinction as the most undervalued writer of that distinguished company. Compared with the industrial-sized scholarship that Eliot, Pound, Stevens, Williams, and others among her contemporaries have been accorded, including most recently her friend H. D., Moore has suffered relative neglect. She still awaits a full-scale critical biography. In the Rosenbach Museum and Library, her voluminous correspondence rests unedited and unpublished, as do her extensive reading, conversation, and poetry notebooks. Her edition of the *Complete Poems* (1967) is anything but complete, and the poems she did choose to include are often greatly revised (perhaps one should say, gravely resectioned), as was her wont. Responding to the severe amputations Moore performed on "our" favorite poems, Randall Jarrell long ago remarked that "we can protest just as we could if Donatello cut off David's left leg"—and we feel, if not a variorum edition, at least a reprinting of the original volumes is scandalously overdue. Like the famous latter-day image of the becaped eccentric which has helped obscure Moore's more fundamental originality, it is yet another unfortunate irony that such a fastidious poet devoted to accuracy of vision should be represented by the distorted versions of the Incomplete Poems. It is perhaps not surprising, however, that, compared with her peers, Marianne Moore has been misperceived and poorly attended.

Commenting on the *Collected Poems* of 1951 in *Poetry and the Age*, Jarrell noted it was "a neat little book," so small at 138 pages "a reader could, with a reference to size, rather easily put her into her minor place, and say—as I heard a good or even great critic say—that it is easy to see the difference between a poet like this and a major poet. It is; is so easy that Miss Moore's real readers, who share with her some of her 'love of doing hard things,' won't want to do it—not for a century or two, at least, and then only with an indifferent, 'I suppose so.'" (And I suppose Moore's real readers will recall her statement concerning another slender volume: "The book is small in the sense that Napoleon was a little corporal.") But its relatively diminutive quantity aside, the reason Moore's poetry has provoked less critical attention than that of the Big Four Modernists may be, as Jarrell suggested, this "love of doing hard things"; though it is not obvious that her male colleagues present fewer "difficulties." Still, Moore does have her rigors (to use a term she favored), and these account for her differences. "Miss Moore's prose-seeming, matter-of-factly rhythmed syllabic verse," Jarrell summarized, "the odd look most of her poems have on the page (their unusual stanzaic patterns, their words divided at the ends of lines, give many of them a consciously, sometimes misleadingly experimental or modernist look), their almost ostentatious lack of transitions and explanations, the absence of romance and rhetoric, of acceptedly Poetic airs and properties, did most to keep conservative readers of our age from liking her poetry."

From the start, Moore presented challenges to conventional thinking, and liking, and so it was perhaps to be expected that she should be rejected at first, like the other rule-breaking Modernists, or under-appreciated in the long run. One of the major motifs of her work is courage, a quality she not only professed but exemplified, along with hope, "hope, which in being frustrated becomes fortitude." A student of paradox, Moore proved, in her life and her art, that restrictions or limitations could—indeed, did—become ways to self-fulfillment. In the early teens, while still a young industrial-school teacher in Carlisle, Pennsylvania, she independently discovered and ingeniously applied the principles of what would be called the New Poetry. As Pound said of Eliot—and more remarkably, considering her relative isolation—Moore "modernized" herself on her own. Rejected by the major magazines of the time, she persisted, and her unusual poetry submissions were finally accepted for publication by the *Egoist* in London and *Poetry* in Chicago. Only after these first appearances in print, in 1915, did she encounter another writer in person. Through Alfred Stieglitz and Alfred Kreymborg, she was introduced to the New York avant-garde, particularly the authors and artists who gathered about Kreymborg and his *Others* circle. Meanwhile, through the pages of such little magazines, she was "discovered" by her other peers, notably Pound, who immediately hailed Moore for her extraordinary talent. In what precisely that talent consisted proved harder to pronounce.

As poet and essayist, Moore has continued to be difficult to define. Moore's first critics, those conservatives who were unreceptive to the New Poetry in general, took exception to Moore's variety in particular, many going so far as to assert it was not poetry at all. Moore herself did not completely deny the charge; she told Donald Hall in 1961, "What I write, as I have said before, could only be called poetry because there is no other category in which to put it." Her work still resists placement into a neat literary pigeonhole; early or late, most of her poems have to be considered as special cases, so various and unexpected are her strategies. While she exhibits the hallmarks of Modernism—precise imagistic detail, concision, fragmentation and ellipsis—it is hard to mistake Moore for any of her contemporaries. Reviewers of her early work noted its idiosyncrasies, principally the stylistic devices Jarrell lists, and especially the poetry's prose qualities. Moore's unprecedented degree of quotation, and that primarily from nonliterary sources, everything from newspapers and government pamphlets to "business documents and // school-books," and her apparently arbitrary arrangements of such materials, led even presumably enlightened readers, including editors of literary journals, to wonder about her procedures. In 1918 Margaret Anderson of the *Little Review* found Moore's experimental forms "intellectual," and thus not properly poetry. Though she gave Moore her first professional publication in America, Harriet Monroe then had second thoughts, and expressed doubts particularly about her stanzaic patterns after the unauthorized *Poems* appeared in 1921. Friends like William Carlos Williams, H. D., Kreymborg, and Eliot were steadfast in their admiration and published praise. Pound actively promoted her, as well, but also warned in 1919 that, since her poems demanded "mental attention," they would not sell.

In 1924, Moore presented her own first collection, *Observations*, and received the Dial Award for "distinguished service to American letters." The following year she was appointed Editor of the *Dial*. During her tenure, until the magazine's demise in July 1929, and for two-and-a-half years thereafter, she published no poetry. At Eliot's urging, she allowed her *Selected Poems* to be printed in 1935. In his foreword, Eliot declared, "she is one of the few who have done the language some service in my lifetime." Despite the praise and though the volume included "The Steeple-Jack," "The Jerboa," "No Swan So Fine," "The Fish," "Marriage," and several other masterful poems, the work sold poorly, as Pound had predicted, and was remaindered. But the lack of popular acclaim was counterbalanced by increasing critical recognition, as the accolades of her poet friends were augmented by serious appraisals, particularly through scrutiny of her technique, by such eminences as R. P. Blackmur, John Crowe Ransom, and Moore's erstwhile colleague at the *Dial*, Kenneth Burke. In 1941 *What Are Years* appeared, followed in 1944 by *Nevertheless*. As she had accorded them important notice early in their careers, Williams, Wallace Stevens, and Elizabeth Bishop returned the compliment to Moore in her maturity. In 1948, the *Quarterly Review of Literature* added to the praise with a special "Marianne Moore Issue."

In 1947 occurred the major trauma of Moore's life, the death of her mother. Perhaps principally as a distraction from her grief—Mrs. Moore was not only a parent but the poet's companion and first critic all her life—Miss Moore laboriously translated all of *The Fables of La Fontaine*. The book was finally published, to mixed reviews, in 1954, and was followed in 1955 by *Predilections*, Moore's selection of essays and reviews drawn from her extensive work as a critic since 1916. In 1951, the *Collected Poems* had won the National Book Award, the Bollingen Prize, and the Pulitzer. She then received wide notice from the popular and literary press alike. Even the acerbic Mr. Jarrell (who had parodied her in the early forties) came to gush, as we have seen. Winthrop Sargeant wrote a profile for a February 1957 issue of *The New Yorker*, which a few months later also published Miss Moore's correspondence with executives of the Ford Motor Company, who had requested the poet's aid in naming their new automobile.

Honors continued to flow: the Gold Medal for Poetry from the National Institute of Arts and Letters, awards from the Poetry Society of America, several honorary degrees, the *Croix de Chevalier des Arts et Lettres* from the French government. To these official acknowledgments—she was even named "Senior Citizen of the Year" by the State of New York—popular fame was added. The American poet became especially well known for her love of baseball, so much so that she was asked to throw out the first ball on opening day at Yankee Stadium in 1968. (With typical thoroughness, she showed up in midseason of 1967 to practice with the team.) The image that George Platt Lynes helped create through his dramatically lit portraits was now touched up and colorized by the photographers from *Life*. After her well-publicized visits to the Bronx Zoo, all that remained to make Marianne Moore a household name was an appearance on *The Tonight Show*, and that too was arranged. Whether she was read as widely as she was watched is another matter.

"It felt queer to see all over again this year, in English reviews of Miss Moore's *Collected Poems*, those sentences, once so familiarly American—saying that she isn't a poet at all," Jarrell observed in 1951. "Nowadays, over here," he continued, "Miss Moore wins all the awards there are; but it took several decades for what public there is to get used to her—she was, until very recently, read unreasonably little and praised reasonably much." After the *Collected Poems* and *The Fables*, Moore brought out a new poetry volume regularly—*Like a Bulwark* (1956), *O to Be a Dragon* (1959), *The Arctic Ox* (1964), *Tell Me, Tell Me* (1967)— and *A Marianne Moore Reader* was issued in 1965. As her public exposure increased, it is arguable that the quality of Moore's poetry declined; perhaps without her mother's counsel she released what earlier would have been restrained. She was now read reasonably more and praised unreasonably much, or, rather, for the wrong reasons.

Nonetheless, by the time of her death, in 1972, all the individual poetry books had been allowed to go out of print (as were *Predilections* and the *Reader*), the much truncated *Complete Poems* (reissued in 1981) allowed to stand for them. George Nitchie's and Donald Hall's introductions to the poetry had recently been published, as well as Charles Tomlinson's collection of critical essays. Three years before her passing, Moore left an enormous archive to the (now renamed) Rosenbach Museum and Library in Philadelphia—workbooks, letters, manuscripts, and her heavily annotated library. Since then, more accurate studies have been possible. Besides Laurence Stapleton's well-researched, and beautifully written, *Marianne Moore: The Poet's Advance*, one may also mention the more recent critical books: Bonnie Costello's *Marianne Moore: Imaginary Possessions*, Grace Schulman's *Marianne Moore: The Poetry of Engagement*, and Taffy Martin's *Marianne Moore: Subversive Modernist*. In 1986, Patricia C. Willis's invaluable edition of *The Complete Prose* was also published, a major event for Moore scholarship.

Only now perhaps, with the more thorough examination of primary documents and the perspective of time, are we coming to appreciate the complexity of Marianne Moore. The present volume is offered as a contribution to the continuing revaluation of this masterfully independent Modernist. To commemorate the centenary of the poet's birth in November 1887, *Poetry* asked several poet-critics and -scholars for their reconsiderations of Moore as artist, critic, and literary personage; they responded with aesthetic reappraisals enhanced by their practical experience as working poets and students of contemporary American poetry. The essays they have contributed to the following pages were centerpieces in a month-long celebration under the title "Marianne Moore: The Art of a Modernist Master" sponsored by the Modern Poetry Association, publishers of the magazine that introduced the poet in this country. This series of public programs, which included recitations from the poet's work and informal discussions, was inaugurated with a reading by Maxine Kumin in the University of Chicago's Regenstein Library at the opening of two exhibits: "Vision into Verse: Marianne Moore and the Modernist Poem," primary materials and personal artifacts from the collections in the Rosenbach Museum and Library; and "Marianne Moore and Harriet Monroe: The Poet, the Critic, and *Poetry*," early manuscripts and author-editor correspondence from the magazine's archives, which are housed in the Regenstein's Department of Special Collections. All but the first and the last of the essays in the present collection were presented at a two-day symposium at the Newberry Library in Chicago.

In addition to the authors represented in this volume, the editor wishes again to thank the Curator of Special Collections, Robert Rosenthal, who first suggested that *Poetry* present a centenary celebration of Marianne Moore and who, with John C. Baum, Jeff Abt, and other staff members of the Regenstein Library, hosted the first program at the University of Chicago, inviting the magazine to share in the honor of opening the exhibitions. Besides assembling the extraordinary "Vision into Verse" travelling exhibition, Patricia C. Willis, then Curator of Literature at the Rosenbach Museum and Library, also delivered a talk on the poet's many-sided career in the first of three programs presented at the Chicago Public Library Cultural Center. Following in this informal lecture series, Amy Clampitt examined Moore's several and subtle influences on contemporary poets; and Grace Schulman discussed aspects of Moore's technique, with illustrations drawn from interviews she recorded with the poet during the last years of their long friendship. To these writers and to our hosts at the Chicago Public Library, particularly Rosemary Dawood and Nancy E. Harvey of the Literature and Language Division, we remain truly grateful. We are further indebted to the Newberry Library and to Charles T. Cullen, President; Karen Skubish, Director of Events; and Richard H. Brown, Academic Vice President, whose many kindnesses to the magazine now also include hosting the two-day symposium and the reception which followed at the Library.

Special acknowledgment is made to Richard Avedon, who granted permission to reproduce his photograph of Marianne Moore on both the poster and the pamphlet which accompanied the original programs and on the cover of this book.

From the earliest planning stages, the Board of the Modern Poetry Association offered enthusiastic support of the project, and special thanks are due to the President, Patrick Shaw, and to Martha Friedberg, Anstiss Hammond Drake, William O. Hunt, Jr., Andy Austin, and the other Trustees. However inadequately, I should also like to express my gratitude to my colleagues at *Poetry*: Nadine Cummings, for the extra burdens she assumed during the several stages of the project; former staff member Jim Elledge, for research and other help; Stephen Young, for careful preparation of the text of the symposium discussions and scrupulous assistance with several other editorial tasks; and Helen Lothrop Klaviter, for tireless effort at every phase of the activities, particularly in helping draft the original proposal, in handling correspondence and permissions, and in managing the innumerable details essential to the success of the original programs and the preparation of this text.

From the initial discussions of the idea for a Marianne Moore celebration through this final product of the program series, we have been fortunate to have the expert suggestions and patient guidance of Thomas C. Phelps: our sincere thanks to him, Wilsonia E. D. Cherry, and the other Program Officers at the National Endowment for the Humanities, whose generous support made the original presentations and this publication possible.

J. P.

# Acknowledgments

W. H. Auden: From "In Memory of Sigmund Freud" in *Collected Shorter Poems: 1927–1957*, by W. H. Auden. © Copyright, 1966, 1960, 1959, 1957, 1955, 1954, 1953, 1952, 1951, 1950, 1949, 1947, 1946, 1945, 1941, 1940, 1939, 1938, 1937, 1934, by W. H. Auden. Copyright, 1937, by Random House, Inc. Copyright 1934, by The Modern Library, Inc. Copyright renewed, 1961, 1964, by W. H. Auden. Reprinted by permission of Random House, Inc.

Elizabeth Bishop: Excerpts from "Manuelzinho," "In the Waiting Room," "Roosters" from *The Complete Poems*, by Elizabeth Bishop. Copyright © 1983 by Alice Helen Methfessel. Copyright © 1941, 1956, 1971 by Elizabeth Bishop. Copyright renewed 1968 by Elizabeth Bishop. Reprinted by permission of Farrar, Straus & Giroux, Inc. Permission to quote the letters of Elizabeth Bishop given by Alice Methfessel, Literary Executrix, and by the Rosenbach Museum and Library, Philadelphia.

Denise Levertov: "A Poem at Christmas" from *The Freeing of Dust*. Copyright © 1972 by Denise Levertov. Reprinted by permission of New Directions Publishing Corporation.

Edna St. Vincent Millay: Excerpts from "E. St. V. M." by Edna St. Vincent Millay. From *Letters of Edna St. Vincent Millay*, Harper & Row. Copyright © 1952 by Norma Millay Ellis. Reprinted by permission.

Marianne Moore: Excerpts from *The Complete Prose of Marianne Moore*, by Marianne Moore. Copyright © Clive E. Driver, Literary Executor of the Estate of Marianne C. Moore, 1959, 1960, 1961, 1962, 1963, 1964, 1965, 1986. Introduction copyright © Patricia C. Willis, 1986. Copyright © Marianne Moore, 1941, 1942, 1944, 1946, 1948, 1955, 1958, 1959, 1960, 1961, 1962, 1963, 1964, 1965, 1966, 1967, 1968. Copyright renewed Marianne Moore, 1969, 1970, 1972. Copyright renewed Lawrence E. Brinn, 1974, 1976. Copyright renewed

# 1

# Marianne Moore and the Monkey Business of Modernism

*Richard Howard*

There is only one figure, a single poet (and of course a single woman) in the entire cavalcade of the American literary vanguard who from the first—and in some instances, from well before the first—was acknowledged, was prized, was in fact and in fancy *adored* by a plurality of eminences in that critical and poetical company, on both sides of the Atlantic, which we now, with some readiness, some show of conviction, call Modernism. By its exemplars she was greeted and ingratiatingly seized upon as one of their own: by Ezra Pound, who dubbed her—invoking a specifically Modernist desideratum—"a protagonist for the rights of vitrification and petrifaxis" (for had she not admitted: "my writing is a collection of flies in amber"?); by T. S. Eliot, who said she was "too good to be appreciated anywhere" (and had she not remarked of her utter isolation: "the cure for loneliness is solitude"?); by Wallace Stevens, who called her "not only a complete disintegrator, but an equally complete reintegrator" (and had she not observed: "the objective is architecture, not demolition"?); by William Carlos Williams, who called her poetry "a multiplication of impulses, distressingly broken up, which by their several flights, crossing at eccentric angles, might enlighten" (and had she not admitted that "to doubt is merely a part of liking and of feeling"?); by Kenneth Burke, who delightedly recorded how she, "by the gentle mastery of her ways of writing, had terrified me over and over again" (and did she not confess that "willingness to baffle the crass reader sometimes baffles the right one"?); and by R. P. Blackmur, who defined hers as "a sensibility which constitutes the perfection of standing aside" (for had she not all apodictically announced that "those who have the power to renounce life are those who have it"?). Even Gertrude Stein, as we discover with some surprise in her recently published correspondence with Carl Van Vechten, was eager to have her admiring respects wafted to the author of, at the time, a single book of fifty-three poems published in 1924, the poet then being thirty-seven years old.

I have woven a tendentious chaplet from the unweeded garden of accolades which sprouted around Marianne Moore at the very inception of her poetic career and which has tended to hypertrophy and overgrow the embowered personage it was intended to honor and embellish; let me lead you up that garden path only a moment longer, and perhaps out of the precincts of encomium—always a little stifling, a little blinding—by noting that there is, simply, no comparable instance of such unanimity of favor among our canonical Modernists and their substantiating critics (as the mere mention of Gertrude Stein may remind us: just consider the bouquet of hostilities these same gentlemen, as well as the rest of the reading world, presented to Miss Stein, whose monolithic insistence that you were with her and for her, or else out of the running altogether, made her so much less likely to be honored as a literary master, or even as a literary mascot, than the decorous Miss Moore. Indeed, I believe we are entitled to some small wonder that the subject of our musings—for all her propriety, her gentility—was not *subjected,* just so, to a share in the mass of obloquy and derision visited upon her three notable contemporaries—Gertrude Stein, Eleanor Roosevelt, and Martha Graham—so monumentally mocked in their prime for all the eventual homage accorded them in their superannuation). There is no analogous instance of such general recognition, reverence, and *commitment* as that showered upon Marianne Moore by those masters whom my high-school English teacher, Miss Gail Wickwire, used to call, in fear and trembling, "the Moderns."

They appeared, those Moderns, at about the same time in the spring term as short sleeves, and to us they seemed, at Shaker Heights High School, to bulk or to bulge large chiefly by their differences and disparities, their mutual repulsions, and even more by their differences from everything which had preceded them. Thus, it was all the more astonishing to encounter—by the time I made it to Columbia University in Miss Moore's own New York, where in another borough the poet was a frequently visible specimen in the literary zoo, and even in the zoo itself—such a concord of approval and even veneration as was evidently hers. Not that we understood, precisely, what she was being praised for. It was hard to know what to make of Mr. Blackmur's entrancement with her method, what he called "her system of counting which stands for more than it shows, and shows, when you are on to it, more than it can possibly stand for." We could see that she was concerned with an attention to detail, to observable experience which seemed, often, pathological. Her strategies were so evasive, so deliberately oblique, for all the immediacy of her concern with the animal kingdom. Her splendor, as Geoffrey Hartmann was to point out years later, was menagerie. She had discovered in the world of creatures a vocabulary, a nomenclature of analogies, for herself. The trouble was that her poems were not really about animals—they were about the poet and about themselves, of course. She used this extraordinary manner of apparently exact description to render, in what we might call a zoophrasty or a zoophrasis, a world of suffused statement about herself. It was the most personal poetry ever written, yet it had become so by a refusal to be autobiographical. There was always a double resistance—on the one hand, to what she called "this disease, myself" and, on the other, to external menace. The animal poems, which Miss Wickwire was so eager to call to our attention and which the Moderns had so praised, were the confessions and acknowledgments of a compromised and vulnerable self. They were not a bestiary at all, or not like any other bestiary we could read. As for these praise-givers, our Miss Wickwire had known, of course, who they were, the concurring Moderns. She had recognized them—as she recognized the subject of their concurrence and the object of their delectation, Miss Marianne Moore herself—just because they were so different, altogether dissimilar, and even discrepant from the Elizabethans and the Augustans and the Romantics and the Victorians she had been "doing" with us every day, all year long. The Moderns, it was true, may not have appeared quite so different from the Metaphysicals, or from the Mad Poets at the end of the eighteenth century, but neither madness nor metaphysics, I should tell you, buttered much hay with Miss Wickwire, who had us and the warm weather to contend with, and the syllabus to get through, *including the Moderns,* by June 10, 1947. . . .

For Miss Wickwire, by and large, any poet was modern—and consequently was modern for us, looming up on the other side of the Great Divide of literature as she professed it: disaffected, alien, dumb—if he (and even if *she,* a relatively singular instance) sustained or suffered an apparent scission from the poetry of the past; and all the more modern if he (and she) insisted upon the appearance and the publicizing of that scission. Such insistances upon a discontinuity with past masters, an excision from the acknowledged fabric, struck Miss Wickwire— and struck us—as particularly ominous in matters of form, for matters of form were so much more than merely that: were in poetry (and were we not reading poems, even if they were modern poems?) and in our transactions with poetry so very distinctive. Matters of form, after all, were how we managed to know it was poetry, and we clung to those formal recognitions with the desperation of the shipwrecked, discovering our vessel coming apart at the joints and the seams, just when we had learned—however sketchily, however academically—its anatomy, its framing. So that even though I believe Miss Wickwire enjoyed being able to dissert, as she had disserted earlier in the year upon the recognizable achievements of Christina Rossetti or of Emily Dickinson—for after all, she was Miss Wickwire, as they were Miss Rossetti and Miss Dickinson, with a certain emphasis: she was Miss Gail Wickwire, part of that American Maiden Tradition to which, from Louisa Alcott to Amy Clampitt, we entrust the instruction of our young people and the ecstatic impulse of our lyric selves—there was, nonetheless, in the encounter with the poetry of the Moderns, and chiefly in the collision with the poetry of Miss Moore, an interval of panic obstruction, for unlike the poetry of any earlier Miss, this poetry was unlike ANY POETRY WHATEVER! How, Miss Wickwire asked, flinging out her short-sleeved arms in a pretty gesture of despair—how were we to know that it was poetry at all?

Even if a certain assurance of harmlessness (much to be desired, in dealing with the responses of midwestern high-school seniors) was apparently vouchsafed by Mr. Blackmur's assertion that "there is no sex anywhere in her poetry, no poet has been so chaste; but it is not the chastity that rises from an awareness—healthy or morbid—of the flesh, it is a special chastity aside from the flesh, a purity by birth and from the void"—was this much help to Miss Wickwire, when it was her task to persuade us—even to bully herself into acknowledging—that these verbal objects Miss Moore had produced with such apparent detachment were or must be poems, even as Shakespeare's sonnets and Shelley's "Ode to the West Wind" and Swinburne's "Hymn to Proserpine" were recognizably and identifiably and *even in their titles* poems? Nor was it much more help when Miss Moore herself, from whom help should certainly be forthcoming, told us (or told someone; everything gets repeated: the walls have ears): "it never occurred to me that anyone might think I imagined myself a poet; if what I write is called poetry it is because there is no other category in which to put it." Really no help at all! This was, lamentably enough, poetry by default, and it cut a preposterous swath, a pitiful figure indeed, in the world of bards and laureates. . . .

Yet there it was: Marianne Moore's poems were precisely the ones which elicited, it appeared, among the very figures we so mistrusted and so misconstrued, among the mysterious Moderns, a perfect anthem of approbation and advocacy, a paean which was to echo down through the generations of American poetry, with confirming *fioriture* appended by Auden and Lowell, by Jarrell and Merrill and Ashbery, by Kenner and Davenport. . . . And what was unanimity among such disparate, even such discordant voices if not—as Miss Moore herself had said in another connection—a good sign if not always a good thing!

Miss Wickwire has gone to join Miss Moore among those gracious, life-enhancing presences who enable us, if we listen to their voices, to fend for ourselves in their absence. No longer am I faced, as I was at Shaker High, with four or five anthology favorites (if that is the word, given our mystification, our muddle when confronted with "No Swan So Fine" or "An Octopus"), but with the crisp Penguin that purports, in a plausible mendacity of 247 pages, to be *The Complete Poems of Marianne Moore.* This is a scandal, comparable to the seizure of revisionary zeal which appears to have overcome John Crowe Ransom, too, in his eighties; perhaps old writers cannot let their early poems alone because they cannot endure the revelations they believe they have permitted. In Miss Moore's case, the choppings and changings are disastrous, and I must urge any reader not to believe the old poet against her younger, wiser self. She warns us, the old poet, taking a whole page for the ominous four-word message, that "omissions are not accidents," a notification that has all the demure severity of a message from Hamlet's father's ghost: we are to put up with excisions, with renamings, with revisions out of all recognition—in short, with losses that no poet's achievement should be compelled to sustain. Let me remind you—and Miss Moore's editors and publishers, if ever my voice could reach so far—that what we need is not this absurd (though self-inflicted) travesty of the poet's accomplishment, nor even its superior predecessor of 1951, the so-called *Collected Poems*, which includes none of her mascot poems that so disfigure the later book, poems written, or assembled, when she had become resigned to the absurd charm of her appearance among us—her costume, her correspondence with the Ford Motor Company about the naming of the damn Edsel, her fanaticism about baseball, her general adorableness. For she had become a kind of Mary Poppins in our literary life, brutally irrelevant; and even someone who admired and understood her truly subversive and wrenchingly emotional qualities, someone like Elizabeth Bishop, did the remaining work great harm with her "invitation to please come flying," that invocation to a kind of benevolent witch, Glinda the Good, who might visit Manhattan and fix everything up with her "glittering collection of morals." No, what we need is a textual reprint of the 1924 *Observations* and of each subsequent book *as it first appeared*, without the deleterious cutting and fussing which the misguided and somewhat craven poet perpetrated upon her true genius.

There are, as it happens, three phases in the natural history of a poet: the phase of the constitution of the poetic canon; then the phase (occasionally elided) of the prose canon; and finally the phase of the poet's letters, sometimes not quite prose or poetry, but poetry torn up by the roots, as in the case of Emily Dickinson. Those of us who have developed an appetite for Marianne Moore's major work have learned to assemble the poems of the first phase for ourselves, without the help of their author or of the Viking Press; and in this centennial year, by a happy labor, Patricia Willis has assembled the complete prose of the second phase, which must make a great difference, a great accrual, in our estimation of the poet. Not in our reading of the poetry, of course, but in our appraisal of the mind and heart, and indeed the body, which created it. From my own experience, I should suppose that the third phase will be quite as vital, quite as rewarding as the second. Back in 1947, not long after I had slid from Miss Wickwire's hands, the editors of *Columbia Review* invited Marianne Moore to judge their annual Boar's Head Poetry Content. This was the year, I believe, when Miss Moore's mother, with whom she had lived her whole life (the poet was then sixty years old), was in failing health. Miss Moore wrote us (I was one of the editors) a note explaining in some detail why she could not take part in our revels—a postcard it was, inspissated with capitals and distributed with astonishing axiological intention over its entire surface: the mysterious thing was an unmistakable message from the poet. For like Henry James, Miss Moore was always entirely present, entirely herself, whether she were meeting a friend (or a dog) in the street, or writing a note of social obligation, or a poem, or a review. She never put "something of herself" into what she wrote—she put it all. I deduce from the note refusing our invitation—a note I stole from the archives of the *Columbia Review,* for I coveted the resemblance of contours to the late poems of Stéphane Mallarmé—that the letters of Marianne Moore will amount to an overpowering affair, an enlargement of this deceptively modest figure who insisted that "she would rather be told too little than too much," for whom "the power of implication" (to which I shall return, for it is a key to her mystery, that implicative power) "was insured by compactness," and who readily acknowledged: "writing is difficult—at least it is for me." In other words, the woman who said she would like to have invented the zipper.

But until the texts of phase three are collected (from private hands, from restricted library collections, and from the Rosenbach Foundation holdings of Moore papers in Philadelphia), we cannot altogether speak of Marianne Moore the poet in the way in which we speak of Yeats, or Stevens, or Hart Crane. It appears that a poet's letters constitute a crucial dimension of the poet—Pope thought so to the point of editing and rewriting and publishing his own—one we cannot well do without, though we are perhaps compelled to do so, or to make believe we do so, for a very long time. Since we have also had to make do with a pernicious selection of the poems, how consoling (her word, one she uses almost as often as *elate,* as *rapt*) that we have, this year, so full and fulfilling an edition of Marianne Moore's prose. Here I have fed, and found the kind of pasturage which the poet's own debilitations of her poems have so frequently denied me. That is, "superlatives and certainties so sanguine as somehow to seem like uncertainties," as well as "a naturalness so studied as to annihilate itself," and the claim that "we must have the courage of our peculiarities" simultaneous with the insistence that "we must be as clear as our natural reticence allows us to be."

What is it we can learn about Moore and modernity (so nearly synonymous, as I intend further to assert) in these hundreds of pieces, often confronting for the first time new works by Yeats, by Pound, by Stevens, by Eliot, by Williams, by Stein? Marianne Moore did not have a great mind, but she aspired to have a whole one, and a whole mind is rarer still, and more important than mere greatness. It is this wholeness of mind, this integrity of Being, which enabled her to say, with such exemplary fierceness: "the thing is to see the vision and not deny it; to care and admit that we do." Everyone knows, by now, those great ethical crystallizations which occur like geodes in her poems, culminating in the volume—and the poem—*What Are Years* (1941). They have become a significant part of the poetic morality of our time. Here are the ones that come to me, merely by murmuring her eminent name and letting the fine words float to the surface:

hope not being hope / until all ground for hope has /vanished

the project / of wings uniting levity with strength

The chasm-side is / dead. / Repeated / evidence has proved that it can live / on what can not revive / its youth. The sea grows old in it.

the haggish, uncompanionable drawl / of certitude

his byplay was more terrible in its effectiveness / than the fiercest frontal attack

as if a death mask ever could replace / life's faulty excellence!

complexity is not a crime, but carry / it to the point of murkiness, and nothing is plain.

the dismal / fallacy that insistence / is the measure of achievement and that all truth must be dark

when one is frank, one's very presence is a compliment

one detects creative power by its capacity to conquer one's detachment

The passion for setting people right is in itself an afflictive disease. Distaste which takes no credit to itself is best.

Ecstasy affords / the occasion and expediency determines the form.

He sees deep and is glad, who / accedes to mortality / and in his imprisonment rises / upon himself as the sea in a chasm, struggling to be / free and unable to be, in its surrendering / finds its continuing.

The power of the visible is the invisible

To explain grace requires / a curious hand

Victory won't come / to me unless I go / to it

The weak overcomes its / menace, the strong overcomes itself

As if, as if, it is all ifs

When what we hoped for came to nothing, we revived.

memory's ear / that can hear without / having to hear

There never was a war that was not inward

A formula safer than an armorer's: the power of relinquishing /what one would keep; that is freedom.

But in *The Complete Prose of Marianne Moore*, we are discovering how such wisdom was come by. Classical in its emphasis—as when she says, "in any matter pertaining to writing we should remember that major value outweighs minor defects"—it is also stoical in its submission to humility and concentration and steadfastness—as when she says, "if one cannot strike when the iron is hot, one can strike *till* the iron is hot." There is, further, in this prose, the spirit that, as Wallace Stevens described it, wears the poem's guise at last. It is, though without the stiffening of doctrine, a spirit profoundly Christian, for it is the spirit which invokes the strength "to surmount defeat by submitting to defeat"; and again, it is the spirit which acknowledges that "to be hindered is to succeed." At its greatest reach, it is the spirit (and I note that Helen Vendler has already seized upon this passage as rising to the passion of religious oratory while keeping its distance from the conventionality of predictable religious utterance) which says: "We need not be told that life is never going to be free from trouble and that there are no substitutes for the dead; but it is a fact as well as a mystery that weakness is power, that handicap is proficiency, that the scar is a credential, that indignation is no adversary for gratitude, or heroism for joy. There are medicines." No religion in history has enabled such *sagesse* except Christianity, though this is a strain of Christian sentiment not to be found over Dante's gate, nor over Saint Peter's portal. It is quietism, and it is a sentiment which has enormous aesthetic— or poetical—consequences, for it makes Miss Moore say that "no work of art is old which was ever new, as no one is dead who was ever alive."

Here, I think, is manifest the consciousness which makes Marianne Moore speak so frequently, and so zealously, as if she had failed; as if for all the admiration and honor of her fellow Moderns, she were not with the elect; "I seem to myself an interested hack," she once said, "rather than an author." She abided by such humility because she believed authorship had to do with continuity, had to do with perpetuation and with union. In this she was with Miss Wickwire. "Insofar as a thing is really a work of art," Miss Moore believed, "it confirms other works of art." So here was the issue. It was the issue Miss Wickwire and her class of seniors at Shaker Heights High School perceived in their confusion. Indeed, it is the issue which even Robert Lowell perceived, quite as confused, when he referred to her "terrible and private and strangely revolutionary poetry." For whatever Modernism may be, we know this much about it, that its modes and mechanisms are those of fragmentation, dissociation, erasure, and opposition. In a word, of collage, an abrupt dispersal without modulation, without continuity, functioning not by transformation but by . . . transgression, very likely. The mosaic of citations and shifting focuses which constituted Marianne Moore's poems from the first was, of course, a device of what might be called primitive Modernism, immediately recognized by more sophisticated—less isolated—practitioners. What they recognized was the inmost struggle to reassemble a whole, to reconstitute ecstasy, to regain, by a project of faceting and assemblage, that rapt elation which Yeats inveterately called unity of being. Characteristically, Miss Moore quotes another author when she wants most succinctly to identify her own enterprise: "One cannot too much encourage artists," she cites Christian Zervos as saying, "who strive to bring back unity, who perceive new sources of ecstasy, who all their lives love something not to be found in this world."

I believe this invoked (and unattainable) unity is the cause, or at least the source, of Marianne Moore's immitigable self-distrust, her conviction that "everything added is something taken away" (one of her rare iambic pentameters). How reticent, how wary she was about the originality so often, and so rightly, attributed to her by her peers! She did not want to be original; she wanted to be whole. As she said, "originality is not a thing sealed and incapable of enlargement, but that an author may write newly while continuing the decorums and abilities of the past." And again, with searching self-knowledge: "we cannot ever be wholly original." One understands that this is said with relief, not with regret. Placing together two things perceived as unrelated but capable of creating a third, indissociable thing—this is the characteristic Moore operation, an enterprise of salvage, a venture toward that integrity she so much adored. Indeed, the invention of the zipper.

"The emended theme compels development," she said, and not till we have a proper edition of all her poems shall we comprehend the extent of her emendation. When I say she was a primitive Modernist, I use the adjective in the sense used when we speak of primitive Christianity; nothing unconsidered or crude is meant. Miss Moore was always eager to seek out the consolations of an order, a discipline, a restraint, and though she loved spontaneity and cherished impulse, she mistrusted the tendencies of pleasure ("satisfaction is a lowly / thing, how pure a thing is joy"). They tended to get out of hand—tendencies indeed. We all remember the famous dismissal: "nor can we dignify confusion by calling it baroque," though I suspect that is just what we can do, and in her case as in others, what some of us, as classifying readers, have done.

This matter of the senses, and ultimately of sexuality, is one which recurs in any consideration of this poet. "Some are not interested in sex pathology," she writes with characteristic impersonality, though we know who is meant, do we not? She even extends the figure of a disease I have already quoted in her terrible condemnation, "innate sensuality is a mildew." By 1928, four years after *Observations* was published, and during the five years as editor of the *Dial* when she wrote no poetry, she mustered her editorial "we" to decisive effect: "We confess to admiring instinctiveness, concentration, and tentativeness; to favoring opulence in asceticism." *Opulence in asceticism*—it is a memorable phrase, and to its memory must be added that stoic corollary: "We fail in some degree, and know that we do, if we are competent; but can prevail." The point was not pleasure, or even gratification. The point was joy. Indeed, I believe the only sexually revealing (or betraying) locution Marianne Moore makes in the seven hundred pages of her prose—the only Freudian slip, if you like—is in this discrimination. "Pleasure," she asserts, "is not joy, it is a strangling horror—the serpent that thrusts forward rigid—and does not know it ever was anything else." What a reproof to the phallic consciousness! No wonder she observed—speaking of versification, or course— "the interiorized climax usually pleases me better than the insisted-on climax." It was joy, it was unity, it was wholeness which was the issue, the ecstatic outcome, the event, and she discerned that she could not reach it by what she once called "the courage of too much nudity on the part of waitresses conveying champagne to clothed patrons."

There is a sense in which the history of Modernism is precisely the history of those figures whom we initially read as if they had no erotic charge—like Henry James, like Virginia Woolf, like Santayana—and whom we ultimately, learning to read better, come to find suffused with erotic life. After all, the use of language itself is a manifestation, an expression of eros. And Marianne Moore is not only no exception to this law (as Mr. Blackmur had supposed); she is a thrilling *example* of a writer charged with erotic energy, sometimes with specifically sexual energy. As I perceive it, her sexuality is expressed in terms of the observed pulsion and response of tissues within the self rather than in terms of the exchange of epidermal sensations between two selves; but such writing is nonetheless as erotic, or as eroticized, as any I know, and has a kind of sensuous enchantment or gusto, to use a word she lingered over. I am uneasy, of course, in discussing the eroticism or the lack of it in Marianne Moore. I think we all are. As with Dickinson or O'Keeffe, I feel that in talking about women artists—or in talking about men such as Henry James or George Santayana—we have not yet devised or developed a vocabulary in which we can readily express or understand the erotics of withdrawal or recessiveness or obliquity, or the refusal of explicit sexual gesture. And consequently, I don't believe any of us can easily say: this is, or this is not, a fulfilled and rewarding sexual life. Nor is it correct for us to deny such a possibility to a life we ourselves perceive as unpromising.

Yet I have my mite to add to the confusion, for I would make an observation or two about Marianne Moore's life with her mother. Like that other primitive Modernist, like Constantine Cavafy, Moore lived until she was sixty with her mother. Yet in a sense she was the converse of the great Alexandrian poet, for it was the entire drama of Cavafy's apparently placid life that, although he shared his social and domestic existence with Fat One, as he called his extraordinary mother Harikleia, he never once revealed to her that he wrote poems. He never showed her his work, whereas Moore never wrote a word, or at least never wrote a poem, which did not pass—in every sense—her mother's austere scrutiny. This is what she meant by *implicative*, I believe. And when she said, "the iron hand of unconvention can be heavier than the iron hand of convention," I suspect she was speaking, in her characteristically oblique way, of the rewarding sense of Mary Warner Moore's approval. According to commonly acknowledged schemes of development, the mother is seen as powerful, and her power is seen as one that must be overcome, outgrown, escaped. Whether nurturing or smothering, the mother's power is perceived as a threat to autonomy. And, of course, autonomy has come to stand as the very structure of maturity. Any theory of identity which sees maturity as the achievement of separation is bound to regard the mother's power as inferior to—and as less desirable than—the father's power, which stands for distance and the world, whereas the mother's power stands for closeness and the home. According to this popular hierarchy of development, a woman who lives with her mother all her life would by definition never achieve full maturity. But perhaps such development to maturity is being measured here by the standard of only one gender. Perhaps we should reconceive the notion of maturity to include more of the spectrum of relationships than an idealized—and largely male-oriented—version of autonomy. A tolerance for incomplete separation (to put it negatively) could be perceived as differently mature from an insistence on total independence, on separation. I invoke these clinical reflections because it seems to be the one real blunder Marianne Moore ever made in her literary life was related to—was occasioned by—the death of her mother. For it was in her grief, casting about for some sort of prop or stay in the period of mourning, that she hit upon La Fontaine. Her decision, her determination to translate the *Fables,* and her commitment to doing so, "rendering" every last one, produced one of the most dispiriting failures in the history of verse translation. Howard Nemerov put it correctly, over thirty years ago: as poems to be read in English, Moore's *Fables* are "irritatingly awkward, elliptical, complicated and very jittery as to the meter"; as renderings of the French, they "vacillate between pedantic strictness and strange liberty." We know the labor must have been long and hard, and indeed it was required to be so, for these translations were not of La Fontaine at all, but of grief. They are the labor of mourning, and implicate the poet's needs, not her narrative intentions or nonchalant originals. "The mind resists a language it is not used to," Miss Moore wrote in another connection, and added what is the best judgment I know on this task we do not call Herculean only because Hercules could not have done it: "The conflict between the tendency to aesthetic anarchy and the necessity for self-imposed discipline must take care of itself." It has taken care of itself, and finally it released Marianne Moore for the last decades of her life's career in literature. Work done during this period is not equal to the style or standard of the remarkable poems created before her mother's death. The way of writing has become something of a tic, the product of *books and verisimilitude,* as she liked to say. But she did not project as valuable—this is what she once remarked of Pavlova, and it goes for herself twice over—the personality from which she could not escape. There was something more that she wanted, something further that she was trying for. "Nothing so eludes portraiture as ecstasy," she once observed, and that is her great truth. It was her felicity and her flaw—it was her fate—to create a poetry of Modernism which was the fruit of ardor, of diligence, and of refusing to be false. Yet all the while her impulse was toward ecstatic wholeness, unity of being, and what she called "the vision." Her struggle was a great one, and it is responsible for the supple tension, the resilience of her finest poems, which "move themselves with spotlight swiftness / into the crevices— / in and out, illuminating." The conflict, the opposition between what I have called the monkey business of Modernism—its dissociations, fragmentations, abrupt juxtapositions, and entangling oppositions—and the mind enamored of wholeness is Marianne Moore's immense arena, the proving-ground which she filled with grand work, ineluctably unlike anything ever written before or since. It is her doom to have cultivated an imaginary garden, in which she has become, for our literary histories, a misapprehended shibboleth. The garden happily remains—an imaginary garden with a real token in it.

# 2

# Marianne Moore:
# Idiom and Idiosyncrasy

*Robert Pinsky*

Marianne Moore's poems have a social presence, you might even say a sociable
presence. That presence is distinct from Moore's tiresome public caricature as a
genteel, fey, impishly brilliant old lady in a peculiar hat—and yet gentility and
idiosyncrasy are unquestionably part of the true social presence in the poems.
Like many stereotypes, this is one we can neither quite feel comfortable with, nor
altogether reject. In Moore's best work, the outer force of manners penetrates
beyond a charming or complacent gentility, to become a profound moral force, as
in the great novelists; and the inner force of idiosyncrasy becomes the sign of a
passionate, obdurate selfhood. I think that to understand the peculiar strengths
or limitations of this poet, we have to look at her work in the light of such matters
as the relation of language and poetry to social life and even to social class. These
matters seem all the more important because Moore was a Modernist, one of the
generation of poets that raised new questions about the kind of poetry that might
be suitable for an American and democratic culture.

Partly because of our own social habits and predispositions, we readers often
respond to Moore's work in social terms: people dote on her poems, or find them
annoying, a little as if responding directly to a person and her remarks. Here is a
very slight but relevant early poem that presents itself explicitly as a social action.
The poem (omitted from the *Complete Poems* of 1967) has the pleasing title "To
Be Liked by You Would Be a Calamity." It begins with a quotation from Thomas
Hardy:

> "Attack is more piquant than concord," but when
>   You tell me frankly that you would like to feel
>     My flesh beneath your feet,
>       I'm all abroad, I can but put my weapon up, and

Bow you out.
Gesticulation—it is half the language.
Let unsheathed gesticulation be the steel
Your courtesy must meet,
Since in your hearing words are mute, which to my senses
Are a shout.[1]

One thing this little epigram demonstrates is that Moore can write in the mode of colloquy without writing colloquially. That is, address and something like exchange take place, but not vocally, and not in words much like any conversational language of twentieth-century America: the words "I can but put my weapon up, and / Bow you out" represent part of an exchange, but an exchange imagined in the terms of another century. Like the deliberately period metaphor of swordplay, the "steel" that is "unsheathed" and "put up," this period voice is a defensive and offensive weapon, a way to keep anger and hatred at some distance while striking at them. Even "My flesh beneath your feet," because of "flesh," is a bit stagy and unreal. The most spare, "natural" language and the most memorable phrase coincide on the phrase "Gesticulation—it is half the language." And that moment in the poem is the most clearly inward: self-addressed, not directed toward the imagined interlocutor at all. The poem is indeed about conversation that does not take place, words that are withheld, language as a social weapon that goes unused except in Moore's powerful imagination.

The artificiality, in other words, is the point. We can picture the actual gesture with which Moore politely and hostilely bowed someone out of her office—personally, I believe such a moment did actually happen—but the address is not only highly, but pointedly, artificial, an invention that represents its underlying true action of silence or reserve. She creates an artificial dialogue to dramatize, and to protect, her inward poise. The poem attains a feeling of social superiority through artifice and the weapon of refusal, the submerged sharklike intelligence that conceives both the unsheathed steel of gesticulation and the "put up" weapon of actual speech. The poem is, in short, an elaborate way of saying "I am not speaking to you"—or, more accurately, "I am not speaking to that person."

Repeatedly and characteristically, Moore's poems construct an elaborate social presence that contrives to disguise or protect, just as manners sometimes do in life. Moore's ambivalent attraction toward the idea of communal life expresses itself, then teasingly cancels itself, characteristically, in a conversation that is not conversation. Reticence and withdrawal, as in "To Be Liked by You Would Be a Calamity," often underlie apparent engagement. Moore's two most characteristic rhetorical modes, apostrophe and quotation, amount to a kind of parody, or at least a blatantly artificial reconstruction, of discourse between people.

In this mock-colloquy, her quotations invoke the possibility of heeding the voice of another, while the poet contrives to manipulate and assign meanings. And in the other direction, her apostrophes often invoke the possibility of addressing another only to suggest the unreality of such address. In *Observations*, there are poems grammatically addressed to an intramural rat, to a chameleon, to a prize bird who is G. B. Shaw, to the sun, to Disraeli, to military progress, to a steam roller, to a snail, to George Moore, to Molière, to the ibis as statecraft embalmed, to a pedantic literalist, to the son of the author of a history book, to critics and connoisseurs, to one by whom it would be a calamity to be liked, to Ireland, and to roses. In none of these poems does the second-person pronoun have the kind of reality it has in poems like, say, Yeats's "Adam's Curse" or Bishop's "Letter to N.Y."

The unreality of the second person is skillfully exploited in some of these poems, often with comic effect, and often aggressively. In "Critics and Connoisseurs," the polysyllabic, first-person sentences describing the swan are artfully contrasted with an abrupt, monosyllabic turn toward the one addressed, "I have seen you":

> I remember a swan under the willows in Oxford,
>     with flamingo-colored, maple-
>         leaflike feet. It reconnoitered like a battle-
> ship. Disbelief and conscious fastidiousness were
>     ingredients in its
>         disinclination to move. Finally its hardihood was
>             not proof against its
>         proclivity to more fully appraise such bits
>             of food as the stream
>
> bore counter to it; it made away with what I gave it
>     to eat. I have seen this swan and
>         I have seen you; I have seen ambition without
>     understanding in a variety of forms.[2]

This is very shrewd writing. The sentence "It reconnoitered like a battleship," while itself terse and plain, introduces the comically ponderous quality that the next sentences embody, "its hardihood was not proof against its proclivity," and "such bits of food as the stream bore counter to it," and so forth, a deadpan irony of inflation, just a little as if mouthed by Robert Morley. By contrast it gives the cutting social edge to "I have seen this swan and I have seen you."

There are many contrasts at work here: polysyllabic abstract moral terms played against the brilliantly observed, specific feet of the swan; the first person against the second person; sentences like Latin played against sentences like abrupt speech; abrupt compression played against unexpected flourishes of elaboration. All of these are part of the larger contest between idiom, Moore's acute and rather satirical sense of a communal speech, and idiosyncrasy, her equally sharp sense of language as the weapon of her private self which observes the swan and the ant, the critic and the connoisseur. She addresses herself to these objects of attention, and also addresses them grammatically, in a formal way—but not actually, not socially, or even anything like it. You might call these two poems "mock satires," in that they present personal, inward meditations in the outward form of a social clash.

Idiom is the sameness of the language customarily used by people in a particular place. Idiosyncrasy, with its first half from the same root, is in language the sameness of a particular person's *crasis* or constitution. Considering these two elements as partially opposed is a way to understand the dry, skeptical reservations, the rock-hard mistrusts, that stand behind some of Moore's relatively warm-looking, humanistic passages. The opening stanza of "The Steeple-Jack" (*CP*, 5–6) illustrates the double quality I mean:

> Dürer would have seen a reason for living
>     in a town like this, with eight stranded whales
> to look at; with the sweet air coming into your house
> on a fine day, from water etched
>     with waves as formal as the scales
> on a fish

The line ending emphasizes the phrase "reason for living" in isolation: a kind of sardonic undertone that emphasizes, not habitation ("living in this town"), but a reason to stay alive. Dürer would have seen a reason for living; do you, or I? Especially in a town like this? That undertone of laconic desperation is not farfetched, since an ocean turbulence affects both the actual stars and their religious representation:

> whirlwind fife-and-drum of the storm bends the salt
>     marsh grass, disturbs stars in the sky and the
> star on the steeple; it is a privilege to see so
> much confusion.

"Confusion" is followed by an extended, hyperbolically long catalogue of flowers, a profuse list so eclectic and long that it is dizzying, even inchoate, and becomes bilious, imaginary, "not-right," animal, before it is punctuated at the end by an apparent apothegm of small-town virtue:

> Disguised by what
>     might seem the opposite, the sea-
> side flowers and

trees are favored by the fog so that you have
        the tropics at first hand: the trumpet vine,
foxglove, giant snapdragon, a salpiglossis that has
spots and stripes, morning-glories, gourds,
        or moon-vines trained on fishing twine
at the back door:

cattails, flags, blueberries and spiderwort,
        striped grass, lichens, sunflowers, asters, daisies—
yellow and crab-claw ragged sailors with green bracts—toad-plant,
petunias, ferns, pink lilies, blue
        ones, tigers; poppies; black sweet-peas.
The climate

is not right for the banyan, frangipani, or
        jack-fruit trees; or for exotic serpent
life. Ring lizard and snakeskin for the foot, if you see fit;
but here they've cats, not cobras, to
        keep down the rats. The diffident
little newt

with white pin-dots on black horizontal spaced-
        out bands lives here; yet there is nothing that
ambition can buy or take away.

This garden is brilliantly disturbed, with its nasty-sounding "salpiglossis that has
/ spots and stripes." The bravura gaudiness and excess of lines like "yellow and
crab-claw ragged sailors with green bracts—toad plant" establish the mood of a
centerless, sinister profusion even before a stanza begins with the words "is not
right," and the establishment in the homely Eden of a domestic, unspectacular,
apparently even innocuous serpent.

　　But serpent the diffident little newt is, though not "exotic" or tropical. At the
apparent climax of an undecipherable abundance, the serpent is there, "yet there
is nothing that / ambition can buy or take away." This is the tone and language
of a plain, morally stringent provincial sufficiency and calm, but like the opening
lines about seeing a reason to live, this Spartan formula has an ironic undertow:
the town's garden profusion as rich as the tropics offers nothing that can be used
outside of it. Ambition is either enclosed within this place and its terms, or
frustrated. Nothing is for export. The student, in the poem's next sentence, sits
with his "not-native books" and watches the boats as they progress "white and
rigid as if in / a groove."

　　In this bleached, rigid, self-contained place, economy of gesture governs
flux and turbulence, as in a woodcut or engraving. Seagulls rise around the clock
or lighthouse without moving their wings—a slight quiver of the body. Even the

storm that disturbs the stars in the sky and the star on the steeple does not shake or transform anything; rather, it provides a significant spectacle: "it is a privilege to see so / much confusion." Turbulence without change, abundance without harvest, elegance without bravado, and character without discourse or incident: it is a community, but one in which Moore's characters do not touch or address one another. The president repays the sin-driven senators by not thinking about them, and the college student with his books sees across a long perspective, as in the background of a Dürer woodcut, the central figure of the steeple-jack, who "might be part of a novel," but for us, is not.

The steeple-jack, the title figure in the first poem in Moore's *Complete Poems*, embodies the poet's relation to social or community life. He is not exactly isolated from the town: he serves the town by gilding its paramount symbol, and he also has posted two signs, one in black and white announcing his name and profession, and one in red and white that says "Danger." The steeple-jack is both prominent—he wears scarlet, he has a bold sign, he is high above—and also a small, attenuated figure, letting down his rope as a spider spins a thread. In his remoteness which is a measure of his courage, he resembles other figures, vulnerable and potentially lonely, who have in common their difference from the ambitious and gregarious. The stanza begins with the word "Danger," but the town offers relative safety for those who live with risk and rely on an inward reserve:

> This would be a fit haven for
> waifs, children, animals, prisoners,
>          and presidents who have repaid
> sin driven
>
> senators by not thinking about them.

Relative safety is a governing ideal in Moore's haven. Those who are as Moore says "each in his way" at home here—the hero, the student, the steeple-jack— live familiarly with the risk of failure. They are at home with that risk, and with countervailing hope, and thus they strive, provisionally. Manners, compared to morals, are more or less by definition provisional, and "The Steeple-Jack" is a poem powerfully, subtly contrived to construct a model of the world of manners, our communal arrangement.

Here, the gap between Moore's personal utterance and the shared language of idiom serves to make the emotion all the stronger. In this secular world, the poet's voice mediates between the ordinary and the mysterious. It is a voice sometimes informal, yet never quite demotic; it is nonjudgmental, yet couched in the grammatical terms of the moralist: what "would be fit" or "is not right" or "what might seem" or "if you see fit." Her formal inventions bracket a capitalized "Danger" between stanza break and period, or stretch over line and stanza a phrase—"the pitch / of the church // spire, not true"—defining the boundary between secular imperfection and religious hope, or between the provisional and the absolute:

> Liking an elegance of which
> the source is not bravado, he knows by heart the antique
> sugar-bowl shaped summer-house of
>                 interlacing slats, and the pitch
> of the church
>
>     spire, not true, from which a man in scarlet lets
>     down a rope as a spider spins a thread.

Because this figure puts out his danger-signs, "It could not be dangerous to be living / in a town like this." Up on the untrue spire gilding the solid-pointed star which on a steeple stands for hope, the steeple-jack is an artist at home in the town without being precisely in it. He leaves his laconic words of identification and warning behind, and puts the possibly deceptive gilding on the representation of a possibly justified communal hope. Though his very name, Poole, denotes a shared aggregate, and though he performs a communal service in a highly visible manner, he also embodies solitude and remove.

The aggressive mock-satire of "Critics and Connoisseurs" and "To Be Liked by You Would Be a Calamity" enacts a highly artificial, almost parodic version of social discourse. The poems deal with fury and incomprehension: "ambition without understanding" in the first poem, and, in the second, words which to the person addressed are "mute, [but] which to my senses / Are a shout." The fury in "The Steeple-Jack" has been transformed into "the whirlwind fife-and-drum" of a storm that disturbs, but remains highly localized, though something like repressed anger courses through the ambiguities about reasons to live, the thwarting of ambition, the untrue pitch and the double-edged standing for hope. The incomprehension or distance between people, the motivating force of the earlier colloquy-poems, has become part of Moore's peculiarly allegorized, but enigmatic, town. This brilliant invention, freighted with symbolic meanings but resolutely particular down to its proper names, "Ambrose," "C. J. Poole," supplies a way for the poet to be present and emphatic, yet elusive. It allows her language to be familiar and sociable, yet never bound by the idiomatic. She has imagined a quiet, communal haven for idiosyncrasy, and put it at the beginning of her complete poems.

Marianne Moore touches on the question of idiom in her *Paris Review* interview with Donald Hall. She begins with admiration for a stage play she has seen:

> The accuracy of the vernacular! That's the kind of thing I am interested in, am always taking down little local expressions and accents. I think I should be in some philologi-

cal operation or enterprise, am really much interested in dialect and intonations. I scarcely think of any that comes into my so-called poems at all.[3]

This is an elaborately complicated response, a maze of false and genuine modesty. However, the description of her poems as reflecting hardly any of the vernacular is basically true. In her next response to the interviewer, Moore talks of taking as an elective at Bryn Mawr a course called, remarkably, Seventeenth-Century Imitative Writing—Fuller, Hooker, Bacon, Bishop Andrewes and Others. One thing that animates the language of the "The Steeple-Jack" is the way it takes us into her imagined place without being the language of a place. Moore's language in its full power is not what she calls "the vernacular"—has little to do with the speech of a place, or with that word based on *verna*, a slave born in the master's household; rather, her poetic medium is partly a reflection of the ruminative, capacious discourse of seventeenth-century prose and partly an assertion of the freedom of her own, autocratic *crasis*.

When Moore does reflect the speech of an actual American group or place, it is with an effect of conceivably deliberate distortion, getting things so thoroughly wrong that we wonder nervously if that is the point. That embarrassment is generated, for example, by her poem on the Brooklyn Dodgers, recklessly calling Duke Snider "Round-tripper Duke" or writing of teammates: "Ralph Branca has Preacher Roe's number; recall?" Whether deliberately or not, the mangling of baseball jargon, on one level comical, on another defines the gap between the shared language of the community and the separated, no matter how benign, utterance of the poet, isolated above.

That isolation has many corollaries, and invites speculation. From a viewpoint to do with social class, a strong drama of Moore's work is her effort to accommodate democracy, her egalitarian and patriotic American side, with what seems the unavoidable gentility of her language. This is a matter of manners that shades into politics, but in a complex way. Moore would be incapable of writing as convincingly "spoken" a passage as Bishop's, from "Manuelzinho":

> You paint—heaven knows why—
> the outside of the crown
> and brim of your straw hat.
> Perhaps to reflect the sun?
> Or perhaps when you were small,
> your mother said, "Manuelzinho,
> one thing: be sure you always
> paint your straw hat."[4]

That "one thing" with its colon is not part of Moore's range. Because it is part of Bishop's range, she can write this passage in a poem about a woman and her

servant or dependent, a passage and poem that some readers have found condescending and cruel, and that some have found deeply understanding and humane.
Either way, Bishop is in a theater of operations, a social place, that Moore does
not enter.

From a feminist perspective, Moore's declining to reproduce something like
the social art of conversation in her poems, even parodying that art by an autocratic system of apostrophe and quotation, is a way of refusing the realm traditionally or stereotypically assigned to women of intelligence and force: polite conversation, the little room in which Jane Austen's heroines must exercise their wills.
There is another sense in which Moore is, in Sandra Gilbert's cogent phrase, a
"female female impersonator," exaggerating and exposing expectations related to
gender. The refusal of assigned terms characterizes some of her most memorable
lines cast in the feminine grammatical gender, from "The Paper Nautilus" (*CP*,
121–22):

> For authorities whose hopes
> are shaped by mercenaries?
>     Writers entrapped by
>     teatime fame and by
> commuters' comforts? Not for these
>     the paper nautilus
>     constructs her thin glass shell.
>
>     Giving her perishable
> souvenir of hope, a dull
>     white outside and smooth-
>     edged inner surface
> glossy as the sea, the watchful
>     maker of it guards it
>     day and night, she scarcely
>
>     eats until the eggs are hatched.
> Buried eight-fold in her eight
>     arms, for she is in
>     a sense a devil-
> fish, her glass ram's-horn-cradled freight
>     is hid but is not crushed.

"Hid but . . . not crushed": this treasured, painstakingly insulated "freight" is not
merely the kernel of emotion at the center of the poet's art, it seems to be the
accomplished burden of her personality itself. What gives emotional power to the
images of protection and nurturing, what gives the "souvenir of hope" its dignity,
is the way courage is evoked by images of transparency, delicacy, the "dull / white

outside." All of these images, because they evoke the nautilus's shell from its outward border, foreshadow the action of the eggs as new life coming out and away from it, to "free it when they are freed." The papery shell is compared to a "fortress," but a fortress less strong itself than the idea of "love," the "only fortress / strong enough to trust to."

This resolution would be sentimental in any poet less fortresslike than Marianne Moore. The amply dramatized isolation and remove, constituted in large part by the idiosyncratic, quasi-archaic, quasi-colloquial turns of word and syntax, all combine to give dignity and penetration to the idea of a shell opening trustfully in love. Depth of protective reserve and the gesture of opening inform the image in the last stanza of "The Paper Nautilus": the white-on-white grooves, "close- // laid Ionic chiton-folds" left in the shell when the eight arms have relaxed their watchful protective embrace.

This is the characteristic action of language and feeling in Moore, and it is a particularly complex or indirect one. Broadly speaking, one can think of poets as having characteristic turns of energy: Dickinson pitting wonder against despair; Yeats fitting together what has been broken; Williams peeling back integuments. The limitations of such quick tags are obvious, and yet it helps me to find the source of feeling in Moore's work if I think of her as constructing, exposing, and disassembling an elaborate fortress. The materials of the fortress are idiosyncrasy and manners, manners of speech, and the social manners they reflect. The town of "The Steeple-Jack," which is referred to as a "haven," does not present actual, kinetic manners between people, but it is depicted in sentences that tease and yearn toward idiomatic speech, then away from it. The town itself is like a newly painted set, ready for the play of social life to commence, with its church columns of stone "made modester by whitewash," and:

> The
> place has a school-house, a post-office in a
> store, fish-houses, hen-houses, a three-masted
> schooner on
> the stocks.

The town, with one figure alone with books on a hillside and another isolated above, is as if poised for the ordinary activities of communal life, below its star which stands for hope—the same quality as in the paper nautilus's "perishable souvenir of hope."

Hope for what? Among other things, hope for the give and take of life, which in both poems is presented as if just about to begin—in the phrase from Henry James that ends Moore's poem on New York, "accessibility to experience." This action of declining a fortress, and welcoming experience, is profoundly moving. The staircase-wit of the mock-satires with which I began consign social experience to a kind of eternal previousness, addressed from behind the walls of idiosyncrasy. In fuller poems like "The Paper Nautilus" and "The Steeple-Jack," a protected and protective shell frees and is freed, a "fit haven" is imagined in a moment of anticipation. Even the poem "Marriage" can be read as a dialectic between the two ideas of that enterprise as a form that contains and as a form that mediates.

The idea of a shell that is first constructed, then disassembled, freeing what was inside and becoming free of it, provides a way of seeing Moore's work. We do not merely identify Marianne Moore by her protective shell of peculiarities, but value her for them. She is not one of those writers about whom we can say she is best when she is least idiosyncratically herself. Utterly to prize idiosyncrasy would be condescension, and yet to suppress or disregard it would reject an essential action of her poetry and the moral energy that drives her work. Overcoming or mastering a social manner that intervenes between the person and "accessibility to experience" provides a central drama in that work.

From one perspective, that drama has to do with a determined, persistent movement toward the demotic and the democratic, cutting against the genteel elements in Moore's idiom. From another, it is the drama of a woman artist alternately refusing and parodying both of the alternate social stereotypes: female charm and male assertion. From the biographical viewpoint, Moore's work reaches outward from the circumstances of her family. The father's insanity and absence from before Moore's birth left a kind of three-person social fortress: the mutual protection of a religious, middle-class family, economically insecure and socially exposed by the absence of the traditional patriarchal head. Dealing with that perpetual deprivation, and that immense embarrassment, gave the truncated family a delicately hardened protective architecture.

The visible forces in Moore's work are peculiarity and generalization, reticence and asseveration, and, in language, the eccentricity of the scholar and the central idiom of the marketplace. These forces bring together what is closed, like a shell or a provincial town, and the open seas of experience. Her evocation of these forces merits, and meets, the standard for art Moore proposes in the concluding line of "When I Buy Pictures":

It must acknowledge the spiritual forces which have made it.

This acknowledgment is exactly parallel to the beautiful ionic grooves, the aftermark of a measured, protective pressure that is relaxed. In language, the line enacts its proposition: to "*acknowledge* the spiritual forces which have made it." The verb "to acknowledge" is subtly and appropriately social; it implies an other: one acknowledges a gift, a compliment, an obligation. That is, social forces acknowledge spiritual forces, in their own terms, and thereby take on spiritual power. What Moore depicts, at her best, is the solitary and laborious approach to that attainment: the trek, you might say, through knowledge to acknowledgment.

The sudden, even unexpected penetrations of emotion in Moore's work flare up from the tireless pressure of the poet negotiating and considering between her own way of talking and our way of talking, between discourse and discourse's imaginary re-making, the suspended life of a town and that life's forever hoped-for resumption. These oppositions embody the shared, socially visible quality of peculiarity underlying the peculiarity of each distinct human soul.

**Notes**

1.  Marianne Moore, "To Be Liked by You Would Be a Calamity," in *Observations* (New York: Dial Press, 1925), 37.

2.  Marianne Moore, "Critics and Connoisseurs," in *Complete Poems of Marianne Moore* (New York: Macmillan/Viking, 1981), 38–39. Hereafter, poems from this collection will be documented parenthetically within the text with *CP* followed by the pagination of the poem under discussion.

3.  Donald Hall, "The Art of Poetry: Marianne Moore," in *Marianne Moore: A Collection of Critical Essays*, ed. Charles Tomlinson (Englewood Cliffs, N.J.: Prentice-Hall, 1969), 23.

4.  Elizabeth Bishop, "Manuelzinho," in *The Complete Poems* (New York: Farrar, Straus & Giroux, 1969), 116.

Marianne Moore, ca. 1922
Photo by Marjori.
*(Courtesy of the Rosenbach Museum and Library)*

# 3

# Marianne Moore as
# Female Female Impersonator

*Sandra M. Gilbert*

*It is a dangerous lot, that of the charming, romantic public poet,
especially if it falls to a woman.*
> Louise Bogan, review of *Huntsman, What Quarry?*

*Family, I discover that I have nothing to give readings in, I must
have long dresses, trailing ones. The short ones won't do.*
> Edna St. Vincent Millay, 22 Sept. 1917

*In the late Forties Marianne Moore walked into a milliner's shop
and asked to be fitted as Washington Crossing the Delaware.*
> Bonnie Costello, *Marianne Moore*

In October 1917, at New York's Neighborhood Playhouse, the Wisconsin Players performed a new one-acter by the poet Wallace Stevens. Set in a curiously surrealistic seventeenth century, *Bowl, Cat and Broomstick* is a facetious piece of literary criticism in which the three oddly named titled characters, exploring the idea that "there is a special power in the poetry of a beauty," meditate on the portrait of a French poetess called Claire Dupray.[1] Significantly, however, the play goes on to deconstruct both the image and the imagination of the hapless Claire. In doing so, as I shall argue, Stevens's minidrama simultaneously underscores the surprising fetishization of the woman poet in a twentieth century of which the work's "seventeenth century" is a bizarre reflection, emphasizes the aesthetic dissonance that marked the careers of male and female poets in the period, and indicates the intensity of the irony with which contemporary male *litterateurs* confronted these new developments. Perhaps more important, the play's action points to a situation that twentieth-century women poets both exploited and resisted in their struggle to transform themselves from art objects to artists.

When *Bowl, Cat and Broomstick* begins, Bowl, an ascetic aesthete, is translating Claire Dupray's verses for his admiring disciple Cat, but with the entrance of Broomstick, a "hard-looking" skeptic, the three turn their attention to the picture of the writer that decorates the frontispiece of her book and begin to speculate on Claire's age, as well as on the relationship between her age, her sex, her beauty, and her art. "She cannot be more than twenty-two," declares Bowl, adding that that "is an age when . . . a girl like Claire Dupray, becomes a poetess." "Say poet—poet. I hate poetess," remonstrates Cat, but Broomstick sardonically observes that "poetess is just the word at twenty-two!" (25) Further analysis of Claire Dupray's work seems to prove the justice of his claim, for the verse of this beauty sounds as extravagantly sentimental as any produced by the "female writers" with "three names" whom most Modernists deplored.[2] "This emotional waste," Broomstick notes, "is all thirty years old at the least. . . . What I hold against Claire Dupray, above everything else, is just that she is not herself in her day" (32). Finally, moreover, the play proves his judgment correct: when the three friends read the preface to Claire's collection, they discover (to the mortification of Bowl and Cat) that Claire Madeleine Colombier Dupray is really fifty-three years old—and "Damn all portraits of poets and poetesses," cries Cat in chagrin.

On the surface, of course, the stylish intellectual farce these characters enact is intended to instruct audiences in the distinction between appearance and reality even while, through the monitory figure of Broomstick, it advances a self-consciously "twentieth-century" aesthetic: poets should "make it new" and even old Broom(sticks) should sweep the world clean of the past's trashy sentimentality. But why does the fastidious *philosophe* of "Sunday Morning" dramatize his allegory of art in terms of male critical gullibility and female poetic pretentiousness? A line spoken by Bowl, as he struggles to balance erotic admiration with aesthetic evaluation, suggests a clue: "It is a new thing that the eyes of a poetess should bring us to this" (27). For although Broomstick ironically responds that "We are not living in the seventeenth century for nothing," the creator of this bemused trio of (miss)readers would certainly have noticed that in just the year when he was composing his playlet "a new thing" was happening on the New York literary scene: Bowls and Cats all over town were talking about "the poetry of a beauty" that was thought by all to have a very "special power."

Edna St. Vincent Millay—whose name, interestingly enough, rhymes with that of Claire Dupray—had actually begun a meteoric career as "poetess" in 1912, when she was twenty years old and her long poem "Renascence" won a prize in a contest sponsored by the *Lyric Year*. Taking the literary world "by storm," the talented ingenue from Camden, Maine, was immediately taken up by a series of wealthy benefactors, who arranged for her to attend Vassar College on scholarship, and who joined in fêting her at parties in New York. And this astonishing debut was quickly followed by further triumphs about which Stevens would certainly have known—for throughout her college years Millay continued publishing poetry and, already Vassar's best-known undergraduate, she garnered even more attention for her acting.[3]

That this youthful poet was as physically lovely as *Bowl, Cat and Broomstick*'s Claire Dupray can only have contributed to her success: in the spring of 1916, the photographer Arnold Genthe posed her against a background of magnolia blossoms for a portrait which later made its way into the Museum of Modern Art and which might well have served as the frontispiece on which Stevens's harried critics brood. But that Millay was as productive as she was attractive may have contributed even more than her notoriety to the ambivalence she must have aroused in some male contemporaries. It seems relevant here that her first collection, *Renascence and Other Poems*, appeared in the fall of 1917, shortly before Stevens's play was performed and six years before the author of *Harmonium* had published his own first volume. And it seems equally relevant that the works in *Renascence and Other Poems* could be either praised or blamed for their use of poetic strategies that were all "thirty years old at the least."[4]

Millay continued to forge a brilliant public career throughout the twenties and thirties. In 1920 her bravura *A Few Figs from Thistles* was published to such acclaim that she became, in one critic's words, "the It-girl of the hour, the Miss America of 1920," and by 1936 few readers would have questioned Elizabeth Atkins's assertion that—rather than being at least thirty years out of date, like Claire Dupray—"Edna St. Vincent Millay represents our time to itself."[5] Besides representing what Atkins also called "the incarnation of our *Zeitgeist*," however, Edna Millay might be said to have stood for another phenomenon: the rise of a group of women poets whose fame was as theatrical as it was literary. Where even the most notable precursors of these women—Elizabeth Barrett Browning, Emily Dickinson, Christina Rossetti—had achieved their reputations in spite of (or, indeed, in some cases because of) lives of radical seclusion, such early twentieth-century poets as Amy Lowell, Edna Millay, Elinor Wylie, and Edith Sitwell ascended lecture platforms as exuberantly as they gave readings in private salons. Costuming themselves to reflect the self-definitions their poems recorded (Lowell in "high-collared dresses sprinkled with beads" that made her look like "Holbein's Henry VIII," Millay in floating chiffon, Wylie in heavy silver "armor," Sitwell in quasi-Elizabethan robes), they literalized the dream of the "poetess" as dramatic *improvisatrice* that had captivated the nineteenth-century imagination in Madame de Staël's *Corinne*.[6]

Not surprisingly, many men of letters decided that, as F. R. Leavis quipped about Sitwell, such female aesthetic careers belonged "to the history of publicity rather than of poetry," and quite a few longed, with the skeptical ferocity of

Stevens's Broomstick, to sweep away their debased, publicity-seeking women rivals.[7] Raging against Lowell's famous transformation of Imagism to "Amygism," Ezra Pound labeled the cigar-smoking New Englander a "hippopoetess," while Thomas Wolfe, in *The Web and the Rock*, produced a savage portrait of Elinor Wylie as a babyishly narcissistic ice queen.[8] More generally, T. S. Eliot, in an early draft of *The Waste Land*, sketched a composite portrait of a modern "poetess," a woman named Fresca whose lineaments limned all the faults—critical acclaim, sexual depravity, a derivative style—with which he and his contemporaries associated the Amy Lowells and Elinor Wylies, the Edna Millays and Claire Duprays.[9] With Stevens's Broomstick, Eliot appears to have felt that serious (male) readers ought to sweep art clean of the commercially compelling "emotional waste" excreted by such popular artists before men of letters themselves were swept away.

As literary history records, of course, male Modernist poets were emphatically *not* swept away by the witches' brooms they may have associated with some of their female contemporaries. On the contrary, though Millay in her own day functioned as a kind of American Poetess Laureate, it was *her* achievement, along with the accomplishments of the women constellated around her, which was rapidly dismissed by the canonizing judgment of time. That these "poetesses" *have* been "eliminated" from critical consideration is dramatically revealed by their absence from most major anthologies as well as from most of the "serious" studies of twentieth-century poetry which have appeared in recent decades. William Pritchard's *Lives of the Modern Poets* (1980), for instance, contains not one reference to Millay, Wylie, Lowell, or Bogan, nor does Jerome Mazzaro's *Modern American Poetry: Essays in Criticism* (1970).

   To be sure, there were at least a few women poets whom the taste-making theorists of Modernism did not so rapidly consign to oblivion. Most strikingly, Marianne Moore was widely treated as an icon of the new, a kind of anti–Poetess Laureate whose work avoided the emotional excesses to which female flesh was generally thought to be heir. In fact, Wallace Stevens, the playwright who had in 1917 vented his spleen on Claire Dupray, magisterially opined that Moore was "A Poet That Matters," and William Carlos Williams, too, continually celebrated her achievements. In addition, T. S. Eliot and Ezra Pound were among a number of other crucial figures who found her work compelling.[10]

   Can there have been two canons formed by twentieth-century women who wrote verse—the canon of work produced by "poetesses" and the canon of art created by anti-"poetesses"? Must contemporary female poets choose between radically opposed literary matrilineages, one which is poetically "incorrect" from the Modernist perspective, and one which is aesthetically respectable? If Millay stands for a female poetic tradition that descends from "bad" (blatantly sentimental) nineteenth-century poetasters, does Moore stand for a female poetic tradition that descends from such a "good" (intellectually vigorous) nineteenth-century artist as Emily Dickinson? I want to suggest that though this may at first seem to be the case, there are a number of surprising similarities between the representative figures of Millay and Moore, similarities which reveal yet again the problematic situation of the woman poet in the twentieth century even while they dramatize the comparably sardonic strategies through which *both* writers translated the "handicap" of "femininity" into an aesthetic advantage.

To begin with "femininity": both Millay and Moore were early fetishized as *women* poets. As early as 1923, in just the years when Millay had become the "It-girl" of popular American verse, T. S. Eliot was implicitly defining Moore as the "It-girl" of the avant-garde intelligentsia, pointedly celebrating her not for the absence but for the presence of "femininity" in her *oeuvre*.[11] And that this appropriately "modern" artist *looked* as "feminine" as Genthe's tenderly girlish Millay was continually emphasized by Williams, who liked to remember the "two cords, cables rather, of red hair coiled around her rather small cranium," and by the many other admiring observers who became as obsessed with her tricorne hat and cape as Millay's fans had been with her trailing gowns.[12]

Interestingly, too, as Moore's reputation among intellectuals began to decline during the fifties and sixties, even positive analyses of her work increasingly emphasized its stereotypically "feminine" qualities. M. L. Rosenthal spoke of her "precious and recherché impressions"; Roy Harvey Pearce noted her "propriety," her "polite and lady-like presence."[13] Nevertheless, in just these years Marianne Moore had become exactly the kind of public "incarnation of the *Zeitgeist*" that Millay was earlier. According to one observer, when Moore read at the Boston Arts Festival in 1958, "a crowd of something like five thousand persons" were waiting to applaud her "in the semi-darkness under the elms."[14] In her tricorne hat and "great cape," she had become an icon of eccentric but distinctively female art, and perhaps it was inevitable, therefore, that—like Millay—she would be entirely excluded from Pritchard's *Lives of the Modern Poets*.

But Millay and Moore had more in common than feminizing publicity. In particular, though both may have thought of the poetic imagination as "gender-free," both were ultimately brought to en-gender it; in fact, whether or not they felt as "naturally" feminine as their admirers and detractors thought they were, both deliberately adopted the mask of "the feminine" as an equivocally empowering one, a stance that allowed both to work from the positions of fetishized femininity in which critics had placed them, using the newly public roles of twentieth-century "poetess" laureate or anti-"poetess" laureate as "free" (precisely because "female") spaces from which they could ironically question many of the conventions of their culture. In doing this, both were employing a characteristic female strategy defined in the forties by Karen Horney. In a study of this analyst's "social psychology of women," Marcia Westkott explains that the woman whom Horney classifies as an "onlooker" simultaneously participates in and detachedly analyzes the drama of her own life. "Critically observing herself and others," writes Westkott, summarizing Horney's argument, "may be the way that a woman is looking at herself being looked at. She becomes the omniscient observer of her own sexualization, the voyeur of the voyeurs of her . . . body."[15] As such, she complies with male demands for stereotypical "femininity" even while she rebels against them, "her superiority logged in stinging . . . observations and judgment."[16] More recently, the French theorist Luce Irigaray has spoken of the "masquerade" of femininity, drawing on ideas put forward by the psychoanalyst Joan Rivière in the twenties.[17] While Irigaray sees such a masquerade as a consequence of the fact that in patriarchal culture women are inevitably "exiled from themselves," I am suggesting, as Horney did, that for women like Millay and Moore such a self-exile, such an ironic estrangement, was in some sense deliberate.

To be sure, as their reputations imply, Millay and Moore masqueraded as— that is, they simultaneously impersonated and analyzed—very different sorts of "feminine" personalities. A comment by the poet-critic Elder Olson indicates the degree of consciousness with which both adopted public characters that also infused and facilitated their verse: "Marianne Moore was very much the spinster schoolteacher. And Edna Millay was the medieval princess, fatigued by too many chivalric romances."[18] Thus Millay, as most readers noticed, generally presented herself as a prototypical *femme fatale*; Moore, as many observed, depicted herself as a paradigmatic "old maid." But the self-consciousness with which they responded to, and reinforced, their own female reification is evident not only in their verse but also in their most casual sketches of themselves.

In 1920, for instance, Millay-as-"onlooker" scribbled what she described as "a lewd portrait of myself" for Edmund Wilson:

> Hair which she still devoutly trusts is red.
> . . . . . . . . . . . . . . . . . . . . . . . . . . . . . .
> A large mouth,
> Lascivious,
> Asceticized by blasphemies.
> A long throat,
> Which will someday
> Be strangled.
> . . . . . . . . . . .
> A small body,
> Unexclamatory,
> But which,
> Were it the fashion to wear no clothes,
> Would be as well-dressed
> As any.[19]

Decades later, Moore produced a similarly high-spirited self-analysis, though one that suggested a very different female image. For where Millay had depicted herself as seductive, Moore, gazing at a photograph of herself, transformed her physiognomy into a comically spinsterish menagerie:

> I'm good natured but hideous as an old hop toad. I look like a scarecrow. . . . I look permanently alarmed, like a frog. I *aspire* to be neat, I try to do my hair with a lot of thought to avoid those explosive sunbursts, but when one hairpin goes in, another seems to come out. . . . My physiognomy isn't classic at all, it's like a banana-nosed monkey. (She stops for a second thought.) Well, I do seem at least to be awake, don't I?[20]

Dissimilar as these self-portraits are, they suggest what was for early twentieth-century women poets an increasingly inescapable link between female anatomy and literary destiny, between the perceived body of the "feminine" poet and the body of her work. And although such a link had been in the first place at least partly forged by both positive and negative male reactions to female aspirations, it ultimately made the achievements of these writers especially vulnerable to attacks by Modernist male theorists, for whom "good" poetry involved what Eliot called an "escape from personality."[21] In fact, the critical struggles associated with the emergence of poetic modernism were consistently sexualized: "bad" verse was stereotypically "feminine" (i.e., formally conservative, sentimental, lacking in aesthetic or intellectual ambition), while "good" poetry was stereotypically "masculine" (i.e., formally innovative, "hard," abstract, ambitious). Or, as William Carlos Williams once put it:

> And what is good poetry made of
> And what is good poetry made of
> Of rats and snails and puppy-dog's tails
> And that is what good poetry is made of
>
> And what is bad poetry made of
> And what is bad poetry made of
> Of sugar and spice and everything nice
> That is what bad poetry is made of[22]

Thus, as the Modernist aesthetic was gradually institutionalized during the first half of the century, the accomplishments of Millay and Moore as representative figures came to seem increasingly marginal, so much so that younger women who might have turned to them as heartening examples instead fled in disgust. Traditional "poetesses" like Millay had been defined as offensively emotional and anachronistic; ostensible innovators like Moore were seen as "precious" and "recherché." The canon reflected in Pritchard's *Lives*—Hardy, Yeats, Robinson,

Frost, Pound, Eliot, Stevens, Crane, Williams—had become *the* canon of the respectably modern. Yet if we reread the apparently disparate but now similarly noncanonical works of Millay and Moore, bearing in mind these writers' paradoxical but courageous deployment of "the feminine" as a sardonic response to the feminization-as-trivialization with which contemporary literary culture greeted them, we will discover that they were part of a separate but equally strong poetic tradition, one whose deliberate dramatization of femaleness was to issue in the achievements of such mid-century women as Sylvia Plath, Anne Sexton, Adrienne Rich, and Elizabeth Bishop, among many others.

Millay's posthumous *Mine the Harvest* includes a poem that significantly links the "It-girl" of the anti-Modernists with the unlikely contemporary who was the "It-girl" of the intellectuals. "The Strawberry Shrub" offers a close analysis of a plant that is "quaint as quinces" and "duller / Than history."[23] Interestingly, moreover, the poem praises this emblematic shrub for just the apparently "ladylike" virtues of "modesty" and "humility" that the self-effacing and ironically "spinsterish" Moore celebrated throughout her career: "You must bruise it a bit: it does not exude; it yields."

It is not unlikely that Millay had been reading Moore when she wrote these lines, but the question of direct influence is not directly relevant. For what Millay might well have intuited in the work of her apparent aesthetic opposite was a sense that such details, humble and "duller / Than history," incarnate the durability and the deliberately ironic differentness of that quality which has been labeled "the feminine." Readers have, of course, long noted the ways in which Marianne Moore's observations of the natural world tended to emphasize the paradoxical strength of supposed weakness. Perhaps most famously, the late "His Shield" meditates on the mythical salamander, who triumphs by being willing, like Millay's strawberry bush, to "yield."[24] Beyond the will to self-aggrandizement that constructs history, he understands "the power of relinquishing / what one would keep; that is freedom" (144). It is a freedom, however, that Moore at least subtextually associates with a female alienation from—or, to put the case more strongly, a female refusal to be complicitous in—history. And, I would argue, it is a freedom that this poet learned to imagine through her self-creation as a "spinster" outsider, that is, through a process of "female female impersonation" which paralleled (though it differed from) Millay's.

Even in some of Moore's first published poems we can see this process beginning. For just as Millay's early *A Few Figs from Thistles* often seems designed to taunt male suitors by flaunting her charms as a *femme fatale* who is indifferent to their wiles, so Moore's early verses frequently seem meant to daunt male readers by forcing them to attend to the acerbic lessons taught by a "spinster schoolteacher" who is as apt to scold as to reward little boys for what they regard as their chief achievements. Such 1915 poems, for instance, as "To Statecraft

Embalmed," "To Military Progress," and "To a Steam Roller" are fierce in their chastisings of masculinist swagger. "To Statecraft Embalmed," for instance, begins with pure contempt—"There is nothing to be said for you" (35)—and "To Military Progress" excoriates the masculinist "mind / like a millstone" (82) while "To a Steam Roller" compares such a mind to a grotesque machine which "crush[es] all the particles down / into close conformity, and then walk[s] back and forth on them" (84).

This overt misandry was associated with a clear commitment to the feminist movement. When she wrote these verses, Moore and her mother were members of the Woman Suffrage Party of Pennsylvania, and many years later, remembering Moore's reports of this and other events, Elizabeth Bishop became heatedly defensive in her friend's behalf. Citing "several references critical of her poetry by feminist writers," Bishop asked, "Do they know that Marianne Moore . . . paraded with the suffragettes, led by Inez Milholland on her white horse, down Fifth Avenue?"[25] Equally to the point, in the same memoir Bishop noted that Moore's "Marriage" is "a poem that says everything . . . Virginia Woolf has said."[26] Her insight was acute, but besides elaborating the feminism embodied in Moore's early epigrammatic verses, "Marriage" helps us understand this poet's continuing construction of a "female" mask which both complemented and contradicted Millay's. For, deeply feminist though it is, this complex meditation on a central patriarchal institution, a work which the poet herself called "an anthology" of quotations, is also a crucial statement of alienation spoken by a "spinsterish" outsider. Indeed, it is more specifically through its noncommittal alienation than through its committed feminism that this extraordinary text reveals the direction in which Moore's pose as "spinster schoolteacher" would take her.

To be even more specific: "Marriage" is obviously spoken by someone to whom what Adrienne Rich has called "compulsory heterosexuality" has simply never seemed either "compulsory" or compelling.[27] Not that it is what Rich might call a "lesbian" poem; it is simply a soliloquy that stands entirely outside sexuality to look at its conventions from, as it were, an extraplanetary perspective—or, perhaps more accurately, from the point of view of an entirely self-sufficient, apparently asexual creature, a genius of an amoeba, say. With scrupulously objective phrasing, the first lines of the poem establish this perspective even while, through the reiteration of the neutral pronoun "one," they promise to take no sides:

> This institution,
> perhaps one should say enterprise
> out of respect for which
> one says one need not change one's mind
> about a thing one has believed in,
> requiring public promises

of one's intention
to fulfill a private obligation:
I wonder what Adam and Eve
think of it by this time.

(62)

Some of the changes Moore made in the poem as she worked through various drafts emphasize her own intention to remain at least superficially nonpartisan. Laurence Stapleton observes that as Moore's "thinking about Adam's . . . desire for power continues, a conclusion is made: 'this division into masculine and feminine compartments of achievement will not do. . . . One is a particle / in an existence to which Adam and Eve /are incidental to the plot.'"[28] In fact, what the writer evidently comes to understand is the degree of her own puzzlement at "this institution," a puzzlement issuing in profound indifference. For although marriage may require "all one's criminal ingenuity / to avoid" (62), it is nevertheless an "amalgamation which can never be more / than an interesting impossibility" (63).

Of course, as Bishop claimed, Moore—writing five years before the publication of *A Room of One's Own* and thirteen years before the appearance of *Three Guineas*—does make a number of proto-Woolfian points: Adam treads

" . . . chasms
on the uncertain footing of a spear,"
forgetting that there is in woman
a quality of mind
which as an instinctive manifestation
is unsafe,

(64)

forgetting, that is, the irony naturally deployed by those who are subordinated. And though, like some of Woolf's patriarchs, Adam deludes himself into believing that he has achieved "the ease of the philosopher" paradoxically "unfathered by a woman," he "stumbles over marriage," the bizarre contrivance of "Unhelpful Hymen!" (65). More to the point, when five o'clock comes and "'the ladies in their imperious humility / are ready to receive you,'" Moore, like Woolf, interjects her opinion of such gatherings: "experience attests / that men have power / and sometimes one is made to feel it" (67), adding further, in a quotation from M. Carey Thomas that anticipates the photographs of male leaders in official regalia which Woolf used as illustrations in *Three Guineas*,

She says, "Men are monopolists
of 'stars, garters, buttons
and other shining baubles'—

unfit to be the guardians
of another person's happiness."

(67)

Ultimately, however, Moore dispassionately withdraws from both parties to the pact of "Unhelpful Hymen," noting that while "he loves himself so much, / he can permit himself / no rival in that love," she "loves herself so much, / she cannot see herself enough," and wondering,

What can one do for them—
these savages
condemned to disaffect
all those who are not visionaries
alert to undertake the silly task
of making people noble?

(68)

Her declared intention to assemble the poem out of "Statements that took my fancy which I tried to arrange plausibly" (271) is therefore revealing, for the collage of quotations that Moore has constructed persistently supports her own pose as a bemused researcher. Indeed, where the verbal shreds of history accumulated by the speaker of *The Waste Land* all become parts of *his* sensibility, so that, as Hugh Kenner once suggested, his "Voice" represents all voices—"the European mind" articulating itself—the shards of language brought together by the author of "Marriage" seem more like three-by-five cards, notes for a dissertation on a subject the writer is trying, with difficulty, to understand.[29] Thus, where Eliot's art of allusion is an act of assimilation, Moore's involves an activity of alienation.

By the end of "Marriage," then, the very notion of "marriage" has been reduced to a rhetorical gesture, one whose hollowness fails to reconcile the equally hollow rhetorical debate that "he" and "she"—Adam and Eve—have carried on throughout the poem: "'the statesmanship / of an archaic Daniel Webster,'" observes the poet, "'persists to their [the married couple's] simplicity of temper / as the essence of the matter,'" yet that "statesmanship" turns out to be mere oxymoronic sloganeering ("'Liberty and union / now and forever'") objectified in empty symbols and theatrical gestures: "'the Book on the writing table; / the hand in the breast pocket'" (69–70). Well might such an institution require "all one's criminal ingenuity / to avoid," not for political (that is, feminist) reasons but because, from this disaffected perspective, it is so absurd.

As more biographical material about Moore's family becomes available, psychoanalytically inclined readers will no doubt begin to draw some conventional conclusions. Certainly the series of playful animal names with which she, her mother, and her brother rechristened each other (after the publication of *The Wind in the Willows* in 1908, Mrs. Moore was regularly "Mole," Marianne was "Rat," and Warner was "Badger") would seem to have perpetuated an asexual childishness.[30] At the same time, though, such a participation in an ingenuous alternative life, with its elaboration of stereotypically "spinsterish" eccentricities, must also have reinforced Moore's feminist inclination to deconstruct patriarchal history from the perspective of a nonparticipant in crucial sexual institutions even while it allowed her to reconstruct a history of her own—a *natural* history in which she and her familiar familial animals played a central part. Thus, coming at the questions which concerned Millay as well as Virginia Woolf—the relations between the sexes, the course of events that constituted "Western culture"—from a radically different position, the author of "Marriage" was eventually to express a notably similar point of view on such issues.

That perspective is perhaps most splendidly articulated in one of Moore's most brilliant meditations on history—"Virginia Britannia," a poem that begins quietly, with an evocation of the natural landscape in which America's earliest drama of colonization was played out, but moves gravely toward a key image of the grave of one of the English interlopers who, as the poet will later tell us in an ironic understatement, were at least as "odd" as the Indians whose land they usurped:

> The now tremendous vine-encompassed hackberry
> starred with the ivy flower,
> shades the church tower;
> And a great sinner lyeth here under the sycamore.
>
> (107)

Though Moore's note reports that the inscription on one Robert Sherwood's gravestone piously describes him as "a great sinner who waits for a joyful resurrection" (279), her text emphasizes the imperialistic sinfulness, rather than the Christian piety, that he represents, for, reviewing the history of "England's Old / Dominion," she notes simultaneously the absurdity and the evil of colonial voracity, declaring in one of her most forceful political statements,

> Like strangler figs choking
> a banyan, not an explorer, no imperialist,
> not one of us, in taking what we
> pleased—in colonizing as the
> saying is—has been a synonym for mercy.
>
> (110)

Similarly, "Too Much," the first section of "The Jerboa," turns to the Roman and Egyptian origins of western civilization to consider, with detached contempt, the lives of "those with, everywhere, // power over the poor" (12). The more complex a culture, Moore suggests, the more it deforms nature, first, by attempting to possess what should be free, and second, by perverting natural purposes. The Egyptians, who "understood / making colossi and / how to use slaves,"

> had their men tie
> hippopotami
>     and bring out dappled dog-
>     cats to course antelope, dikdik, and ibex;
>         or used small eagles. They looked on as theirs,
>         impalas and onigers,
>
> the wild ostrich herd
> with hard feet and bird
>     necks rearing back in the
>     dust like a serpent preparing to strike, cranes,
>         mongooses, storks, anoas, Nile geese;
>         and there were gardens for these—
>
> (10–11)

Diverted by "Dwarfs here and there," Egypt's "Princes / clad in queens' dresses" and "queens in a / king's underskirt" were served by depersonalized attendants who

>             were like the king's cane in the
>         form of a hand, or the folding bedroom
>         made for his mother of whom
>
> he was fond.
>
> (12)

Nor were these people who "liked small things"—who "kept in a buck / or rhinoceros horn, / the ground horn; and locust oil in stone locusts" (11)—an historical anomaly, for the opening stanzas of "Too Much" tell how "A Roman had an / artist, a *freedman*" (italics mine) devise a grotesquely huge "pine cone / or fir cone—with holes for a fountain," which, significantly, was to be placed on Rome's notorious Prison of St. Angelo and "which is known // now as the Popes'" (10). Moore's sardonic remark that this bizarre object "passed / for art" expresses her disdain for the way in which the Roman master who ordered it distorted the creative energies of the "freedman"-artist and misrepresented nature (10). At the same time, her emphasis on the endurance of the absurd cone—"known // *now* as the Popes'"—indicates her sense that all history, perhaps all culture, has been shaped by such deformations of nature.

After an afternoon spent with Marianne Moore, the journalist Marguerite Young wrote in 1946 that "She has a box of wild bird feathers of all kinds wrapped in tissues and a blue-jay claw. She offered me some eagle down, which she says is getting scarcer. She offered me a blue-jay claw."[31] Against the extravagant nature of the art produced by hierarchical culture, Moore set, in her life as in her work, the economical art of anti-hierarchical nature. The second section of "The Jerboa," entitled "Abundance," continues the celebration, begun late in the first section, of the jerboa, "a small desert rat, / and not famous, that / lives without water" but "has happiness," explaining that "one would not be he / who has nothing but plenty" (13). And lest readers mistake the poet herself for a zoological connoisseur not unlike the lords and ladies of ancient Egypt, she makes her moral explicit:

> Africanus meant
> the conqueror sent
>   from Rome. It should mean the
>   untouched: the sand-brown jumping-rat—free-born; and
>     the blacks, that choice race with an elegance
>     ignored by one's ignorance.
>
>                                                   (13)

Possession and enslavement, arrogance and ignorance—these are the fruits of "civilized" history, and only those outside history (the creatures who have a timeless natural history of their own like the mockingbird, the wren, and the jerboa) or marginalized by history (the "choice race" of the blacks, or the forgotten race of Powhatan and Pocahontas) are free of cultural pollution. Moreover, it is the endurance of the freest of these creatures—the nonhuman ones—which "dwarfs" human arrogance. The jerboa still "has a shining silver house // of sand" (13), but the Pharoahs, as Millay once put it, only "nearly had" their way: the king (of Egypt) is dead.[32]

In the only seriously negative passage that Moore's admirer Randall Jarrell ever wrote about her, the usually astute Jarrell complained that in idealizing certain animals the author of "The Jerboa" was falsifying the nature of a Nature which is after all, he reminded his readers, red in tooth and claw. His critique is worth quoting at some length:

> The way of the little jerboa on the sands—at once True, Beautiful, and Good—[Miss Moore] understands; but the little shrew or weazel, that kills, if it can, two or three dozen animals in a night? the little larvae feeding on the still-living caterpillar their mother has paralyzed for them? We are surprised to find Nature, in Miss Moore's poll

of it, so strongly in favor of Morality; but all the results are implicit in the sampling—
like the *Literary Digest*, she sent postcards to only the nicer animals.[33]

Jarrell's observation is in a sense correct, but the point he makes is precisely one
that Moore herself, a college biology major, might have made. Seeking to imagine
alternatives to the voracity and ferocity of history, the jerboa's celebrant strives
to depict the alternative history that might be constructed by what Jarrell contemptuously calls "the nicer animals." That Jarrell goes on to wish that "Miss Moore
had read a history of the European 'colonization' of our planet (instead of natural
histories full of the quaint animals of those colonies)" reveals the surprising depth
of his misunderstanding. Moore had carefully studied *both* histories and wished
to substitute one for the other.

But if one reads Moore's natural history with care, it becomes plain that the
animals through whom she critiques culture are often female, like females, or
associated with females. In "He 'Digesteth Harde Yron,'" for instance, the ostrich
"watches his chicks with / a maternal concentration" (99). In the face of such
quasi-feminine commitment to nurturance, human excess ("Six hundred ostrich
brains served / at one banquet") becomes particularly vicious (100). At the same
time, the watchfulness of the paper nautilus, who, we are told in the poem of that
name, does not "construc[t] her thin glass shell" for "authorities" (121) but to
shelter her eggs because "love / is the only fortress / strong enough to trust to"
(122), represents the historically marginalized but triumphant endurance of the
female of the species. Finally, two of Moore's images of women underscore the
implicit feminism of her natural history. The early "Sea Unicorns and Land
Unicorns," with its enthralled portrait of the unicorn, notes that, as the old legend
suggests, this miraculously elusive beast can be "tamed only by a lady inoffensive
like itself— / as curiously wild and gentle" (78). Similarly, the idealized vision
of a woman that is at the center of the late "A Carriage from Sweden" praises the
beauty of a woman "with the natural stoop of the / snowy egret . . . [and with] split
/ pine fair hair, steady gannet-clear / eyes and [a] pine-needled-path deer- / swift
step" (131–32). Consistently compared to those natural creatures whom Moore
values so much more highly than cultural artifacts, it is this innocently queenly
female figure whose potential potency haunts even the poet's most "spinsterish"
lessons in zoology and botany. And it was Moore's deliberate "female female
impersonation" that made it possible for her to articulate such a fundamentally
feminist possibility.

For, refusing to comply with the exigencies of romance, coolly distanced from
"Marriage," this poet was liberated to imagine civilizing alternatives to "civilization." Thus, playfully dressed as "Washington Crossing the Delaware"—wearing
a skirt *and* a cloak *and* a tricorne hat—and thereby signaling her "old maid's"
freedom from heterosexualized femininity, Moore was casting herself as the leader

of a new kind of war for independence. As president of the apparently whimsical but really fantastically serious state of ostriches and nautiluses, unicorns and virgins and deer-swift women, she would lead her creatures across the Delaware into a different history. Her New World would be the old order of birds, beasts and flowers, of alienated women and enslaved peoples, resanctified.

To add a brief coda to this discussion of female impersonation: It is arguable that for Moore, as for Millay, the artifice, even the eccentricity, of the verse genre in which she chose to write functioned, metaphorically, just as the costumes of both women literally functioned—to dramatize *and* question the artifice of female poetic identity. Millay's love sonnets, for example, allowed her to enact an erotic role reversal comparable to the one Christina Rossetti defined in her prefatory note to "Monna Innominata," letting her show what might have happened "Had such a lady [as Beatrice or Laura] spoken for her self."[34] But because, unlike Rossetti, Millay was working in this form at a time when, to male Modernist contemporaries, it seemed (to quote Stevens again) "thirty years old at the least," the genre itself became a kind of archaic costume in which this rebellious poet parodically attired herself so as to call attention to the antiquated garb of "femininity." Also, whether the corset of form in which Millay encased her ideas was Shakespearean or Petrarchan, the very process of rhyming and measuring that the composition of any sonnet entails would in effect let her become "the voyeur of the voyeurs" of the "body" of her work.

Similarly, though Moore's innovative and, for an English poet, almost unprecedented use of prosaic-sounding syllabics would seem to place her at the other end of the aesthetic spectrum from the sonnet-writing Millay, her generic choice, too, let her call attention to the arbitrariness of female poetic identity, as well as to the artifice of "poetry" itself. Frequently insisting that she was not really "a poet," Moore famously documented that claim in "Poetry," where she declared "I, too, dislike it" (266), and where she responded to Tolstoy's assertion that "Poetry is verse; prose is not verse. Or else poetry is everything with the exception of business documents and school books" by impudently remarking that it is not "valid / to discriminate against 'business documents and // school-books'; all these phenomena are important" (267).[35] To be sure, this self-presentation can be, and has been, attributed to Moore's notorious "humility." As Bonnie Costello puts it, in this writer's work "the prosaic, conversational tone, the long, meandering, run-on lines and shifts of figurative level, give the impression of nonchalance. She is not, she seems to suggest, writing anything so grand as a poem."[36] At the same time, however, by transforming "prose" into "poetry," Moore questions the historically privileged status of "poetry" even while, not with humility but with a kind of quiet arrogance, she proves that *she* can make anything—including a business document or a school book—into "poetry." In addition, just as the process of metrical and formal mastery allows Millay the sonneteer to become a voyeur of the aesthetic victory at which readers will also gaze, so Moore's use of syllabics lets her watch herself being watched as her meticulous counting converts "prose" into "poetry."

What can we learn from what might be called the sardonic heroism with which Marianne Moore, as much as the more obviously theatrical Edna St. Vincent Millay, deployed "the feminine" as both defense and offense—defense against trivialization, offense against masculinism? Among other lessens, I think we can learn a great deal about the specifically female tradition out of which much contemporary poetry by women has arisen. For one thing—and this is perhaps a painful truth that Millay and Moore, in their separate ways, dramatize—the female female impersonation or "masquerade" practiced by these two artists reminds us that, as Marcia Westkott remarks in her incisive commentary on Horney, woman's "alienation is informed not only by her visualized presence, her being taken as a fetish by others, and therefore by herself" but also "by her marginality."[37] Yet, to put the case more positively, such alienation means that, to quote Westkott again, the woman—in this case, the woman poet—"is the outsider who can see through the pretensions of the powerful" and, I would add, construct aesthetic modes which seek, at least implicitly, to deflate those pretensions.[38]

Most crucially, such aesthetic modes seek to address the main issue that, if we return to the seventeenth century inhabited by Stevens's Claire Dupray, we will find couched in Broomstick's defensive irony, Bowl's determined naïveté. Staring at the vexed portrait of the poetess, Broomstick asks, "Does the voice of tragedy dwell in this mouth?" And Bowl answers, "I was not thinking of that. I was thinking merely of the expression it gives to the portrait. That expression is vitally biographical" (27). Stevens is plainly being comic here, but his characters are as correct about Edna St. Vincent Millay and Marianne Moore as they are about Claire Dupray, for both of these women appear to have worked out of a secret feminine assumption that "the personal is the poetical." True, Moore declares in "To a Giraffe" that it is "in fact fatal / to be personal"—but by this, she explained, she meant that it is "undesirable // to be literal" (215), so that both she and Millay, as avatars of that new being Claire Dupray, attempted a mode of female female impersonation that was "vitally biographical" even as it subverted biography by suggesting its artifice.

A poem by Elizabeth Bishop, one of her finest works, suggests precisely the cultural arbitrariness to which these poets were addressing themselves. In "In the Waiting Room," the seven-year-old Bishop—or the construct "Elizabeth"—attends her "Aunt Consuelo" at a dentist's appointment, reading a *National Geographic* that contains bizarre pictures of a dead man labeled "Long Pig" and naked African women with "horrifying" breasts as she endures her time of "waiting." But when "Suddenly, from inside, / came an *oh!* of pain / —Aunt Consuelo's voice—," the child has a remarkable epiphany, an insight into the artifice of identity which reflects many of the points I have been making here:

> . . . I felt: you are an *I*,
> you are an *Elizabeth*,
> you are one of *them*.
> *Why* should you be one, too?

And, glancing around her at "trousers and skirts and boots," she confesses,

> I knew that nothing stranger
> had ever happened, that nothing
> stranger could ever happen.[39]

There is, says Bishop, "nothing stranger" than being a human being, than being, specifically, a *female* human being ("those awful hanging breasts"). And, like Millay, Moore, and others, Bishop may have felt that such "strangeness," intensified by the gaze of a voyeuristic public, could only be confronted through the deliberate estrangement of literal or figurative costume—"long dresses, trailing ones," or a tricorne hat and a "great cape." For her, as for her precursors, a central imperative of the woman poet's career in the twentieth century was eventually to be summarized by the advice that, in the wonderful poem entitled "Pink Dog," she offered to a naked and hairless female dog in Brazil: "Dress up! Dress up and dance at Carnival!"[40]

### Notes

1. Wallace Stevens, *Bowl, Cat and Broomstick*, in *The Palm at the End of the Mind: Selected Poems and a Play*, ed. Holly Stevens (New York: Vintage, 1972), 28. All references will be to this edition, and page numbers will be included in the text.

   For a valuable discussion of this play from another perspective, see A. Walton Litz, "Introduction to *Bowl, Cat and Broomstick*," in *Quarterly Review of Literature* 16 (1969): 230–35.

2. For a sardonic discussion of "female writers" with "three names," see Nathanael West, *Miss Lonelyhearts* (New York: New Directions, 1969), 13–14.

3. While she was at Vassar, Millay published poems in the *Forum*, *Poetry: A Magazine of Verse*, and the *Yale Review*; her most gratifying part was in a play of John Masefield's about which the Laureate himself wrote her a fan letter.

4. Whether Millay's admirers decided, with Arthur Ficke, that in "Renascence" she had "a real vision, such as Coleridge might have seen" and, with Floyd Dell, that her poem was "comparable in its power and vision to 'The Hound of Heaven,'" or whether, with Edward Davison, her detractors deplored the "girlish pretty-pretty-ness" of some of her lines, they were defining her as a literary anachronism just like Stevens's Claire Dupray. Ficke is quoted in Millay's *Letters*, 118; Dell and Davison are both quoted in Norman Brittin, *Edna St. Vincent Millay*, rev. ed. (Boston: Twayne, 1982), 33.

5. Elizabeth Atkins, *Edna St. Vincent Millay and Her Times* (New York: Russell & Russell, 1964), 70, vii.

6. On Lowell, see C. David Heymann, *American Aristocracy: The Lives and Times of James Russell, Amy, and Robert Lowell* (New York: Dodd, Mead, 1980), 228; on Wylie, see Judith Farr, *The Life and Art of Elinor Wylie* (Baton Rouge: Louisiana State University Press, 1983), 13.

7. Leavis is quoted in James D. Brophy, *Edith Sitwell: The Symbolist Order* (Carbondale: Southern Illinois University Press, 1968), xii.

8. Pound is quoted in Heymann, 198; Thomas Wolfe, *The Web and the Rock* (New York: Harper and Brothers, 1939), 482–83; cited in Farr, 19. Millay was also fictionalized as Rita in Edmund Wilson's *I Thought of Daisy* (New York: Farrar, Straus & Giroux, 1953).

9. *The Waste Land: A Facsimile and Transcript of the Original Drafts Including the Annotations of Ezra Pound*, ed. Valerie Eliot (New York: Harcourt Brace Jovanovich, 1971), 27.

10. Indeed, in letters to friends, Stevens confided that her innovative art "is a good deal more important than what Williams does" and that "she is one of the angels: her style is an angelic style." See *The Letters of Wallace Stevens*, ed. Holly Stevens (New York: Knopf, 1966), 278, 290; Ezra Pound, "Marianne Moore and Mina Loy," in *Marianne Moore: A Collection of Critical Essays*, ed. Charles Tomlinson (Englewood Cliffs, N.J.: Prentice-Hall, 1969), 46–47; and T. S. Eliot, "Marianne Moore," in Tomlinson, 48–51. Interestingly, in the last paragraph of his brief piece, Pound significantly qualified his praise by remarking patronizingly that "these girls have written a distinctly national product, they have written something which could not have come out of any other country, and (while I have before now seen a deal of rubbish by both of them) they are interesting and readable (by me, that is)." (47)

11. Eliot, "Marianne Moore," 48.

12. *Selected Essays of William Carlos Williams* (New York: Random House, 1954), 121, 292. In *The Autobiography*, Williams similarly recalls "her red hair plaited and wound twice about the fine skull" ([New York: Random House, 1951], 146).

13. M. L. Rosenthal, *The Modern Poets: A Critical Introduction* (New York: Oxford University Press, 1960), 142; and Roy Harvey Pearce, "Marianne Moore," in Tomlinson, 150. Pearce added that "Her yes! is muted, cautious, and somewhat finicking . . . but it is as authentic as Molly Bloom's" (157–58).

14. See T. Tambimuttu, ed., *Festschrift for Marianne Moore's Seventy-Seventh Birthday* (New York: Tambimuttu & Mass, 1964); for equally dramatic evidence of Moore's charismatic public "image," see also "The Ford Letters," in *A Marianne Moore Reader* (New York: Viking, 1961), 215–24.

15. Marcia Westkott, *The Feminist Legacy of Karen Horney* (New Haven: Yale University Press, 1986), 190.

16. Ibid., 191.

17. Luce Irigaray, *This Sex Which Is Not One*, trans. Catherine Porter (Ithaca: Cornell University Press, 1985), 133; see also Joan Rivière, "Womanliness as a Masquerade," *International Journal of Psychoanalysis* 10 (1929): 303–13.

18. Quoted by Peter Brazeau in *Parts of a World: Wallace Stevens Remembered* (New York: Random House, 1983), 211.

19. Millay, *Letters*, 99–100.

20. Bonnie Costello, *Marianne Moore: Imaginary Possessions* (Cambridge: Harvard University Press, 1981), 15.

21. T. S. Eliot, "Tradition and the Individual Talent," in *Selected Essays: 1917–1932* (New York: Harcourt, Brace, 1932), 10.

22. William Carlos Williams, "The Great American Novel," in *Imaginations*, ed. Webster Schott (London: Macgibbon & Kee, 1970), 169.

23. Edna St. Vincent Millay, "The Strawberry Shrub," in *Collected Poems*, ed. Norma Millay (New York: Harper and Row, 1956), 455.

24. *Complete Poems of Marianne Moore* (New York: Macmillan/Viking, 1967), 144. All references will be to this edition, and page numbers will be included in the text.

25. Elizabeth Bishop, "Efforts of Affection," in *The Complete Prose of Elizabeth Bishop* (New York: Farrar, Straus & Giroux, 1984), 144.

26. Ibid.

27. See Adrienne Rich, "Compulsory Heterosexuality and Lesbian Existence," in *Blood, Bread, and Poetry* (New York: Norton, 1986), 23–75.

28. Laurence Stapleton, *Marianne Moore: The Poet's Advance* (Princeton: Princeton University Press, 1978), 39.

29. See Hugh Kenner, *The Invisible Poet: T. S. Eliot* (New York: McDowell Obolensky, 1959).

30. See Stapleton, xii.

31. Included in Tambimuttu, 70.

32. On the dead pharaohs, see Millay, "Epitaph for the Race of Man": 6, "See where Capella with her golden kids," in *Collected Poems*, 706; for "the king is dead," see Moore, "No Swan So Fine," in *Complete Poems*, 19.

33. Randall Jarrell, *Kipling, Auden & Co.: Essays and Reviews, 1935–1964* (New York: Farrar, Straus & Giroux, 1980), 128.

34. Christina Rossetti, "Monna Innominata," in *The Complete Poems of Christina Rossetti: A Variorum Edition*, Vol. 2, ed. R. W. Crump (Baton Rouge: Louisiana State University Press, 1986), 86.

35. Donald Hall, to whom Moore admitted "influences from prose," somewhat disingenuously explains that "what she means is that she admires certain felicitous phrases which she encounters in prose and which she often includes with full attribution in her poetry" (Hall, *Marianne Moore: The Cage and the Animal* [New York: Pegasus, 1970], 56).

36. Bonnie Costello, "The Feminine Language of Marianne Moore," in *Women and Language in Literature and Society*, eds. Sally McConnell-Ginet, Ruth Borker, and Nelly Furman (New York: Praeger, 1980), 225.

37. Westkott, 193.

38. Ibid.

39. Elizabeth Bishop, "In the Waiting Room," in *Geography III* (New York: Farrar, Straus & Giroux, 1976), 3–8.

40. Elizabeth Bishop, "Pink Dog," in *Complete Poems: 1927–1979* (New York: Farrar, Straus & Giroux, 1983), 191.

Marianne Moore, 1968
*(Courtesy of the Rosenbach Museum and Library)*

# 4

# Marianne Moore, the Maternal Hero, and American Women's Poetry

*Alicia Ostriker*

I want a hero: an uncommon want," writes Byron in the opening salvo of *Don Juan*, noting that heroes are a dime a dozen these days:

> I want a hero: an uncommon want,
> When every year and month sends forth a new one,
> Till, after cloying the gazettes with cant,
> The age discovers he is not the true one.[1]

There follows a list of some two or three dozen British and French military and political heroes, whom Byron politely calls "Followers of fame . . . 'farrow' of that sow," including, of course, both Lord Nelson and Napoleon, none of them quite agreeable to the poet's purpose. For as Byron well knew, and we know still, the hero in Western history and art is primarily a warrior, the embodiment of power, prowess, and patriotism. Alternatively he may be tragic, a sublime being destined to be destroyed. He may be an adventurer, an Odysseus, a Lawrence of Arabia. Or he may be Promethean, the Satanic or Byronic hero, darkly rebellious, vibrantly and excitingly sinful, whose purest avatars at the present moment are probably rock stars. Then there is the poet-hero, from at least Dante onward, including in English and American poetry Milton, Blake, Wordsworth, and Whitman, among others.

Among Marianne Moore's contemporaries, the hero as poet assumes a variety of postures. Eliot disguises himself at first as J. Alfred Prufrock, the definitively modern antihero, and ends up as the poet whose role is to "purify the dialect of the tribe,"[2] apotheosize an England at war, and direct our spirits toward that still point of the turning world which is beyond the world and redeems us from the world. The warrior Coriolanus and the Christian martyr Thomas Becket are among

Eliot's exemplary heroes en route. The young Ezra Pound, equally enthusiastic over the adventurous and beauty-loving troubadour and the vigorously bloody-minded Renaissance soldier ("Damn it all! all this our South stinks peace"),[3] later champions such figures as Odysseus, Jefferson, Adams, Confucius, certain Chinese dynastic rulers, Mussolini. Williams creates Paterson, the sleeping giant. Wallace Stevens proposes the artist-hero as metaphysician. Can one, in such a heterogeneous array, find heroic points in common? The *large* gesture is one, perhaps, for the heroisms imagined by our poets tend to cover amplitudes of territory in space and time. The hero represents an embattled Truth, an embattled transcendence, an ideality to which reality is enemy. Needless to say, he is masculine, although he may be accompanied by a female or females as objects of love and/or sources of inspiration—Eliot's virgins, Pound's ladies, goddesses and muses, Williams's Park, Stevens's interior paramour—who are either more natural or more supernatural than the poet-hero himself. For the world of the hero in our tradition is strangely gender-marked, so that, or perhaps in order that, females in it cannot occupy the same plane of existence as males; the American Adam is not the American Eve. Finally, the hero is distinguished from us who read about him; that is the point. *He* is sublime; *we* are our sweating selves.

I make these unremarkable observations in order to draw attention to the peculiar oddity of Marianne Moore's "The Hero." Originally the third part of a three-part poem published in the June 1932 *Poetry*, called "Part of a Novel, Part of a Poem, Part of a Play" (the first two parts were "The Steeple-Jack" and "The Student"), it was revised for the 1935 *Selected Poems* and ultimately published as a separate poem.

Formally, "The Hero" consists of stanzas emphatically marked by closure and linkage—the first and the two final lines of all but the third stanza rhyme with "hero"—combined with some quintessentially playful Marianne Moore run-on and divagation, or apparent divagation and eccentricity. It is a poem evidently antithetic to linearity, moving sidewise or crabwise as it does into its task of defining the hero, which is not actually announced as its task until the poem is over. The first stanza seems to have nothing to do with heroism, only with "personal liking"; and when "the hero" appears in the second stanza, he sounds not at all heroic, for he is merely like us in experiencing personal dislike and fear. "We do not like some things, and the hero / doesn't." In the mid-third stanza begins a minimally linked sequence of attributes and figures from the Old Testament, history, art, and anecdote, which are presumably supposed to exemplify heroism, until in the last stanza "the hero" is defined not by his action but by, so to speak, his ingestion and perception: by his *form* of perception and by *what* he perceives:

> It is not what I eat that is
> my natural meat,
> the hero says. He's not out

> seeing a sight but the rock
> crystal thing to see—the startling El Greco
> brimming with inner light—that
> covets nothing that it has let go.[4]

This definition is, it would be safe to say, elliptic, cryptic, even a shade mystic. Yet as if her exposition had been entirely logical and clear, and with the strong closing gesture of an extra rhyme word in the sequence *El Greco, let go, know, hero,* the poet dismisses us with a prim summarizing nod: "This then you may know / as the hero."

What is the "this then" that we "may know" (or may not)? By their fruits ye shall know them, possibly. But despite the poet's final apparent firmness, Moore's hero is indeterminate rather than determined. We may "know" him not in essence or abstract but by some or all of the previous signs. He is like us, motivated by personal liking, disliking, fear and steadfastness—but who are "we," and why have we become "you" at poem's end? Does Moore's pronoun shift mean the hero is special and unique, above and unlike us, or not? He is, and here is a jump, "vexing" like Jacob and Joseph, two Old Testament dreamers and outsiders, but also like Cincinnatus and Regulus, two Roman soldiers and leaders, the first of whom may have reminded Moore of George Washington, as a patrician who preferred retirement to rule, and the second Lincoln, as he was assassinated. The hero is patient and hopeful despite despair, like Pilgrim in his progress. He is furthermore, and here comes another of Moore's videolike cuts, exemplified by a Negro groundskeeper at Mt. Vernon who answers a shrill tourist decorously, with a "sense of human dignity / and reverence for mystery" (George and Martha Washington's dignity? His own?) along with the self-effacement of a shadow. In the last of Moore's Biblical references, the hero like Moses "would not be grandson to Pharoah," which may mean that he would reject power and wealth in a society based on slavery, would conduct an exodus from slavery (and is thus perhaps linked with the dignified frock-coated Negro), or would prefer spiritual reality to material appearance. As someone who is "not out / seeing a sight" but seeing the "inner light" in objects, he is what he sees; William Blake might put it that he becomes what he beholds. Lastly, he is generous rather than greedy. Like the El Greco of its final stanza, the refracted and refractory idea of heroism this poem suggests is startling, but perhaps the most startling element in it is an analogy I have so far omitted to mention. In stanza 4, the hero is said to be

> lenient, looking
> upon a fellow creature's error with the
> feelings of a mother—a
> woman or a cat.

As at the outer edges of "The Hero" occurs a pronoun shift, at its crux occurs a gender and species shift. The hero as "a mother—a / woman or a cat" has no analogies so far as I know among Moore's forebears or male contemporaries, nor is leniency a typical attribute of heroes in the twentieth century or elsewhere.

To foreground the figure of the maternal hero in Moore might lead us in the direction of biographical speculation; Moore after all lived with her own mother for much of her life, and adopted behavior which might reasonably be considered maternal (if not always "lenient") toward other poets and as editor of the *Dial*.[5] However, my interest here is in Moore's poetry, and in suggesting that our usual view of Moore as an eccentric whom we expect to charm rather than disturb us, an observer concerned with objects rather than self, and a ladylike moralist preaching only the most conventional and respectable morals, stands in need of modification. Here is Randall Jarrell's judgment, stated with characteristic verve:

> Some of her poems have the manners or manner of ladies who learned a little before birth not to mention money, who neither point nor touch, and who scrupulously abstain from the mixed, live vulgarity of life. . . . We are uncomfortable—or else too comfortable—in a world in which feeling, affection, charity, are so entirely divorced from sexuality and power, the bonds of the flesh.[6]

For Roy Harvey Pearce, Moore's early poems are "so cautious and cautionary, so essentially uncommitted," while her late poems seem to him "brilliant exercises in rhetoric" which "are not quite poems" and the critic remarks on "the poet's polite and lady like presence. . . . She is most certainly not tormented . . . by things as they are."[7] These are the judgments of admirers, as is the conventional wisdom of the *Norton Anthology of Modern Poetry* editor whose preface describes Moore as "unassuming," "unpretentious," and says her "humility is vast."[8] I have argued elsewhere that criticism like poetry is often gender-marked, and these quotations are eminent examples. No major male poet would be praised in these faintly condescending terms, although for Anne Bradstreet, Emily Dickinson, H. D., and other women poets "*ad feminam* criticism" has until very recently been the rule more often than the exception.[9] Moore's foes also complain of her decorum. Here, for example, is Gilbert Sorrentino in an essay entitled "An Octopus /of ice:"

> Miss Moore has never looked beneath the first layer, because what is there is ugly, corrupt, and filled with the kind of life and turmoil that eccentricity cannot grapple with. . . . The product of such hysterical safety measures is the hysterical, safe poem. . . . A poet, presented as "major," who has worked for half a century, has avoided confronting, even once, in her entire body of work, the fact that the nation is brutalized, corrupted, and perhaps hopelessly psychopathic . . . since the poet had no emotion save that of the most bitterly conformist, no response but that which is the expected one.

Sorrentino does not fail to add the observation that "there is no sexuality."[10] To her supporters and detractors alike, Moore is first and last a proper lady.

There would be no point arguing that modesty, propriety, restraint, and the celebrated virtues of surface order are unimportant for Moore; clearly their importance is tremendous. As an artist, she is dazzling in part precisely for her mastery of surfaces, just as within her literary milieu she beguiled her peers by the lifelong performance—doubtless heartfelt and sincere—of the role of lady. Nonetheless, I want to propose a more complicated and even contradictory Marianne Moore whose authentic modesty veils an equally authentic arrogance (Donald Hall finely demonstrates this in his book *Marianne Moore: The Cage and the Animal*), whose visible propriety and decorum mask a less visible subversiveness and anger, whose morality, far from being conventional, is radical enough to irritate some of her readers—a poet who admired William Blake and the Hebrew Prophets, and whose force is, in her words, "Disguised by what / might seem the opposite."

The Marianne Moore who intrigues me is a doubled creature, simultaneously highly civilized and, in Adrienne Rich's phrase, "disloyal to civilization."[11] Unlike some of her more renowned Modernist contemporaries, she expresses no nostalgia for the hierarchic structures of past literature, religion, and social order, nor does she yearn toward hierarchy in the present. She dislikes "that which is great because something else is small" ("When I Buy Pictures," *CP*, 48). Ever the fan of democracy, she despises power, authority, and empire. She attacks ancient Egypt and ancient Rome in "The Jerboa," the France of Louis XIV in "No Swan So Fine," imperial China in "Critics and Connoisseurs," and imperial England in "Sojourn in the Whale." This last poem is one which metaphorically identifies England's righteous colonial swallowing of Ireland with patriarchy's oppression of women. A half century before feminists influenced by Marx and Fanon began describing women as a preeminently colonized class, here is how Moore addresses Ireland:

> you have lived and lived on every kind of shortage.
>     You . . . have heard men say:
> "There is a feminine temperament in direct contrast to ours
>
> which makes her do these things. Circumscribed by a
>     heritage of blindness and native
>     incompetence, she will be wise and will be forced to give in.
> Compelled by experience, she will turn back;
>
> water seeks its own level":
>     and you have smiled. "Water in motion is far
>     from level." You have seen it, when obstacles happened to bar
> the path, rise automatically.

(CP, 90)

Pitying and mocking the central institution of patriarchal culture, marriage, Moore anatomizes the Adam who "experiences a solemn joy / in seeing that he has become an idol," the Adam who finds marriage

> "a very trivial object indeed"
> to have destroyed the attitude
> in which he stood—
> the ease of a philosopher
> unfathered by a woman.

Moore's Eve "attests / that men have power / and sometimes one is made to feel it," and that

> "Men are monopolists
> of 'stars, garters, buttons
> and other shining baubles'—
> unfit to be the guardians
> of another person's happiness."

> (*CP*, 62–70)

The stars and garters are, of course, insignia of a ruling class, while the shining baubles possessed by men may be either jewels or women. Moore's critique of patriarchal self-inflation parallels that of Virginia Woolf in *A Room of One's Own*; her critique of marriage reminds one of Woolf's in *To the Lighthouse*, only it is a little less charitable. This same Moore who, we are told, evades issues of power and sexuality, asks at the close of "Critics and Connoisseurs":

> What is
> there in being able
> to say that one has dominated the stream in an attitude of self-defense;
> in proving that one has had the experience
> of carrying a stick?

> (*CP*, 39)

If this were not so extremely polite it would be extremely vicious. It is of such work that the young poet H. D. may have been thinking when, in a review of Marianne Moore's poems published in the August 1916 *Egoist*, at the outset of a lifelong friendship, she portrayed Moore as the "perfect swordsman, the perfect technician" who confronts the dull adversary with pity: "my sword is very much keener than your sword, my hand surer than your hand—but you shall not know that I know that you are beaten."[12]

More recently the adversarial or combative Moore has been described by Helen Vendler, who observes that male critics make her "more shrinking and squeamish than she is" and suggests that "perhaps Moore's contempt for the world of male power provokes a counterattack on what may seem to some her miniature version of life." Vendler notes the "asperity" of Moore's poems in her late twenties and early thirties, which "display a whole gallery of self-incriminating fools—self-important, illiterate, unimaginative, sentimental, defensive, pompous, cruel." However, Vendler adds, "Hers is the aggression of the silent, well-brought-up girl who thinks up mute rejoinders during every parlor conversation."[13] Well said; yet here I fear we are back to a diminished Moore: not a strong-minded angry woman but an overgrown girl, whose critiques are personal and private rather than generic, social, political, and historical. Everyone is so fond of the Marianne Moore who is a sort of household pet that it seems somehow criminal to point out that she bites. One worries that her admirers will stop *liking* her then. Yet bite she does. And I should point out that it would be unthinkable to describe any poet we considered major as a large child; imagine seeing Robert Lowell's aggression as that of a spoiled boy, or T. S. Eliot's representations of sex in *The Waste Land* as those of a frightened boy.

Besides recognizing more fully Marianne Moore's adversarial inclinations, I believe we need to apprehend her as something of a feminine visionary. Secular as her writing may be when we compare it with, for example, that of H. D., Moore is nonetheless a poet who imagines alternatives to the way we live, think, feel, and does so in modes which we may identify as gynocentric and discover as well in the work of other women poets. Let me list, very briefly, a few of the more significant qualities which Moore shares with other women writers, not in order to imply that gender is a rigidly determining category for the artist but to suggest the shade of difference it may make and to offer a context which will clarify what Moore attempts to do with the figure of the maternal hero. First, Moore's assertion that "The Past Is the Present" and her inclination to skip and jump among the centuries within a given poem indicate that she deviates from the high-Modernist assumption that the modern world has been sundered from the past; nowhere in her work is the sense of temporal loss we find in Yeats, Pound, or Eliot. Her way of transforming the temporal to the spatial, in museumlike poems which exhibit bits of history as if they were interesting artifacts or fossils, coincides, however, with Gertrude Stein's continuing present, with H. D.'s palimpsests whereby the Trojan War, the conquest of Greece by Rome, and World Wars I and II are recurrences of the same event, and with Adrienne Rich's *aperçu*, "Time is male," each of which exemplifies in different ways what Julia Kristeva has called "women's time," in tacit resistance to "the time of history."[14] Again, her affirmative use of animals as lightly disguised versions of herself harks back to Emily Dickinson and forward to poets as various as May Swenson and Elizabeth Bishop on the one hand, Margaret Atwood, Maxine Kumin, and Anne Sexton on the other, and to the quite widespread tendency among contemporary women poets to represent nature, or the body of the world, as continuous with, rather than disjunct from, our own bodies.[15] Her imagery of disguises, veils, and armor is shared by innumerable women artists. Her style, with its charm, brio, and dash, its elusiveness and its profoundly comic valence, might be threaded back to Anne Bradstreet and Dickinson, in neither of whom does Puritanism preclude humor. "God be with the clown," said Dickinson, and there is a whole story to be written of the ways women writers use humor as a means of resistance and pleasure in a literary culture which privileges tragedy.[16] Then there is the curious way Moore plays with gender distinctions as if, at times, she did not take them quite seriously—and the fact that Dickinson does the same, as does Virginia Woolf in *Orlando*, Anne Sexton when she is "tired of the gender of things," Diane Wakoski when she disguises herself as the "Lady Bank Dick," Adrienne Rich when in "Diving into the Wreck" she sees a mermaid and merman and recognizes "I am she: I am he," Marilyn Hacker when she writes a sequence of gay love sonnets, Jorie Graham in a "Self-Portrait as Apollo and Daphne."[17]

If each of these devices is a way of imagining the world as other than it is (less rigid, less oppressive, less sad, and above all less governed by authorities exterior to personal judgment), it remains the case that Moore is in no sense a poet of explicit protest. On the contrary, her consistent stance toward the world is one of a rather determined affection. Her social or political jibes are not diatribes. Philosophically she prefers admiration to confrontation. But with this we return to the maternal hero, a recurrent figure in Moore's poetry, as affection is a recurrent tone in her temperament, balancing—perhaps explaining—the acerbity which is its countertone. The maternal hero is affectionate, nurturing, protective; she needs to be, for there are enemies at hand. The maternal hero is courageous but also patient; is often an artist of some sort; and is plainly a figure for the poet, Marianne Moore, in her satiric-visionary phase.

I will confine myself to three examples. The pre-war poem "Bird-Witted" invites us by its title to expect a dissertation on folly or triviality. The text of the poem constitutes a rebuke of that very expectation, an implied criticism of our condescending attitude toward both birds and mothers, and a celebration of heroic nurture. The hero in this poem is a mother mockingbird whose once flutelike voice, the observer notes, has grown "harsh" with caring for her fledglings, now grown as large as herself. Most of the poem is preoccupied with a description of the "astute grown bird" and her "feebly solemn" young, but two-thirds through the poem we see "A piebald cat . . . / . . . slowly creeping toward the trim / trio on the tree stem," and the close depicts "the parent darting down, nerved by what chills / the blood" as she

> wages deadly combat,
>     and half kills
>         with bayonet beak and
>         cruel wings, the

```
    intellectual cautious-
    ly c r e e p i n g cat.
```

(*CP*, 105–6)

The poem plays with the idea of feminine instinct or passion versus masculine intellect, and its semi-gossipy tone suggests that it might be a literary as well as an avian anecdote. Unquestionably literary is "The Paper Nautilus," which locates an artist very like Marianne Moore in a literary context we can all recognize:

```
        For authorities whose hopes
    are shaped by mercenaries?
        writers entrapped by
        teatime fame and by
    commuters' comforts? Not for these
        the paper nautilus
        constructs her thin glass shell.
```

(*CP*, 121)

That Moore's armored animals are emblems of the self has long been recognized. In this poem, the nautilus is a creature for whom creation and procreation are fused. Within her carefully constructed and guarded shell, "her perishable / souvenir of hope" with its dull white outside and glossy inside, lie eggs that are "hid but . . . not crushed" until they hatch and "free it when they are freed." The eggs may be poems, or the meanings of poems; words, or the meanings of words. The nautilus as creator is a "watchful / maker," as against the mechanical watch-maker God of the philosophers. She is explicitly a hero, like Hercules; she is also demonic, "a devil- / fish"; and finally she has created "love / [the] only fortress /strong enough to trust to," an image tacitly contrasted to the narcissism of "commuters' comforts" and the financial and military implications of "mercenaries," at the poem's opening. Grace Schulman points out that Moore in 1940 may have had in mind the supposedly indestructible set of fortifications along the eastern border of France called the Maginot Line. In 1967, according to Schulman, Moore tried to describe her feelings about the Vietnam War: "I try to comfort myself with the thought that they are learning better why they are fighting. But when they say, 'This may go on till summer,' we are doomed, I feel." After a digression to other topics, she quoted the last stanza of "The Paper Nautilus,"

```
        round which the arms had
    wound themselves as if they knew love
        is the only fortress
        strong enough to trust to
```

(*CP*, 122)

and added: "Now that is as specific as I can put it. If you felt that way about any people, you couldn't fight them. You couldn't want to kill anyone."[18]

Numerous Moore poems pursue similar lines, as the poet continued all her life to seek a "refuge":

> a refuge for me
> from egocentricity
> and its propensity to bisect,
> mis-state, misunderstand
> and obliterate continuity?

("Tell Me, Tell Me," *CP*, 231)

Let me look, finally, at "In Distrust of Merits," one of Moore's most famous and most controversial poems (*CP*, 136–38). Early admirers in the aftermath of World War II commended it for "sincerity" (Richard Eberhart) and "the direct communication of honest feeling" (Oscar Williams), while Randall Jarrell felt it an excessively literary work of a "timid" and "private spirited" woman safe in her garden.[19] Helen Vendler dislikes it: "Pressed into unwise explicitness by her horror of the Second World War, she wrote a bad poem called 'In Distrust of Merits,' which was monotonously anthologized because of its concurrence with popular sentiment. . . . In that instance emotion overpowered Moore so that implication was sacrificed to banality of outcry."[20] Bonnie Costello, who elaborately describes the figures of combat in Moore, nonetheless concurs, though in milder tones, with Vendler's judgment: "In Moore's best work the conventional wisdom of combat is converted by context into a fresh discovery of the power of art. The poems that pronounce about war and peace show too much the pressure of news."[21]

I do not think this is a bad poem; I think it concurs with popular sentiment in about the same way as the Sermon on the Mount concurs with popular Christianity; and, again, the accusation of banality makes me wonder if there is not a gender bias which enables us to assume that a lady poet is being banal where a gentleman poet is being profound. I wonder, that is, if anyone would dare to hint that the climax of "Little Gidding" concurs with popular sentiment or that the line "history is now and England" is possibly sentimental. Laurence Stapleton demonstrates that Moore was working on "In Distrust of Merits" for years,[22] so it can hardly be considered the spontaneous overflow of powerful emotion. Nor is it self-evident that a poem about art is necessarily better than a poem about war, unless, of course, the point is that girls and ladies may be interested in art but may not be interested in politics. Equally baffling is the notion that "In Distrust of Merits" is simple, easy, or direct. Geoffrey Hartmann astutely calls it a "dialogue of one, an ironic crossfire that continually denies and reasserts the possibility of a selfless assertion of the self."[23] An essay by Susan Schweik on this poem and the issue of gender in war poetry notes its "tension between moral self-confidence on the one hand and felt or feared inadequacy on the other" and argues that it may be read as either an inconclusive or a conclusive "just war" plot, as patriotic or anti-patriotic.[24] "In Distrust of Merits" seems to me a difficult poem both in its indeterminacy and because it contains a moral imperative that I cannot yet follow in my life, though I should like to be able to.

Like "The Paper Nautilus," this poem opens with a rhetorical question which seems to invite a negative response: "Strengthened to live, strengthened to die for / medals and positioned victories?" followed by an announcement:

> They're fighting, fighting, fighting the blind
> man who thinks he sees—
> who cannot see that the enslaver is
> enslaved; the hater, harmed.
>
> (*CP*, 136)

But this confident assertion is more problematic than it sounds. For the "they" who are fighting is undetermined; can we be sure the poet refers exclusively to the Allies? Are we sure of the identity of the blind man? Is he necessarily Hitler or Mussolini? Moore has made the war scrupulously unspecific geographically and historically so as to evoke the idea of pure combat independent of time, place, and particular politics. "They're fighting, fighting, fighting"—each time that refrain is repeated, and it is repeated with increasing desperation throughout the poem, we learn more of what that initial blindness means, where it resides, and why it is so difficult to fight successfully. "In Distrust of Merits" is a poem engaged in wishful thinking, or thinking which wishes things to be other than they are because the way that they are is intolerable. It is a poem which deepens as it goes along, as it seems to me, uttering a series of absurdities which it recognizes as such, at each recognition entering a deeper level of the wish and a more painful sense of its impossibility. Thus,

> They're
> fighting in deserts and caves, one by
> one, in battalions and squadrons;
> they're fighting that I
> may yet recover from the disease, My
> Self; some have it lightly; some will die
>
> (*CP*, 136)

is magnificently compressed, in its ambiguous use of "I" and "My / Self" to mean either Marianne Moore or anyone, and it is exquisitely poised on the line endings which illustrate it. The I / my / die rhyme underscores the lethal potential of the ego, while the inconspicuous splitting of "My / Self" into "some . . . some" implies simultaneously that ego is legion and that it is communal. For a brief almost Whitmanlike moment, the self is both one and many. But the passage is obviously an absurdity because we know, and Moore knows, that the Allied soldiers (as well as the Axis soldiers) are not fighting for the transcendence of the ego in the sense of being motivated by it. How grave the disease of the self is becomes clearer a little later:

> We
> vow, we make this promise
>
> to the fighting—it's a promise—"We'll
>     never hate black, white, red, yellow, Jew,
> Gentile, Untouchable."

Immediately afterward follows the recognition: "We are / not competent to / make our vows" (*CP*, 137). "In Distrust of Merits" swings on these gestures of angry, frustrated recoil against the poet's anguished need to have "the fighting" mean something, come to something. It is bad enough that "we" make ridiculous promises no army asks us to make, but it is worse that we cannot hope to keep them. The fact that "the fighting" here is a syntactically indeterminate term which we can read as meaning "the fighting men" or "those who are fighting," but also as "the *act* of fighting," the war itself as well as those engaged in it, deepens the absurdity. The chiasmic movement of "vow . . . promise— / it's a promise . . . / . . . vows" is a dipping from adult to childish locution—as if "we" were children earnestly trying to make ourselves heard over an adult brawl, promising to be good if they'll stop—and then back, at the point of recoil. Increasingly the poem takes the tack of insisting that war makes demands on the noncombatants. In proportion to our realization that the war is not in itself noble, that the world continues to be an orphan's home—in proportion as we force ourselves to look at the quiet form upon the dust which may be a dead soldier or may be all Europe, so we are driven to do something. But what can we do? The "patience patience / patience" (*CP*, 137) the poet recommends collapses rapidly (like Job's) into despair:

> Shall
> we never have peace without sorrow?
> without pleas of the dying for
>     help that won't come?

(CP, 137–38)

Yet if we insist on somehow extracting life from "these agonies" (*CP*, 138), we can acknowledge and "fight" in ourselves the hate, the selfishness, the intolerance, the arrogance we attribute to our enemies, that which "causes war, but I would not believe it" (*CP*, 138). In 1939 Moore had written her brother a letter mentioning an essay by Reinhold Neibuhr which "reminds us that intolerance is at work in us all *in all* countries—that we ourselves 'persecute' Jews and Negroes & submit to wrongful tyranny. Or at least feel 'superior' in sundry ways."[25] Who is that blind man who thinks he sees? Alas, it is I.

As is so often the case in Moore, there is a complicated play of pronouns throughout this poem, ultimately governed by the inconspicuously uttered wish, "be joined at last, be joined," which at first has a public subject, the three world religions of Judaism, Christianity, and Islam, but by implication a private and more difficult one. "They" (the fighters) are juxtaposed to "I" or "we" the onlookers; between them is a gap which Moore attempts to close, first by attributing her motivation (love) to them, latterly by demanding their reality (war) of herself. Fifteen years later, and on a vastly magnified scale, an almost identical movement structures H. D.'s epic *Helen in Egypt*, another poem which responds to World War II (and all wars which precede it) in female terms, as it shifts from locating "love" within the archetypal warrior Achilles to locating "war" within the archetypal noncombatant Helen.

What of the end of Moore's poem? Some have approved, others have disparaged Moore's rhetoric:

> I inwardly did nothing.
> O Iscariot-like crime!
> Beauty is everlasting
> and dust is for a time.

> (*CP*, 138)

But what exactly do the lines mean? This conclusion is more often judged than it is explicated. How does penultimate self-accusation connect to ultimate affirmation? Does it connect at all? Does Moore's evocation of beauty, so close to that of the conclusion of Stevens's "Peter Quince at the Clavier," deepen her Judas like guilt or mitigate it? Perhaps both, paradoxically, simultaneously, much as the Sanskrit utterance of faith at the close of *The Waste Land* allows itself to be read either ironically or (as Eliot's subsequent career suggests) as an invitation to spiritual renewal beyond the poem's borders. But the accent is on hope rather than hopelessness, and I suspect that it is this, the refusal quite to collapse in despair and self-hatred at the world's evil, the insistence on loving it "nevertheless," that most discomforts Moore's critics. For the correct stance of the Modernist poem is irony and detachment, and Moore is disconcertingly neither detached nor ironic in this poem. Her "I," which troublesomely includes us, her readers, asks us not to lament evil or resign ourselves to it but to fight it inwardly. Well—we are literary people, we think. That's not our job; poetry makes nothing happen; et cetera.

When Elizabeth Bishop in the 1955 "Invitation to Miss Marianne Moore" politely invites the elder poet to "come flying" and imagines her "Mounting the sky with natural heroism," as well as "a slight censorious frown" and the inclination to "bravely deplore," we hear a daughterly mix of affection, admiration, and gentle mockery. Moore many years before had privately urged Bishop to do a bit more deploring herself. While praising the draft of Bishop's story "In Prison," Moore added, "I can't help wishing that you would sometime in some way, risk . . . some characteristically private defiance of the significantly detestable."[26] It was advice which Bishop resisted, and which may have irritated her. Bishop's political poetry is in some ways less oblique than Moore's, in other ways more so; nor is the maternal stance one she adopted for herself. Yet it is worth noting how frequently Moore's sense of maternal heroism surfaces in the poems of postwar women poets who do not on the face of it seem "influenced" by her. Adrienne Rich, in her autobiographical essay "When We Dead Awaken," notes that during her student days Moore was "the woman poet most admired (by men)" but suggests she was too "maidenly" a model for herself.[27] Yet to quote only a single one of the many Rich poems which advocate a Moore-like labor of self-examination connected to the duty of human nurture and human connection, here are some lines from a poem called "Hunger":

> I know I'm partly somewhere else—
> huts strung across a drought-stretched land
> not mine, dried breasts, mine and not mine, a mother
> watching my children shrink with hunger.
> . . . . . . . . . . . . . . . . . . . . . . . . . . . . . . .
> I stand convicted by all my convictions. . . .
> . . . . . . . . . . . . . . . . . . . . . . . . . . . . . . .
> I'm alive to want more than life,
> want it for others starving and unborn. . . .
> . . . . . . . . . . . . . . . . . . . . . . . . . . . . . . .
> Until we find each other, we are alone.

Moore's sense that the noncombatant is as fully implicated in war as the combatant is echoed in a poem written by Denise Levertov during the Christmas 1972 bombing of North Vietnam by the United States. The poet dreams herself dressed as a waitress with cannisters of napalm and other explosives under her apron which she uses against the President and ministers of war. The poem ends like Moore's, with two assertions which point in opposite directions:

> *O, to kill*
> *the killers!*

It is
to this extremity

the infection of their evil

thrusts us.

In another key entirely, Sharon Olds, in "The Language of the Brag," declares that she has wanted

some epic use for my excellent body,
some heroism, some American achievement
beyond the ordinary for my extraordinary self

and has found it in an unexpected place. The thick physicality of Olds's language, here as in all her work, should not obscure the parallels between her vision and Moore's. In Olds as in Moore, the ironic ascends toward the comedic, the personal self at its most intimate is most democratically collective, and the maternal is inseparable from the verbal, in a gesture that is at once defiant and celebratory:

I have lain down and sweated and shaken
and passed blood and feces and water and
slowly alone in the center of a circle I have
passed the new person out
and they have lifted the new person free of the act
and wiped the new person free of that
language of blood like praise all over the body.

I have done what you wanted to do, Walt Whitman,
Allen Ginsberg, I have done this thing,
I and the other women this exceptional
act with the exceptional heroic body,
this giving birth, this glistening verb,
and I am putting my proud American boast
right here with the others.[28]

Poems of this sort are not at present fashionable. In the cool climate of the 1980s, there is something embarrassing, even tacky, about poets who write from a sense of moral urgency, and something ridiculous about poets who would claim that motherhood, of all things, is heroic. All the more may we need such poets, just as we need to believe, in spite of the evidence, that we are responsible creatures in the world. Or as Marianne Moore delicately puts it in "Armor's Undermining Modesty," "There is the tarnish; and there, the imperishable wish." (*CP*, 152).

**Notes**

1. George Gordon, Lord Byron, "Don Juan," in *The Complete Poetical Works* (Oxford: Clarendon Press, 1986), 5: 9.

2. T. S. Eliot, "Little Gidding," in *The Complete Poems and Plays* (New York: Harcourt Brace, 1950), 141.

3. Ezra Pound, "Sestina: Altaforte," in *Personae: The Collected Shorter Poems of Ezra Pound* (New York: New Directions, 1926), 28.

4. Marianne Moore, "The Hero," in *Complete Poems of Marianne Moore* (New York: Macmillan/ Viking, 1967), 8. Hereafter *CP*.

5. Williams rather prettily captures something of Moore's maternal presence for her peers in his portrait of the young Marianne as the "caryatid" or "rafter holding up the superstructure of our uncompleted building . . . our saint—if we had one—in whom we all instinctively felt our purpose come together to form a stream" and in the famous metaphor of poet as housewife: "Miss Moore gets great pleasure from wiping soiled words." See *The Autobiography of William Carlos Williams* (New York: Random House, 1951), 146–48 and *Selected Essays of William Carlos Williams* (New York: Random House, 1954), 292. On her editorship of the *Dial*, see Donald Hall, *Marianne Moore: The Cage and the Animal* (New York: Pegasus, 1970), chap. 5. On her maternal relationship with Bishop, see Elizabeth Bishop, "Efforts of Affection: A Memoir of Marianne Moore," in *The Collected Prose of Elizabeth Bishop* (Farrar, Straus & Giroux, 1984), 121–56; Bonnie Costello, "Marianne Moore and Elizabeth Bishop: Friendship and Influence," *Twentieth Century Literature* 30 (Summer/Fall 1984): 130–49; David Kalstone, "Trial Balances: Elizabeth Bishop and Marianne Moore," *Grand Street* 3 (Autumn 1983): 115–35; and Lynn Keller, "Words Worth a Thousand Postcards: The Bishop-Moore Correspondence," *American Literature* 55 (October 1983): 405–29. The motherless Bishop met Moore in 1934, the year she graduated from college. Moore worried over Bishop's health, promoted Bishop's poetry, and played a personal and literary mentor's role to her throughout the thirties, after which the "daughter" gently distanced herself. I am indebted for my sense of this relationship to Victoria Harrison, whose dissertation-in-progress concerns Bishop's rebellions "in shades and shadows."

6. Randall Jarrell, "Her Shield," in *Poetry and the Age* (New York: Vintage, 1953), 183–84.

7. Roy Harvey Pearce, "Marianne Moore," in *Marianne Moore: A Collection of Critical Essays*, ed. Charles Tomlinson (Englewood Cliffs, N.J.: Prentice-Hall, 1969), 152, 155, 157.

8. Richard Ellmann and Robert O'Clair, eds., *The Norton Anthology of Modern Poetry* (New York: Norton, 1973), 419–20.

9. The phrase is Sandra Gilbert and Susan Gubar's; see their *Shakespeare's Sisters: Feminist Essays on Women Poets* (Bloomington: Indiana University Press, 1979), xx. See also Alicia Ostriker, *Stealing the Language: The Emergence of Women's Poetry in America* (Boston: Beacon Press, 1986), 1–6, 27–33, 47–48. A thorough discussion of gender bias in the criticism of another major Modernist is Susan Friedman, "Who Buried H. D.? A Poet, Her Critics, and Her Place in 'The Literary Tradition,'" *College English* 36 (March 1975): 801–14.

10. Gilbert Sorrentino, "An Octopus / of ice," in *Something Said: Essays* (San Francisco: North Point Press, 1984), 157–59.

11. Adrienne Rich, "Disloyal to Civilization: Feminism, Racism, Gynephobia," in *On Lies, Secrets, and Silence: Selected Prose, 1966–1978* (New York: Norton, 1979), 275–310. The phrase is from Lillian Smith: "Freud said once that a woman is not well acculturated; she is, he stressed,

retarded as a civilized person. I think what he mistook for her lack of civilization is woman's lack of *loyalty* to civilization."

12. H. D., "Marianne Moore," *Egoist* 3 (August 1916): 118.

13. Helen Vendler, *Part of Nature, Part of Us: Modern American Poets* (Cambridge: Harvard University Press, 1980), 62.

14. Kristeva links women's desire for alternative temporalities with mistrust of "civilization" and discomfort with discursive language: "Female subjectivity as it gives itself up to intuition becomes a problem with respect to a certain conception of time: time as project, teleology, linear and prospective unfolding; time as departure, progression and arrival—in other words, the time of history. It has already been abundantly demonstrated that this kind of temporality is inherent in the logical and ontological values of any civilization. . . . It might be added that this linear time is that of language considered as the enunciation of sentences (noun + verb; topic-comment; beginning-ending)." Julia Kristeva, "Women's Time," trans. Alice Jardine, *Signs: A Journal of Women in Culture and Society* 7 (Autumn 1981): 17. The temporalities Kristeva categorizes as feminine, however—repetitious or cyclical time on the one hand and "cosmic time" or "eternity" saturated with *jouissance* on the other—fail to describe Moore's way of spatializing time, although the former is evidently relevant to Stein and the latter to H. D. See my discussion of time in women's mythmaking poetry, and its relation to reevaluation of values and to formal experiment, in *Stealing the Language*, 234–38.

15. See *Stealing the Language*, 114–19; Estella Lauter, *Women as Mythmakers: Poetry and Visual Art by Twentieth-Century Women* (Bloomington: Indiana University Press, 1984), 172–202.

16. See Taffy Martin, *Marianne Moore: Subversive Modernist* (Austin: University of Texas Press, 1986), the final chapter of which is called "And You Have Smiled." See also Judy Little, *Comedy and the Woman Writer* (Lincoln: University of Nebraska Press, 1983).

17. See Anne Sexton, "Consorting with Angels," in *Complete Poems* (New York: Houghton Mifflin, 1981), 111; Diane Wakoski, "The Lament of the Lady Bank Dick," in *The Motorcycle Betrayal Poems* (New York: Simon and Schuster, 1971), 93–97; Adrienne Rich, "Diving into the Wreck," in *The Fact of a Doorframe: Poems Selected and New, 1950–1984* (New York: Norton, 1984), 162–64; Marilyn Hacker, *Love, Death, and the Changing of the Seasons* (New York: Arbor House, 1986), passim; Jorie Graham, *The End of Beauty* (New York: Ecco, 1987), 30–34.

18. Grace Schulman, *Marianne Moore: The Poetry of Engagement* (Urbana: University of Illinois Press), 67–68.

19. Quoted in Susan Schweik, "Writing War Poetry like a Woman," *Critical Inquiry* 13 (Spring 1987): 532–56.

20. Vendler, 61–62.

21. Bonnie Costello, *Marianne Moore: Imaginary Possessions* (Cambridge: Harvard University Press, 1981).

22. Laurence Stapleton, *Marianne Moore: The Poet's Advance* (Princeton: Princeton University Press, 1978), 129–41.

23. Geoffrey Hartmann, "Six Women Poets," in *Easy Pieces* (New York: Columbia University Press, 1985), 111.

24. Schweik, 541, 545.

25. Stapleton, 130.

26.  Moore to Bishop, 1 May 1938, Rosenbach Museum and Library.

27.  Adrienne Rich, "When We Dead Awaken," in *On Lies, Secrets, and Silence*, 39.

28.  A great many poems could be adduced here; those I have mentioned are Adrienne Rich, "Hunger," in *The Fact of a Doorframe*, 230–31; Denise Levertov, "A Poem at Christmas, 1972," in *The Freeing of the Dust* (New York: New Directions, 1975), 38; Sharon Olds, "The Language of the Brag," in *Satan Says* (Pittsburgh: University of Pittsburgh Press, 1980), 44–45.

# 5

# "That Weapon, Self-Protectiveness"

*David Bromwich*

In the following pages, I sketch what I take to be a deep affinity of poetic imagination between Marianne Moore and Elizabeth Bishop. But it is a delicate subject, and, having announced it in this way, I have to add several qualifications. The affinity is temperamental. It shows in the poems that Moore and Bishop wrote. I will be saying nothing about the friendship they maintained outside of poetry. Also, affinity is not quite the same thing as influence. It goes both ways equally, as influence never does; or rather, it convinces us of the reality of some third thing. The effect of reading Moore and Bishop together, it seems to me, is that one can see aspects of their work as part of a shared predicament. Let me begin by saying what that is.

There is a tonality of self-assertion in Moore's early writing which her readers somehow tend to forget. But Elizabeth Bishop never forgot it. Her own most powerful early poem, "Roosters," and the development that followed from it owe a great deal to a pattern of declaration and withdrawal which Moore was the first to exemplify. That poem accordingly has a curious and instructive history. It came to Moore's attention just at the time when she herself had started to reject the side of her work to which Bishop was returning. I am not sure how far either poet was aware of this, and it does not really matter much. What is suggestive in any case is a certain coincidence of motives. At a crisis of their relationship, each poet was driven to attempt a full defense of her own work. And in the course of sustaining that effort, each came close to defining a path of self-revision that the other also would take. So the terms of a contest lead back to terms of mutual identity.

I do not know of another phenomenon like this in literary history. The relationship between Wordsworth and Coleridge, for example, feels different from the start, because it involves so clear a division of labor. While one poet lives and feels, the other teaches a way to think about living and feeling. There was nothing resembling such an arrangement between Moore and Bishop. I offer this account, therefore, partly in a spirit of inquiry. It is, from one point of view, an anomalous record of the commerce that once existed between diverse minds; from another, it makes a general point about the sort of self-knowledge that poems may have—a knowledge both overt and perplexing, which may be another name for the knowledge of others.

A poem by Marianne Moore in *Observations* is called "To Be Liked by You Would Be a Calamity." The phrase, written for Moore's voice, also bears the emphasis of an unsnobbish discrimination which one knows from certain comedies of the period, as in Cary Grant's line about a dull rival, "To hardly know him is to know him well." Moore's poem goes like this:

> "Attack is more piquant than concord," but when
> You tell me frankly that you would like to feel
> My flesh beneath your feet,
> I'm all abroad; I can but put my weapon up, and
> Bow you out.
> Gesticulation—it is half the language.
> Let unsheathed gesticulation be the steel
> Your courtesy must meet,
> Since in your hearing words are mute, which to my senses
> Are a shout.[1]

The opening quotation, "Attack is more piquant than concord," comes, as the notes tell us, from Hardy, and it seems to say that for drama, as for rhetoric, attack makes a more arresting *attitude* than concord. But the poem does not entirely keep the pledge of this beginning; indeed, it does something better than that.

We know there are occasions for which an attitude of attack will simply be improper. And, to judge by her most celebrated poetry and prose, Moore's writing was particularly adapted to such occasions. She armed herself with a shield, and it is her grace that we infer this to be a choice at once of feminine strength and feminine courtesy. So, too, by the end of this poem, her weapon is put up. But though no duel is fought, something striking has happened in its absence. The occasion was in this case proper for a duel, and we are made to see the poet would have been equal to it. Her weapon is the sword after all. Only, she implies, her antagonist is unworthy. In the code of honor that is here invoked, a refusal to do battle is more aggressive than a challenge could possibly have been. It is the untoppable assault, disdaining even the clash of a fight—much as rhetorical silence may be more deadly than any question or answer. One might summarize the action of the poem by saying that, as speech moves from words to shouting to mere gesticulation, so action moves from courtesy to a challenge to the command of "Weapons up!" that calls off a challenge. The last move has great *éclat* since it both presumes and brings about the social nonexistence of one's antagonist.

Every reader, I think, will feel that the person addressed in this poem is a man. But how do we know? The main clue is "My flesh beneath your feet." It is true the form of that phrase is oratorical, almost like a description of heraldry, and to that extent neutral. Yet, together with the authority of "bow you out," it points to a sexual undercurrent that is apparent throughout the poem. For the restraint of "gesticulation" belongs to someone who can choose, and who wants us to see that she can choose, her weapons against his.

This poem represents a strength in Moore which she later kept from display; and she cut it from both editions of her collected poems. Her reason cannot have been solely an estimate of its worth. Among her poems of blame and praise, it has less distinction perhaps than "To a Steam Roller," but is plainly more memorable than some others which she did choose to reprint. Anyway, the rank of the poem may be less interesting now than the quality in Moore that it helps bring to light. The whole look and feel of Moore's poems as they first appeared—the stance a reader would naturally have imputed to them—was quite different from what it has since been supposed to be. Many of the shorter and one of the long poems in *Observations* were cast in the form of compliments or satires, with a Popean discipline of raillery. These include "To an Intra-Mural Rat," "To Military Progress," "George Moore," "Novices," and "Marriage." All these poems were ranged near the front of *Observations*, where they would shape a reader's impression of what the author was up to. By contrast, Moore's 1951 *Collected Poems* moved them to the back; to start with, instead, it offered the genial topographical inquisitiveness of "The Steeple-Jack"; a little further on, with the poem that begins "In this age of hard trying," the poet would be found claiming a particular kinship with one whose

> by-
> play was more terrible in its effectiveness
>     than the fiercest frontal attack.
>         The staff, the bag, the feigned inconsequence
>     of manner, best bespeak that weapon, self-protectiveness.[2]

By then, Moore had come to prize an ideal of intellectual capability in which imaginative or moral virtues shone most brightly from a hidden place of repose—"in an unhackneyed solitude." This is a reversal of emphasis from her satires and, at the same time, a further application of their tactics. Observation itself has now become half the language. The inconsequence may be feigned, the self-protectiveness may be a weapon, but they can be so only to the person who stays for a long look into them. Meanwhile, to others, they have the surface charm of ornamental things. From those others, they are shielded.

In Moore's criticism as much as in her poetry, this stance is often associated with pairs of virtues. Reticence and candor, humility and gusto, are two famous instances, but the rule for them all is that a dominant trait may be known by its antithetical and recessive counterpart. Thus, we are surprised (and it is a sort of surprise Moore connects with genuine imagining) to find that gusto should be an incidental accompaniment of humility; or, again, to find that reticence should sometimes imply a candor of its own. But Moore's interest in such pairs was a gradual and not an easy discovery. In *Observations,* she had been steadily concerned with the expulsion from genial life of certain pretenders to virtue; for, as William James believed, "Not the absence of vice, but vice there, and virtue holding her by the throat, seems the ideal human state."[3] James had the good humor to feign that this view was not his own, but in the early Moore one will find no such pretense. Her predilections there went hand in hand with prejudices.

Elizabeth Bishop read *Observations* when she was a student at Vassar, and later said that it changed her sense of what could be done in poetry. This fact will mislead if we take it to disclose a source of her style. People who call Bishop a disciple of Moore, or "of the school of Moore," whatever that may mean, have got both poets wrong. But Moore did occasionally tease Bishop about the reviewers' cant of schools, sometimes with a rather anxious undertone; and in a letter of 24 October 1954, Bishop sent her a clarifying reply:

> I don't know what *Le Journal des Poetes* is, I'm afraid—you say it says I show your influence. . . . Well, naturally I am only too delighted to—Everyone has said that—I was going to say, all my life—and I only wish it were truer. My own feeling about it is that I don't show very much; that no one does or can at present; that you are still too new and original and unique to *show* in that way very much but will keep influencing more and more during the next fifty or a hundred years. In my own case, I know however that when I began to read your poetry at college I think it immediately opened up my eyes to the possibility of the subject-matter I could use and might never have thought of using if it hadn't been for you.—(I might not have written any poems, I suppose.) I think my approach is so much vaguer and less-defined and certainly more old-fashioned—sometimes I'm amazed at people's comparing me to you when all I'm doing is some kind of blank verse—Can't they *see* how different it is? But they can't, apparently.[4]

This is considerate praise that does not strike a false note of self-depreciation. But it deflects the original question by passing quickly from Bishop's style (which she knows she did not get from anyone) to her subject-matter (where she can admit an uncomplicated debt to Moore). If one looks at Bishop's own subjects, however, one finds that they are nothing at all like Moore's. What resemblance there is occurs in lighter pieces—"Seascape" and "Florida" are the only ones that really seem close.

But suppose one has in view the sort of stance I described in *Observations*: something less pervasive than style, and less foursquare than subject, yet a thing as pronounced as either in its results for poetry. Here one can start to see a cause of Bishop's absorbing interest in the poems of *Observations*. Certainly, the depth of the interest was exceptional. Moore was the first and would remain the only celebrated person whom Bishop ever sought as company. With her, Bishop overcame an ingrained shyness sufficiently to introduce herself; to renew a favorable first acquaintance by suggesting many subsequent meetings; and to attend faithfully to one side of a lifelong correspondence, in the early years by writing as much as a letter or postcard a week. When, in her late twenties, some years into their friendship, she was first invited to address Miss Moore familiarly, as Marianne, she put "Marianne" at the top of her next letter with a fringe of magic lights.

I now want to tell a story about the genesis of "Roosters." It is a story I believe to be true, though the evidence for it is simply interpretative. But it is apt anyway for the present occasion because it connects an important poem by Bishop with the satirical impulse of *Observations*. Imagine, then, Bishop's reading of another poem in that book, called "To a Prize Bird" (*Ob*, 13):[5]

> You suit me well, for you can make me laugh,
> Nor are you blinded by the chaff
>   That every wind sends spinning from the rick.
>
> You know to think, and what you think you speak
> With much of Samson's pride and bleak
>   Finality; and none dare bid you stop.
>
> Pride sits you well, so strut, colossal bird.
> No barnyard makes you look absurd;
>   Your brazen claws are staunch against defeat.

The prize bird's qualities fit the poet, as salamander-skin would later do; they are right for her, as a chosen suit is right. Seen in this way, her subject here makes an oddly masculine emblem. Yet the bird's eloquence is fraught with inconsequence, for what he holds fast to is the bar inside the cage, and he can be colossal only in that cage, his temple. As for his power as a figure of imagination, it is chiefly negative. He is *not blinded* by the chaff he hears and repeats, in the sense that, being indifferent, he can seem superior to dull words or syllables. This mention of blindness leads by association to Samson's "pride and bleak / Finality." I do not think the allusion is meant ironically, and anyone who does think so faces plenty of contradictory evidence from the daughter of John Milton Moore. True, the bird is impressive only in being unconformable. He struts, is colossal or brazen, in the manner of heroic statuary. If he is staunch against defeat, that is not the same as being assured of conquest. Nevertheless, this is the only place I can recall in Moore where pride is allowed to show itself as a virtue without qualifications.

The adjectives *brazen, strutting,* and *colossal* will have caught the ear of any reader familiar with "Roosters." But for those whose memories of the poem go some way back, a brief description may be helpful. It begins as the poet is awakened from sleep by the first grating cries of roosters before the dawn. She treats this daily disruption as an annoyance, but, as the poem goes on, it comes to seem more like an assault. The roosters are fancied as presiding over every bedstead, invading every privacy of the town she inhabits. They strut and swagger, and fight each other for dominance, in a heedless and brutal spectacle, all for the sake of projecting a "senseless order" over the town. But here the poem breaks off, and the poet considers a revised image of the scene, which she calls "the pivot." A cock crowed to signal Peter's betrayal of Christ; and yet, this brought the recognition that saved him: he saw only then that he was guilty. Thinking (not talking) of her own betrayals, the poet wonders if the dreadful cries of the birds may not come to bless after all. Her meditation closes with dawn realized, in what now seems, more plainly than it did before, the setting of an aubade. *How can the night have come to grief?* The conventional question addresses her love and what it has done to itself, as much as it laments the ruin of her dreams by the harsh noises of the morning. But the roosters no longer dominate her thoughts. Instead, there is a gentler bird, the swallow, its belly touched by the pink light; and there is the possibly hopeful image of the sun climbing in her window: a male, like the roosters that heralded him, rather more pagan than Christian, but anyway "faithful as enemy, or friend."

Bishop wrote "Roosters" early in 1940. Until then, she had submitted most of her work to Moore for comment or revision. This was an arrangement of deference, well understood on both sides, and with decorums always carefully observed by Bishop, even when she chose not to take the advice. But I can give a better idea of the implicitness of this side of their friendship by recounting a curious incident. When, without consultation, Bishop sent her story "In Prison" to *Partisan Review* and told Moore she had done so, she received a jesting, maybe only half-jesting, reproof. It had been independent of her, said Moore, to try to publish the story alone, and if it was returned with a printed slip that would be why. The tenor of the comment may suggest a sort of preceptorial gravity from which any sane beneficiary would plot to escape. Yet I think that Bishop for her part sometimes overestimated Marianne Moore's conventionality—or tended to heighten, in her own conception of it, the severity of Moore's sense of imaginative virtue. The story "In Prison," for example, she did eventually show to Moore, after a lot of disclaimers. Moore did not deprecate its Modernist and psychological procedures, as Bishop had feared she would, but wrote a letter full of subtle and discriminating criticism, in which she announced that "You and Dr. Niebuhr are two abashing peaks in present experience for me." The same letter of 1 May 1938 goes on to say that she feels hampered in praising Bishop by a fear of spoiling her; and there follows this extraordinary paragraph:

On the other hand,—Dr. Niebuhr says Christianity is too much on the defensive, that it is more mysterious, more comprehensive, more lastingly deep and dependable than unsuccessfully simpler substitutes which objectors to it offer; and I feel that although large-scale "substance" runs the risk of inconsequence through aesthetic impotence, and am one of those who despise clamor about substance—to whom treatment really *is* substance—I can't help wishing you would sometime in some way, risk some unprotected profundity of experience; or since no one admits profundity of experience, some characteristic private defiance of the significantly detestable. Continuously fascinated as I am by the creativeness and uniqueness of these assemblings—which are really poems—I feel responsibility against anything that might threaten you; yet fear to admit such anxiety, lest I influence you away from an essential necessity or particular strength. The golden eggs can't be dealt with theoretically, by presumptuous mass salvation formulae. But I do feel that tentativeness and interiorizing are your danger as well as your strength.

What most compels notice in this judgment is the warning it gives against self-protectiveness and inconsequence—even "that weapon, self-protectiveness" and the power of "feigned inconsequence"—and the encouragement it gives to "some characteristic private defiance of the significantly detestable." For *significantly* we may read *publicly* detestable. Hence Moore's reiterated emphasis on the strength such a gesture would require.

"Roosters" seems to me an answer to this letter, and to the imperative it contained: so much so that the poem carries a special authority for Bishop's career as a whole. Any reader, but especially a male reader, is bound to think of it as a strong utterance, in something like an objective sense. From beginning to end it covers the whole range from satire to prayer—from, if a parallel is wanted in Moore's work, the register of "To Be Liked by You Would Be a Calamity" to that of "In Distrust of Merits." I can point the moral by saying it is a poem of significantly characteristic private detestation, against all the acknowledged and audible legislators of the world whom the poet arrays against herself, and whom she explicitly identifies as male. Bishop remarked in a letter to Moore that she had written the poem with thoughts of the recent Nazi invasions and the overrunning of small towns in Norway and Finland. Just a glimpse of that motive appears in the fantastic interlude of "Roosters" in which the fighting cocks become fighter planes vying to outmaneuver each other for a kill:

> Now in mid-air
> by twos they fight each other.
> Down comes a first flame-feather,
>
> and one is flying,
> with raging heroism defying
> even the sensation of dying.

And one has fallen,
but still above the town
his torn-out, bloodied feathers drift down;

and what he sung
no matter. He is flung
on the gray ash-heap, lies in dung

with his dead wives
with open, bloody eyes,
while those metallic feathers oxidize.[6]

It is this repulsive image that will prompt the transition, "St. Peter's sin / was worse than that of Magdalene," and lead to the poet's suggestion that the revenge she takes in this poem is short-sighted; that "deny" is not all the roosters cry; that, in her own denials, she resembles them more nearly than she had supposed. But the stanzas above are worth dwelling on a little longer.

Something of their animus came, I believe, from Bishop's reading of another poem by Moore, the satirical ode "To Military Progress." Before quoting it, I have to observe that, though the creature it addresses is never specified, we do know that he grinds chaff, unlike the prize bird who was oblivious to "the chaff / that every wind sends spinning from the rick"; and again, that he is a petty creature or contrivance, with a good deal of just that barnyard absurdity which the prize bird had scorned. Here is the poem:

You use your mind
like a millstone to grind
    chaff.
You polish it
and with your warped wit
    laugh

at your torso,
prostrate where the crow
    falls
on such faint hearts
as its god imparts,
    calls

and claps its wings
till the tumult brings
    more
black minute-men

> to revive again
>         war
>
> at little cost.
> They cry for the lost
>         head
> and seek their prize
> till the evening sky's
>         red.[7]

A striking feature of the poem's movement is the effect of sudden magnification and miniaturization, whereby a gigantic torso that is seen close up yields, without quite fading or dissolving into, the tumult of "black minute-men" who swarm as if framed in an aerial perspective. The same kind of shift occurs in "Roosters," but in a reverse direction: from the distant, small, and merely irritating first crow of the rooster out of the "gun-metal blue dark" to the swelling into the foreground of "protruding chests / in green-gold medals dressed."

The similarities between a minor poem by Moore and an ambitious poem by Bishop would be trivial if they did not somehow catch a resonance from the larger aspirations of both poets. But one does feel the propriety of the echo when one places "To Military Progress" alongside "Marriage," a poem of a comparable scale with "Roosters"—with its knowledge of

> the spiked hand
> that has an affection for one,
> and proves it to the bone

and its testimony "that men have power / and sometimes one is made to feel it." Here we do come back to the life described in "Roosters," and all those

> many wives
> who lead hens' lives
> of being courted and despised.

So when she wrote "Roosters," Bishop was, for once, moving close to the overt subject matter for which Moore's writing was famous. An early and intelligent critic, Randall Jarrell, was not quite right to classify it as an "animal-morality poem" in the vein of Moore; in procedure, it is closer to the severe poems of *Birds, Beasts, and Flowers*, such as "Tortoise Shell" and "The Ass." Yet in relation to all of Moore's early work, "Roosters" feels like a gesture of solidarity, and Bishop could reasonably have expected a sympathetic response. What she got was not exactly the opposite of that. But Moore's dealings with the poem were so characteristic, private, public, and strongly self-protective that the facts had better just be recited.

To test her own scruples, Moore sent Bishop a rewritten version of the poem, entitled "Cocks," a word by comparison with which *roosters* must have seemed to her ear coarse and unclassical. She broke up some of the triple rhymes into twos or ones and elsewhere cut and rephrased—the kind of heavy revision she had occasionally tried when editing the *Dial*, as, for example, with the text of Hart Crane's "The Wine Menagerie." But her minor objections, to what she took to be the poem's faults of impropriety or sophistication, were mixed up in her comments with a partly facetious, partly earnest running disputation between the two poets, concerning the permissibility of Bishop's ever using the word *water-closet*. Moore seems to have been conscious that in this instance her prudence might be taken for prudishness.

In reply, Bishop gave solid reasons for her choices in the poem; and that provoked from Moore a spirited self-defense, in a letter of 16 October 1940:

> Regarding the water-closet, Dylan Thomas, W. C. Williams, E. E. Cummings, and others, feel that they are avoiding a duty if they balk at anything like unprudishness, but I say to them, "I can't care about all things equally, I have a major effect to produce, and the heroisms of abstinence are as great as the heroisms of courage, and so are the rewards." I think it is to your credit, Elizabeth, that when I say you are not to say "water-closet," you go on saying it a little.

The heroisms of abstinence that Moore speaks of would find their proper aphorism near the end of "Armor's Undermining Modesty"; "A mirror-of-steel uninsistence should countenance / continence." But her paradox in the letter I have quoted is still more decisive. The men whom she names are convicted of priggishness from having been too timid to avoid the *duty* of appearing unprudish. She cannot be bothered with their athletic moralism, having "a major effect to produce" for herself. This peculiarly felicitous act of exclusion is carried off in a mood of independence which Bishop would have understood well.

On the face of things, Moore's response only points to an accidental difference over manners. Why then did the major effect of "Roosters" so elude her intelligence? The answer, I believe, is connected with her gradually changing view of her own career, which I mentioned at the start. Throughout the thirties and forties, she was withdrawing from a style of polemical irony which had been vital to her early poems, just as it had been to Eliot's (an analogy she herself might have drawn, for she admired the gusto of *Sweeney Agonistes*). "Roosters," therefore, was calculated to remind her of a part of her imagination that she wanted to be finished with. Indeed, it is noteworthy that in Moore's later work, the commanding moments frequently seem to occur as effects of *revised* satire. These are moments in which an act of moral exclusion does not show the risk of its having been ventured first as an attempt at personal derision. I have in mind, for example, the monstrous setting she built for the apparently pleasant remark, at the end of "Four Quartz Crystal Clocks," that "punctuality is not a crime." The motto, in context, refers back to the salvaged days that may come of minutes saved here and there, and it appears in that light as a *warning* given by "Jupiter or jour pater, the day god" to

> the cannibal Chronos
> (eater of his proxime
> newborn progeny).

It says that every inching forward of the hand of the clock, past punctuality, is an inversion of nature, on a par with the cannibal father devouring his sons. A lot of her milder-sounding jokes are coded warnings of a similar kind.

The design of passages like this, as Moore came to understand them, was finally to "attain integration too tough for infraction." By contrast, "Roosters" was all infraction, all assault, most of the way through. Yet it was following a course marked out by Moore herself, which she was only then beginning to turn away from. It chose, in short, the very weapon that she was in the process of surrendering.

What can one learn about "Roosters" from the perspective opened up by its relationship to Moore? Like "Marriage," it is a protest against the people who most fiercely threaten the poet's imaginings, and who do so with the practical sanction of worldly authority. And those people are: statesmen, businessmen, soldiers, husbands. The poet, who alone can displace them, is a woman not a wife. The grotesque feeling of the poem comes from the deep impression it makes of accurate hatred—an emotion only to be missed by those who have been tricked into insensibility by its rhymes. The pretense which the rhymes signal, of a satisfied striving for the minor effect, is, in fact, crueler in the end, as its ironies return upon the reader, than any comparable "undermining modesty" in Moore's early writing. But, for the reasons I have been tracing, this was an experiment which Bishop's reading of Moore led her to try. The strange thing about the partial retraction on which "Roosters" closes is that it touches just the note of humility that would become familiar above all in Moore's later work. And yet it does so before one can point to a movement as definitive in a single poem by Moore. It needs to be added that humility itself may have a tactical value, as both of these poets recognized. Moore showed what that could mean in the way she chose to rewrite the last stanza or "Roosters." "The sun," Bishop had written,

> climbs in,
> following "to see the end,"
> faithful as enemy, or friend.

Moore changed it to:

> And climbing in to see the end,
> the faithful sin is here,
> as enemy, or friend.

That version is weaker than Bishop's as poetry for the same reason that it is clearer as morality (incorporating, as it does, the Peter-Christ parable, which Bishop left implicit at the end). Moore's revision, however, seems to me in line with the poem's argument in the last several stanzas. For by that point it has become a petition for forgiveness. It is the nature of roosters, Bishop concedes, to annoy, hector, tear, and fight for command. Though they break in to the poet's sleep and the dreaming life that comes with sleep, their denials are not unlike hers; as, for that matter, their "active displacements in perspective" are not unlike hers. One recalls here particularly the sound like the grating of a wet match that first brings their cries to consciousness. In "The Bight," "At the Fishhouses," "The Armadillo," and "The End of March," a similar sensation always seems to be closely linked with the work of a powerful imagining.

As for Bishop's reasons for seeking forgiveness, they will remain obscure only so long as we look at her as a citizen and not a poet. Like the creatures she denounces, she is a reshaper of things in the world, and others will live with what she makes. There is, on this view, one kind of poetry in an inventive reading of maps, another kind in the overrunning of actual places on a map of conquest. Either way, hers or theirs, the aim is to make a senseless order prevail. Thus, Bishop's allusion to "marking out maps like Rand McNally's" is not the innocent detail it seems. It is carefully placed in this poem, by an author for whom "The Map" would become a kind of signature. Her sense, in allying herself with the roosters, of a complicity in all that she hates, may suggest that the withdrawal from satire here allowed Bishop to escape from a much graver turning against herself. A corresponding shift from invective to prayer would enter Moore's work with "In Distrust of Merits." The black minutemen of "To Military Progress" are still there ("O small dust of the earth / that walks so arrogantly"), but the poet goes on to observe, "There never was a war that was not inward." It is a fine summing-up of everything Bishop wanted us to feel at the statuary scene that makes "the pivot" of "Roosters":

> Christ stands amazed,
> Peter, two fingers raised,
> to surprised lips, both as if dazed.

For betrayal haunts all language and all gesticulation, from the most personal acts to those which implicate a whole society.

I have been speaking of the parallels between Moore and Bishop, and the mutual loyalties of their poetry, as if Bishop's own judgment of the essential difference between them ought to be simply granted. So it ought to be by the reader who aims to value them as individuals. Yet there remains a sense in which Bishop, toward the end of her career, drew closer to Moore's pattern than might have been predicted of the author of "Roosters." She, too, came to "dominate the stream in an attitude / of self-defense," to borrow Moore's words from "Critics and Connoisseurs." And there is a feeling both of loss and of tenacious reserve in how she reveals her consciousness of this fact. It will come out plainly, I suspect, when we can read her letters to Robert Lowell, whose self-exertion was as foreign to her and as marvelous as her imagination was to him. But within her own poetry, Bishop left a clue to her development in the latest of her poems that may still be read as an homage to Moore. I mean "The Armadillo," of which the unused, unusable title must have been "Another Armored Animal."

Bishop's personal emblem in that poem has become "a weak mailed fist / clenched ignorant against the sky." No longer staunch against defeat like Moore's prize bird, this creature in its retiring way is successfully blind to the prospect of destruction. As a fable about both poets, "The Armadillo" makes a more poignant tribute than the more explicit "Invitation to Miss Marianne Moore." But the longer and slighter poem (begun as a prose appreciation for the "Moore Issue" of a quarterly) gives a point of its own to the story I have been telling. Bishop there salutes as characteristic properties of Marianne Moore's writing her "dynasties of negative constructions" which, she says, go to form "a long unnebulous train of words." My aim has been to show that the words are unnebulous because they protect the mind of a poet without mass salvation formulae; that the constructions are negative because they often have at heart the purpose of bowing someone out.[8]

### Notes

1. Marianne Moore, "To Be Liked by You Would Be a Calamity," in *Observations* (New York: Dial Press, 1925), 37. Hereafter, poems from this collection will be documented parenthetically within the text with *Ob* followed by the pagination of the poem under discussion.

2. Marianne Moore, "In This Age of Hard Trying, Nonchalance Is Good and," in *Collected Poems* (New York: Macmillan, 1951), 38–39.

3. William James, "The Dilemma of Determinism," in *The Will to Believe* (New York: Longmans, Green, 1897), 169; from a passage in which James ventures, "what I should instantly say, were I called on to plead for gnosticism."

4. Bishop's dutiful tone in this letter is uncharacteristic. More commonly, she used her letters to Moore for descriptions that might some time be worked into poems, as in the following sentences from a letter of 8 December 1953, soon after her move to Brazil: "The fireflies *are* extraordinary, in case I didn't tell you before—large and green and much steadier than ours, and they keep right on even in the heaviest tropical rains. Also there is another variety, quite a large insect, we see

once in a while, that floats steadily towards you with a really big milky blue light—it can be quite frightening, like a burglar, or a distant train, even."

5.    Moore in her notes identifies the subject of the poem as George Bernard Shaw.

6.    Elizabeth Bishop, "Roosters," in *The Complete Poems* (New York: Farrar, Straus & Giroux, 1969), 42.

7.    Marianne Moore, "To Military Progress," in *Complete Poems of Marianne Moore* (New York: Macmillan/Viking, 1981), 82.

8.    For another view of Moore and Bishop, with a different treatment of occasionally similar or overlapping passages from their letters, the reader will want to consult Bonnie Costello's "Marianne Moore and Elizabeth Bishop: Friendship and Influence," in *Twentieth Century Literature* 30 (1984): 130–49.

Marianne Moore, date unknown
*(Courtesy of* Poetry *Magazine)*

# 6

# Observations on
# Moore's Syllabic Schemes

*John Hollander*

Contemporary discourse about poetic form is frequently so inane and, worse, so misleading, that I hesitated somewhat before deciding to discuss Marianne Moore's intricate and original prosody. Writers of verse and some of their sectarian apologists today, ideologues of rhyme and accentual-syllabism on the one hand and of some particular mode of *vers libre* on the other, have so written about the matter of style that the central question of the nature of poetic fictions is totally suppressed. Whitman guessed that the grass, one of his central tropes, was "the flag" of his "disposition," but some of his self-proclaimed acolytes would want to brandish an academic requirement for free verse as the banner of a faction. If Emerson's prophecy in "The Poet," and Whitman's fulfillment of it in the 1855 *Leaves of Grass*, was right, then any follower of Whitman couldn't write like *that* and manifest anything but that betrayal of poetic following, the political follower or clone. Moreover, such apologists for academic *vers libre* (canonized, taught in the schools of verse writing, etc.) confuse the issue by calling accentual-syllabic verse "formal." Thereby they divert attention—perhaps even their own—from their own formalism and deny that all good free verse has formal structure and power, although its forms and ability to play with language are themselves a figure, rather than a literal extension, of those of accentual-syllabism. An additional implication is that form cannot frame, identify, or gloss a mode of poetic discourse. Worst of all, it seems to deny that form, for a poet rather than versifier, is both generative and allusive, and that while students must learn that verse is not poetry—that poetry is a meter-making argument, as Emerson put it—the secret knowledge of poets is of how much argument-making meter there really, and almost inexpressibly, is. But this is such a personal and awkward matter that poets often avoid it, or else say very misleading and often self-misrepresenting things about their private modes of voice when they do indeed consent to do so.[1] I hope it will not be wrong to try to invade some of Marianne Moore's formal privacy for a while.

Moore's formal practice is personal in so obvious a way that it is easy to misconstrue its nature and function. *Observations* has a few short residual accentual-syllabic poems ("To an Intra-Mural Rat," "Reticence and Volubility," "A Talisman," etc.) and some long poems in two different modes of *vers libre*. For example, the long, unwinding strip of that grand poem, "Marriage"—a strip, varying from twelve to about thirty picas in width, unrolling like a path jointly trod, or a term of years viewed as a corridor, not as a chamber, its extent, rather than a more obvious openness, constituting its trope of possibility. Or, on the other hand, the more problematic, accordion-pleated movement of "An Octopus" or "Sea Unicorns and Land Unicorns," in which some lines are so long as to require, in the typesetting of the 1924 volume, turnovers. But it is here that Moore's idiosyncratic isosyllabism emerges as a dominant system for her, providing the pattern of rises, turns, and landings of her particular Emersonian stairway of surprise. I want to look now at a few short poems that are characteristically generated in—and *by*—her schemes in that system. And I should like to consider how her use of them is as original as her way of dealing with the phenomenal world and how her isosyllabism, with its manner of framing English verse and its partitions of written language, correspond in the mixture of familiarity and strangeness with her segmentations—as B. L. Whorf put it—of nature.

But first some observations about syllabism generally and about some of the problems it raises for interpretation. So conventional as to seem natural in languages without tonic stress like modern French and Japanese, or even in those like Czech, Finnish, or Italian (all unrelated), with a clear but clearly predictable stress (initial in the first two, penultimate in the last), it is quite as foreign to English as Greek quantitative prosody was to Latin when Ennius adapted it. The accommodation by strictly accentual Germanic meter—the four-beat alliterative line—of French syllabism at the time of Chaucer yielded, as we know, the great mixed metaphor of accentual-syllabism. But our system is one in which the accentual will tend to dominate, extra unstressed syllables but not stressed ones being allowable by the ear. Strict syllabism, on the other hand, is phonologically mysterious in languages with phonemic or (*pace* Chomsky and Halle) problematically prominent word-stress. It might be likened to the quantitative experiments of the Elizabethans, who could, by the use of rules applicable only to the spelling system of written English, assign ghostly "quantities" to syllables without regard to phonology and produce lines often of puzzling beauty and effectiveness.

For example, a well-known anonymous translation from Ovid's *Heroides* sounds, some archaisms aside, like one mode of beautifully paced modern end-stopped free verse:

> Constant Penelope sends to thee, careless Ulysses.
> Write not again, but come, sweet mate, thyself to revive me.
> Troy we do much envy, we desolate lost ladies of Greece,
> Not Priamus, nor yet all Troy can us recompense make.
> Oh, that he had, when he first took shipping to Lacedaemon,
> That adulterer I mean, had been o'erwhelmed with waters.
> Then had I not lain now all alone, thus quivering for cold,
> Nor used this complaint, nor have thought the day to be so long.[2]

Yet these variously six- or seven-stressed lines, without any regular cadential closure, are, according to a secret rule, perfect Latinate hexameters.

A prosodic system, then, can engage the written language with various consequences for the spoken language therein encoded. This makes for the fundamental problematic of the borrowed system of strict syllabics, first written in English by Moore and Robert Bridges (probably quite independently of one another) and subsequently by W. H. Auden, Richard Howard, and others. The linguistic problem of defining a syllable varies in speech and writing, raising the question—in writing alone—of a syllabic rule. (Is the word *motion* to be considered di- or tri-syllabic, and does the consequent interpretation thus allude implicitly to the accentual-syllabic verse of the seventeenth, or the nineteenth and twentieth, centuries?) Moore, for example, often archaizes in this way, or even more egregiously, as in "Nevertheless": "within the fruit—locked in / like counter-curved twin"—where the archaic "curvèd" is necessary for the hexasyllabic measure, and where its introduction, given the strong rhyme anyway, moves it toward iambic trimeter. But this brings up once more the central question: while the scheme is phonologically neutral, the audible rhythm of any line or lines is ad hoc, a fulfillment but not a prescription of the syllabic rule. Thus, two lines of ten syllables each might be:

> This line will be inaudibly measured,
> But this line's heavy stresses can be heard.

The first sounds like a tetrameter—"This line will be inaudibly measured," and we're tempted to go on, "Its rhythmical riches will always be treasured," which temptation would stem from an aural misprision of the syllabic system. Yet, if the poet were writing syllabic couplets of ten and twelve, this added line would both follow the syllabic rule and work, by a different rule, for the ear. Note also that my sample pair of lines "rhymes" in a syllabic system, *a la manière française*, and not in any normative one for English, in which only stressed syllables can carry a rhyme. Also, note that the shorter the line, the more likely it is to resound accentually, whether by design or not.

But written syllables "rhyme" in a frequently inaudible way, given the fact

of vowel reduction—in languages like English or Russian—on unstressed syllables. The initial *a* in the first syllable of the word *about*—phonemically, / /—can
be treated as if it were /a/ or even /ey/ by a syllabic rhymer. The word *syllable* can
be heard as if "full," or ending in a "bell," or even standing mutely like a "tree"
in a system like Moore's. There is a sort of visionary trope of phonology at work
in this. Thus, consider a poem such as "A Carriage from Sweden" with an *xbbxx*
rhyme scheme and internal rhymes in the first and last lines of the stanza, usually
connecting the first and last syllable in each one. The last line of stanza 2 goes:
"*int*egrity it is a v*ein*" (my italics), where "vein," monosyllabic for the eight-
syllable count of the stanza's terminal line, momentarily breaks into two syllables
of "ve-in" for the *rime riche*.

But the central rhythmic issue of syllabic verse remains the tuning in and
out of the accentual, as in the two-line example given before. The following
passages will be of interest in this regard:

> Perch'd on the upland wheatfields beyond the village end
> A red-brick Windmill stood with black bonnet of wood
> That trimm'd the whirling cross of its great arms around
> Upon the wind, pumping up water night and day
> From the deep Kentish chalk to feed a little town
> Where miniatured afar it huddled on the coast
> Its glistening roofs and thrust its short pier in the sea.
>
> (Robert Bridges)

> Mid the squander'd colour
>     idling as I lay
> Reading the Odyssey
>     in my rock-garden
> I espied the cluster'd
>     tufts of Cheddar pinks
> Burgeoning with promise
>     of their scented bloom
> All the modish motley
>     of their bloom-to-be
> Thrust up in narrow buds
>     on the slender stalks
>
> (Robert Bridges)

Through the open French window the warm sun lights up the polished breakfast-table,
laid round a bowl of crimson roses, for one—a service of Worcester porcelain, arrayed
near it a melon, peaches, figs, small hot rolls in a napkin, fairy rack of toast, butter
in ice, high silver coffee-pot, and, heaped on a salver, the morning's post. She comes
over the lawn, the young heiress, from her early walk in the garden-wood, feeling that
life's a table set to bless her delicate desires with all that's good, that even the
unopened future lies like a love-letter, full of sweet surprise. (Elizabeth Daryush)

Fifty-odd years ago if you were going to see Shoshone Falls, the road was not, God knows, slicked up for the wheeled hordes of Nature-lovers gawking in flowered shirts from Hawaii, and little bastards strewing candy wrappers as they come. No—rough roads then, gravel sometimes and, too, lonesomeness: no pervasive stink of burnt high-test, like the midnight memory of some act of shame long forgotten but now back in sickening sweat. (Robert Penn Warren)

When there are so many we shall have to mourn, when grief has been made so public, and exposed to the critique of a whole epoch the frailty of our conscience and anguish, of whom shall we speak? For every day they die among us, those who were doing us some good, who knew it was never enough but hoped to improve a little by living. . . . One rational voice is dumb. Over his grave the household of Impulse mourns one dearly loved: sad is Eros, builder of cities, and weeping anarchic Aphrodite. (W. H. Auden)

> One rational voice is dumb. Over his grave
> the household of Impulse mourns one dearly loved:
>      sad is Eros, builder of cities,
>      and weeping anarchic Aphrodite.
>
> (W.H. Auden)[3]

The first of the two quotations from Robert Bridges, the opening of his 1921 poem called "Kate's Mother", is in twelve-syllable lines with the accentual six beats so frequently dominating that these read like blank alexandrines. This effect is underlined by the internal rhyme in the second line and the enjambment of "huddled on the coast / Its glistening roofs," with the discovered transivity of the verb reinforced by the reciprocal verb *thrust*. But notice the second passage from Bridges, the opening of his "Cheddar Pinks" of 1924, the same year as Moore's *Observations*. Whatever accentual patterns resound through the parallel syntactic elements in the last four lines, for example, it is obvious that the movement of these lines depends upon what looks like an opening accentual promise being broken: the first two lines suggest that the next two will be something like "Reading moldy Homer / on the first of May," as I have elsewhere argued.[4] There is something programmatic about introducing the syllabic mode in this fashion. As we shall see, Marianne Moore frequently does almost the opposite, letting the poem unroll in pure syllabics, with occasionally prominent rhythmic patterns surfacing here and there, but with a pronounced accentual scheme for cadential closure.

It is always instructive to recast *vers libre* or isosyllabic verse as prose and consider what emerges in the scanning of the prose lines. The third sample, a pure-syllabic sonnet by the British poet Elizabeth Daryush (Bridges's daughter, in fact), starts out with all of the characteristic cadences and periods of a certain mode of novelistic descriptive prose, but the last sentence resounds in clear, rhymed, iambic pentameter. As has been apparent, an iambic pentameter line is a perfectly possible instance of the isosyllabic design, just as a Keatsian pentameter, full of resonant alliterations, is an allowable but unspecified instance of iambic verse.

Included are two other samples of pure syllabism very different in effect from Moore's: Robert Penn Warren's totally prosaic octosyllabics (an experiment that this wonderful poet wisely never repeated) use the resources of the scheme not at all. But the opening of W. H. Auden's poem "In Memory of Sigmund Freud" sets up a movement that prevails throughout the longish poem. The stanza form uses two lines of eleven syllables, one of nine, then one of ten, set up and indented so as to look like, and allude to, a poem of Horace's in the alcaic stanza. The first two lines are heard in roughly accentual pentameters, the last two being lost in the drawn-out clauses of the periodic syntax. Only at the very end, the last strophe, which is included in its correct form, breaks out into the canonical cadence.

Moore's poems present a few additional problems which I shall only list briefly. (1) She revises format totally from time to time (e.g., "Peter," which gets recast into free verse after *Observations*). (2) The frequent turnovers in the setting of the earlier books falsely suggest that the stanzaic form is other than what it is (e.g., the nineteen-syllable line ending each strophe of "Radical" is turned over but with the residue so indented as to suggest that it is a seventh line—the stanza has only six—of a varying number of syllables). (3) Her indention practice seems strange at first; traditionally, strophes of varying line-length indent in decreasing number of feet or, if all lines are the same length, to group rhymes. Moore indents to group rhyming lines, often only two to a six- or seven-line stanza, despite the greatly varying lengths. (4) The look of the stanza can sometimes seem functional, sometimes less emblematically allusive. The early poems keep looking like seventeenth-century lyric stanzas. Perhaps a prototypical one is that of Herbert's "Denial," which may have been an important poem for her. "The Fish" seems to swim down the page, but that poem isn't about fish in any case, and the title and strophic shape make a subtle joke about surfaces and depths, once one has read down to the heavy, dark bottom of things. (5) There are her indeterminacies, the variations, inconsistencies, violated stanzaic and linear schemes that, perhaps like the *abrash* or sudden violation of pattern in certain oriental carpets, may be there as if to ward off the evil eye.[5]

And there is the matter of quotation, of the incorporation of found linguistic objects, in Moore's poetry. With Moore it is not a question of dealing with the inadvertent emblem that nature produces in some trivial occurrence, like the typographical error that yielded the mythological occasion of Elizabeth Bishop's "The Man-Moth." Nor are Moore's quotations like those of Eliot in which he reconstitutes a famous line or phrase by adding or subtracting, with a ringing

ironic gesture—for example, the altered quotation of the first line of Oliver Goldsmith's famous song from *The Vicar of Wakefield,*

> When lovely woman stoops to folly,
> And finds too late that men betray,
> What charm can soothe her melancholy,
> What art can wash her guilt away?[6]

In the rather nasty treatment the poem gives to "the typist home at teatime" in
"The Fire Sermon" section of *The Waste Land,* Eliot's quatrain (lines 253–56)
answers the question of Goldsmith's lines. But by shifting the first word of Goldsmith's second line to the end of the first one, he puts the "and" into stressed—
and what will emerge as rhyming—position, giving it a more emphatic quality, a
sense of *atque* rather than merely *et* in Latin. Moreover, the line becomes one of
the pentameters of Eliot's mock-heroic, rhymed section of the poem, and for us,
his equally famous lines, now about a woman he regards as being so wretched as
to cast doubt upon the possibility of any such thing as a lovely lady existing, revise
and scornfully complete the lost, simple matter of what was framed in Goldsmith's
opening line:

> When lovely woman stoops to folly and
> Paces about her room again, alone,
> She smoothes her hair with automatic hand,
> And puts a record on the gramophone.[7]

Moore's quotations of bits of prose do indeed adapt them formally, in that
they enter into her realm of syllabic counting in many of the poems, but without
the blatant irony that accompanies the device in the example just quoted, in which
seeing a new formal possibility implied finding something wrong with the sentiment it expressed. But she sees her quoted passages as potential pieces of her
own discourse without *that* sort of ironic concern made prominent, and she re-
interprets the passage, or generalizes from it, as if with any found linguistic object
in the vernacular—quotations, private scriptural allusions, or citations from a
vast bible of ordinary discourse. Also, the quoted texts are like her poetic elements, her syllables, insects or tiny organs of the natural history of written language; these fascinate her from the early poems on, and at first she begins to prize
apart the written organ/organism. This botanizing or lepidoptery extends to the
larger formats of poems themselves, I think, and graphic patterns of stanzaic
forms, found on pages of books of poetry, await her inclusions and decontextuali-
zations. And so too, to a degree, with her quoted material.

But before leaving this issue, it should be noted that Marianne Moore is quite capable of complex quotation of the sort that depends on a residue of the original text excluded by the fragment quoted. Two early examples: the indented quotation from Daniel Webster at the end of "Marriage,"[8] itself part of a quotation in Moore's poem (and hence the quotation marks)

> "Liberty and union
> now and forever;"

is made to apply in a strange way to the minimal polity of a couple in the poem, "that striking grasp of opposites / opposed each to the other, not to unity." But the suppression of the rest of the remark, which during my childhood schoolchildren knew, is quite telling: "One and inseparable" completes Webster's proclamation, but the wry originality of Moore's view of the polarizations of marriage has been too dialectical to allow for a trivial notion of the married pair as "one and inseparable." Out goes the last phrase, but with a strong gesture of its being thrown out to mark the event.

An even more complex return of an excised context occurs toward the end of "In the Days of Prismatic Colour" (*CP*, 41–42):

> Principally throat, sophistication is as it al-
>
> ways has been—at the antipodes from the ini-
>     tial great truths. "Part of it was crawling, part of it
> was about to crawl, the rest
>     was torpid in its lair." In the short-legged, fit-
> ful advance, the gurgling and all the minutiae—we have the classic
>
> multitude of feet.

Moore's footnote identifies the quoted phrase as coming the Loeb Library translation of the *Greek Anthology* (tr. W. R. Paton—actually it is not on page 129 of volume 3 as her note, unchanged from *Observations* on, states, but from epigram 129 of Book 9, page 67 of Paton's third volume). The epigram in question concerns not some sort of centipede, but rather a large, thirsting dragon, so thirsty that, putting its jaws into the river Cephisus, it drank it up completely "and horrid gurgling sounded in its throat. As the water sank, often did the nymphs lament for Cephisus that was no more." The "gurgling" is sucked up into the poem, without acknowledgment, and perhaps the lamenting nymphs are reduced to some of the "minutiae." In any event, a consideration of the source of the quotation here reveals the mythographic etiology of the tiny unpleasantness of the personified "sophistication," whose ancestor is a great dragon which consumes a river, perhaps a river of discourse, and perhaps even of poetry.

Most of the peculiarities of Moore's formal practice are apparent almost from the outset, not only in their flexibilities and determinedly ad hoc schemes, but in their revisionary relations to accentual-syllabic modes of rhythmic pattern, rhyming and versification. (One might adapt Yeats's characterization of his own later dramatic lyrics and call much of her work "poems in rhyme perhaps.") An inspection of two short early poems will be of interest here. The first appears in the 1924 *Observations* as "Fear Is Hope." (Left out of subsequent editions, it resurfaced as a poem called "'Sun,'" first in *The Marianne Moore Reader* then, again revised, in *Tell Me, Tell Me* with some important changes and, typically, a shifted pattern of indentation and no initial capitals.) Totally rhymed—the one unrhyming line in the first stanza rhymes within its analogue in the second one—and redolent variously of Donne and Herbert, the poem is nearly prototypical. It commences with a quotation, although, oddly enough, never identified with a note. Its title brandishes the kind of near-oxymoronic paradox so characteristic of Moore's moral discourse: it looks forward, as will be seen, to "What Are Years?" in this respect. Moments in it—for example, the fine phrase about the rising sun and its own inner light as a trope of human inner resources, "Splendid with splendor hid you come"—prefigure her deliberate teasing of specimens of language in the wordplay of the later poetry. But what I wish to point out in "Fear Is Hope" is the prominent accentual-syllabic cast of the verse, audible in spoken performance without forcing:

> "No man may him hyde
>> From Deth holow eyed."
> For us two spirits this shall not suffice,
> To whom you are symbolic of a plan
> Concealed within the heart of man.
>> Splendid with splendor hid you come, from your
>>> Arab abode,
>> An incandescence smothered in the hand of an as-
>>> trologer who rode
> Before you, Sun—whom you outran,
> Piercing his caravan.

> Sun, you shall stay
> With us. Holiday
>> And day of wrath shall be as one, wound in a device
>> Of Moorish gorgeousness, round glasses spun
>> To flame as hemispheres of one
>>> Great hourglass dwindling to a stem. Consume
>>>> hostility;
>>> Employ your weapons in this meeting place of surg-
>>>> ing enmity.

> Insurgent feet shall not outrun
> Multiplied flames, O Sun.[9]

One notices here that, in almost a deliberately Donnelike fashion, Moore seems to pun on her own name at an appropriate turn in the second strophe— "round glasses spun / To flame as hemispheres of one / Great hourglass dwindling to a stem" is, indeed, "a device / of Moorish gorgeousness" (so did she "weave" herself "into the sense"). It is, as has just been implied, a singularly Herbertian trope as well, turned yet once more: Sunday and mundane, doomsday and funday, sunrise and sunset woven together. The "you . . . symbolic of a plan" only emerges as the sun at the end of the stanza. (Whereas the revised version, "Sun," identifies the addressee in the title, displaces the "two spirits" of the early poem onto the figure of the sun itself, and, in the next line, demotes the concealment of the "plan" and most efficiently dissolves the "incandescence" into a far harder "fiery topaz.")[10] The "Fear Is Hope" of the title presents not an emblem which a strange, twisted associative chain—not of argument, but of that highly original discourse we now think of as Marianne Moore–talk—will come up with a reading of. Rather, it is the motto, glossing the *impresa* of the rising sun.

In any event, the poem not only reads aloud well (T. S. Eliot remarked in 1923 that this was generally true of Moore's work), but, more specifically, the versification is itself audible, and pushes the syllabic mode toward its accentual pole. It has already been observed that very short syllabic lines tend to generate such an effect in any case, whether by design or not. But here it is not a question of, say, six-syllabled couplets like those of "Nevertheless." The couplets closing the strophe here, their rhymes in fully stressed position, the past tense of "outran" / "caravan" yielding to the future of "outrun" / "sun," keep the seventeenth-century overtones ringing. What is problematic are the long lines, of fourteen and eighteen syllables respectively, but which fall unambiguously into the accentual cadences of a fourteener and a paired pentameter and tetrameter with the rhyme being carried at the end of the second of these. It is this sort of accentual presence which keeps emerging and receding in the later poems, controlled by a range of metrical, graphic, and other rhetorical devices. For example, the clear accentual rhymed quatrain that emerges at the very end of "In Distrust of Merits" (*CP*, 136–38), the established pattern of 7a, 7b, 7a, 6b having previously provided a purely graphological and typographical scheme, with largely inaudible rhymes: it breaks out into unambiguous cadence, as if the intention all along had been an accentual trimeter quatrain, rhymed *abcb:*

> I inwardly did nothing.
> O Iscariot-like crime!
> Beauty is everlasting
>     and dust is for a time.

This poem, then, syllabic in scheme, is accentual-syllabic in instance, prominently rhymed—*aabccddcc, eebffggff,* with the strophes linked by the *b* rhyme—and weakly enjambed. Its format is also typical: indentation marks rhyming lines, but not equally measured ones, and unplanned-for turnovers occurring in the typesetting occasion the apparent hyphenations and ghost-lines "Arab abode," "trologer who rode," and, in the second stanza, "hostility" and "-ing enmity," which do indeed scan in having four syllables (whereas the first two do not). Whatever sense of stanza format—in both historically allusive and purely phenomenal, naturally historical, zoological dimensions—may have been at work in these early poems, the exigencies of printing may have fiddled with it somewhat.

On the other hand, "To a Chameleon," also from *Observations* and also reprinted much later, with tiny but significant changes (in *O to Be a Dragon*), is quite a bit more problematic in the way its accentual qualities allow a listener to retrieve the versification. A splendid little emblem-poem, it deftly moralizes the chameleon as an icon of the imagination's resourcefulness, a creature whose camouflage is yet one more instance of the kinds of arms, armor, carapace, protective spines, and even certain paradoxical outward fragilities that are her continuing tropes for inner resources. The chameleon is traditionally—at least from Andrea Alciati's *Emblemata* (1531)—the emblem of flatterers. *"In Adulatores"* is its motto, and the epigram in Alciati, and universally translated into vernaculars thereafter, tells us how the chameleon, always open-mouthed, feeds on air and changes in appearance by taking on different colors save red and white. So also, the comparison continues, flatterers of princes feed on the vulgar air *(aura populari)* and, gaping, devour all. But Moore seems almost to be revising this emblem without having known anything of it directly, other than proverbial chameleon-as-insincerity lore. She uses the trope interestingly elsewhere (in "St. Nicholas" and in the fine, early little poem on Disraeli called "To a Strategist," addressed as a "bright particular chameleon" who "regild[s] a shabby fence"), but here it partakes most of the general figure of hard, resourceful purity and integrity with which Moore seems so often to be allegorizing virginity. It is neither the easy changeability of the creature nor its somewhat maculate appearance at stages in its change to which she speaks; indeed, the chameleon is to some degree of the tribe of the ermine, that sixteenth-century emblem of virginity. (As always, Moore writes like a Belphoebe with the kind of moral imagination about the nature of her own armor that only an old, wise Amoret could have.)

Before examining the poem, I should like to add one more observation. Aside from some of the ways in which her unrolling, idiosyncratically periodic syntax overflows the frequently tightly syllabic cups and basins of her stanzas, running down through them like water in a baroque fountain, what makes some of her poems seem rather Horatian is her ongoing argument with Horace's Ode 1.22. Notwithstanding her confessed displeasure with Latin at school, students of her generation would have sung, to a German melody, accentually set, at least the first strophe of

> Integer vitae scelerisque purus
> non egat Mauris iaculis neque arcu
> nec venenatis gravida sagittis,
>     Fusce, pharetra

> [He who is upright in life and pure of guilt
> needs no Moorish darts nor quiver loaded, Fuscus,
> with poisoned arrows][11]

It is just those "Moorish darts" which, thrown aside in Horace's rhetorical disclaimer, so fascinate the Moore-ish mind; she picks up the mere external, facetious literalnesses which one kind of poetry abandons and refigures them in a new, dangerously literal-sounding kind of emblem, of the sort which she is herself, throughout her oeuvre, picking up, turning around, dissecting with "those various scalpels" of her attention.

I shall come back to this Horatian quality shortly, but for now, the matter of the form of "To a Chameleon" requires attention. It starts out with the natural locus of the very colors of dark red and green which the animal appropriates:

> Hid by the august foliage and fruit of the grape vine,
>     Twine
>   Your anatomy
>   Round the pruned and polished stem,
>       Chameleon.
>       Fire laid upon
>     An emerald as long as
>   The Dark King's massy
> One,
> Could not snap the spectrum up for food as you have done.[12]

The fourteen syllables of the opening line resist a stress-ordering, and the rhyme (on the unstressed final syllable of "grape vine") is picked up for the ear only because of the way in which the monosyllabic line "Twine" calls for attention. But as the poem untwines, what is essentially its binary epigram of exhortation and explanation ("O X, do Y; for Z is the case"), a characteristically curious thing happens. Disregarding line length, we observe that the poem's rhyme scheme is *aabxccybcc*, but once the muted rhyme of "grape vine" / "Twine" has gone by, all we *hear* is another, less muted "Chameleon" / "Fire laid upon," a dimeter couplet. But accentually, and prominently so, the poem uncoils from the syllabism of its first half into strong couplets:

> Chameleon.
> Fire laid upon
> An emerald as long as The Dark King's massy One,
> Could not snap the spectrum up for food as you have done.

—two dimeters and two fourteeners. (The alternative word-order, "Could not snap up the spectrum for food as you have done," would have given a six-beat last line and destroyed the inset accentual and rhyming cadence.) The poem itself, as symbolic chameleon, breaks out in a change of phonological color past the mid-point, when fire gets laid on the silent darkness. In the revised form of the poem, Moore was careful, along with making the initial letters all lower-case, to hyphen-ate "grape-vine," to ensure that it would not be intonationally interpreted as the spondee that disyllabic compounds in the process of formation in modern English remain before finally trochaizing, as it were. Combined with a capitalized *August* with its shifts of stress and designation, a spondee there would have pushed the line into the stance of a fourteener, like the last one. This is a tiny although prominent and epigrammatic case of what might be called the momentary allego-rizing of what is rhetorically purely a scheme, and thereby representationally neutral. Major poetry always does this. It is not a matter of what has often been talked of as the expressive effects that verse, framing rhyme, mimetic rhythm, what I. A. Richards called the "interanimation of words," frequently generate. Rather, it is a question of the scheme operating at another level, becoming momentarily opaque—rather than merely doing its expressive work, however sub-tly and strongly—and then being allegorically interpreted by—though not explic-itly in—the course of the poem.

Let me give some examples. Milton works this way with syntactic devices, with the tension between Latinate and English word-order, with his variety of enjambments, and so forth. William Carlos Williams, in a poem called "The Right of Way" in *Spring and All*, explores a range of ways by which enjambment can create a new meaning in a sentence or clause by playing with a syntactic ambiguity *whose very existence has been hidden in its implicitness and only revealed in its deployment:*

> In passing with my mind
> on nothing in the world
>
> but the right of way
> I enjoy in the road by
>
> virtue of the law—[13]

it starts out. These line breaks employ the scheme of cutting syntax and serving up unexpectedly shaped slices of it. But they do not trope the scheme. Only at the very end of the poem does this happen, and with great wit. The word *enjambment* in French, with its visible leg, means striding across, or straddling.

Williams's poem has been taking a little walk, straddling the fences it finds at line-endings, and thereby exercising its own "right of way." Only in the last two lines is this figuration established, with an enjambment of a sentence *au sujet d'enjamber,* a cut that looks sharply surgical, but then, with the *contre-rejet* (as French prosody calls the straddled opening of the next line), immediately is sutured:

> Why bother where I went?
> for I went spinning on the
>
> four wheels of my car
> along the wet road until
>
> I saw a girl with one leg
> over the rail of a balcony

A joke, perhaps, but a deep one for *ars poetica.* Similarly, we might look at a beautiful quatrain of Emily Brontë's, the penultimate one of her posthumously published "Stanzas."[14] The first two lines, expository and reportorial, walk easily through their transparent pentameters. The second two, full of phonological incident and rhythmic excitation, unveil successively scenery and spirit:

> I'll walk where my own nature would be leading:
> It vexes me to choose another guide:
> Where the grey flocks in ferny glens are feeding;
> Where the wild wind blows on the mountain side.

Smooth lines walk; rougher ones create noticeable place, the locus of both vision and freedom. The alliteratively chiasmic "grey flocks in ferny glens" is pictorial; the spondaic build-up of "wild wind blows on the mountain side" is a figure of boundlessness. Yet both, by their position in the quatrain, partake of the figure of opacity as place to be reached, if only by the medium of the regular pace of walking.

What is the scheme, then, that Marianne Moore is troping in this little poem? The chameleon hidden in the foliage and fruit of the vine emerges at first as being twined around it. The accentual rhyming pattern of the chameleon poem emerges into audibility from its own pure-syllabic camouflage. The scheme in question is Moore's own—her stanzaic patterns which, in their fixity, allow of many motions when in use. A final matter is that of the form as *format,* mentioned earlier in these remarks. It is not that the typographical pattern produced by aligning rhymed lines is anything like a shaped or figured poem like the Hellenistic *technopaignia,*

Herbert's altar, or *calligrammes* by Apollinaire or May Swenson. Instead, to use Marianne Moore's own words in 1926 about E. E. Cummings, such a stanza represents "a kind of verbal topiary-work . . . not a replica of the title, but a more potent thing, a replica of the rhythm—a kind of second tempo, uninterfering like a shadow.[15] Not a chameleon-shaped stanza, in short, but a symmetrical form one reads into and then out of. In fact, it is rather like the stanza pattern of Herbert's emblematic "Easter-Wings." And in the slightly shifted indentation of the later version, this pattern is made more apparent, even at the cost of violating the alignment of the rhymed lines—long/short, short/long—of the opening and closing "couplets":

> Hid by the august foliage and fruit of the grape-vine
> twine
>   your anatomy
>     round the pruned and polished stem,
>       Chameleon.
>       Fire laid upon
>     an emerald as long as
>   the Dark King's massy
> one,
> could not snap the spectrum up for food as you have done.

Herbert's stanzaic pattern scans a movement from longer lines down to the words "thin" and "poor" at the center of the two stanzas, where Moore has "Chameleon" and "Fire laid upon." Moore's poem glosses the pattern of diagonal descent through long and short lines—aligned as Herbert, who indented by line length, could not contrive—into a revealed center and then out again into accentual audibility. Her shape narrows and thins, but it is not troped as such. Nor is it true that the schematic emergence of the accentual rhythm and the audible rhyme from pure-syllabic hiding are generally troped this way in her work. Indeed, the tuning in and out of phonological pattern, the occasional accentually marked internal rhymes, are usually transparent, not opaque.

Thus, the breaking-out of audible short concluding couplets in the last two of the three stanzas of the fine poem "What Are Years?" (*CP*, 95) is not itself emblematic of a pattern of action in the poem. But the foregrounding of the rhythmic process as the structure is worked through is related in another, nonmimetic way to its argument. (I use *argument* here not in its modern logical sense, but in the older one—most familiar through Milton and Emerson—of poetic substance or *mythos*.) Its "firm stanzas hang like hives," in Stevens's words,[16] though not here, as with Dante's, in hell. The bees of phrase buzz in and out; the looser, more problematic part of the argument overflows the first of the strophes into the second, while the third, fully possessed of its central trope, is self-contained. Nothing in the strophic scheme (brackets here stand for indented positions)—

6a]
6x
7a]
8x
4x
9x
7x
6b]]
6b]]

—tells us much about what might be done with it, save that, in any poem of Moore's we will not see the stanzas used as narrative moments or as phases of an unfolding or turned aspects of a central trope. But let us turn to the poem itself. Its title poses a question of a puzzling sort: it must be glossed over before it can be answered. *"What are years?"* Well, that would depend upon what *"years" are.* . . . The first strophe opens in a traditional mode of not-quite-answering:

> What is our innocence,
> what is our guilt? All are
>     naked, none is safe. And whence
> is courage: the unanswered question,
> the resolute doubt,—
> dumbly calling, deafly listening—that
> in misfortune, even death,
>     encourages others
>     and in its defeat, stirs
>
>     the soul to be strong? He
> sees deep and is glad, who
>     accedes to mortality
> and in his imprisonment rises
> upon himself as
> the sea in a chasm, struggling to be
> free and unable to be,
>     in its surrendering
>     finds its continuing.
>
>     So he who strongly feels,
> behaves. The very bird,
>     grown taller as he sings, steels
> his form straight up. Though he is captive,
> his mighty singing
> says, satisfaction is a lowly
> thing, how pure a thing is joy.

This is mortality,
this is eternity.

Such a question, given as if in answer—perhaps to evade not a wrong answer but another sort of untruth—comprises a poetic scheme of its own, which I have discussed in detail elsewhere. Here it is used even more obliquely than usual: "innocence" and "guilt" are paired terms, immediately aligned and then perhaps crossed, with nakedness and safety in the next line. But there is no analogous dichotomy between aspects of *years*. Without the question of the title to puzzle us, we read on to the logically plausible next question about the sources of courage, until drawn up again by the first appositive glossing: "courage: the unanswered question, / the resolute doubt." The recursive reference of "unanswered question"—the title's, the first line's, perhaps the one about courage that the very phrase is in the act of helping to propound—is impossible to avoid. That last question, extending its period through the inaudible syllabic rhyme of the unclosing couplet of the first stanza, untouched by any phonological disturbance, comes to interrogative roost only in the second strophe.

From there, the unanswering assertion, Latinate in syntax, Horatian in tone, moves to the figure of containment—the sea rising up in a narrowing chasm—that presents another feature of the relation of sea and rock unfolded at the end of "The Fish." As the stanza moves toward its close in "What Are Years?," accentual patterns start working prominently: "the sea in a chasm, struggling to be / free and unable to be"—here the chime of "be" with the earlier "sea" promotes its syllabic weight at line end, and momentarily suggests that the verb is existential rather than predicative (in Italian, e.g., *essere* rather than *stare*). That suggestion is immediately quenched by the rhyming *contre-rejet* "be / free," although that very line continues something of the indeterminacy of the verb, this time because of the possibility of the previously established periodic syntax—as if "unable to be, / in its surrendering [, *something*]." But no; the second "be" is of that same "be / free." The audible couplet "in its surrendering / finds its continuing" makes sure of that. All we could complete the "unable to be" phrase with is the understood "so." The rhythmic couplet, by the way, is prominent despite its absolute rhythmic ambiguity. Either line could be performed as if scanned either as a dactyllic dimeter—

in its surrendering

—or as a trimeter—

finds its continuing.

In either case, both lines would get parallel stressing and, prepared for by all the preceding *sea*-ing and *be*-ing and *free*-ing, close out simultaneously sentence, strophe, moral paradox, and, ultimately, purported answer to the question about courage.

The "so" opening the last strophe, together with the following "behaves," is elegantly ambiguous. The sentence can mean "thus it is that he who feels things strongly behaves himself, *or* behaves himself thereby." Or it can mean that "he who strongly feels so—that is, strongly also—behaves." And yet the poem's moral stance, apportioning those two readings perhaps to the parties of innocence and guilt, would ultimately reveal them as being identical. The caged songbird, parallel to the previously enchasmed sea, "steels / his form straight up." The assertive declamatory rhythm of this opening accumulates within and across its lineation. Accentually, we get a little unrhymed quatrain:

> So he who strongly feels,
>     behaves. The very bird,
> grown taller as he sings, steels
>     his form straight up.

The rhyme "feels" / "steels" is displaced by the rhythm (cf. "grown taller in singing, steels," which would cause the rhyme to resound), even as we in reading feel the "steel" to be displaced from the bars of the birdcage onto the frail creature imprisoned by them, making of his nakedness a kind of safety. And even as the sea rises up in its chasm, perhaps to produce a spectacular display at high tide, so the bird's "mighty" song rises above the poverty of satisfaction with his lot. The poem avoids the easy expedient of contrasting with the lowly (a Biblical word, as Marie Borroff has suggested)[17] satisfaction, "how high a thing is joy." The chiastic pattern "satisfaction"—"lowly" / "pure"—"joy" not only contrasts but links purity and lowliness, yet not with an oversimple valorization of high and low. This is the purity that Moore continually celebrates.

In one of the *Soliloquies in England* called "Skylarks," Santayana observes, both of songbirds and young men training to be World War I aviators, that "the length of things is vanity; only their height is joy."[18] Moore's joy is neither of mere height nor or of mere length, but of life, perhaps even weirdly, fulfilling itself in its limitations. All of this being the case is our mortality and thereby all the eternity that can be conceived. The final couplet perfectly matches its precursor at the end of the second stanza in rhythm and parallels the gentler paradox of surrendering being continuing with its own sharper and more final one.

Perhaps now that the strange, twisted argument has discovered its own end, we can confront the question of the title. What are years? Terms of imprisonment? As our own years increase, are we doing time or redeeming it? Are years for counting up? Counting out? Does their accumulation build up the prison of our days? Daryl Hine, in writing about verse form itself, observed how "glibly we speak of the sinister forces that shape our existence / When, were it not for their influence, most of our lives would be shapeless."[19] In the case of this poem, the shaping of its very utterance is exemplary. The way it moves through its syllabic frame is parabolic, while not in the least mimetic. The bird's singing is *not* invoked in lines that themselves suddenly break out into the song of accentual cadence, for example, which would have been a low, even more than a lowly, device. Accentual emergence in "What Are Years?" is not troped as song; it is rather employed *en passant* to probe syntactic and semantic depths and, almost conventionally in Moore, for closure, for resolution. She asks, at the end of a later poem called "Saint Valentine" (*CP*, 233), "Might verse not best confuse itself with fate?," invoking the etymological sense of confusion as a mixed outpouring and reminding us yet once more that, for the true poet, verse is not a mold to pour thoughts into nor the badge of style that a literary politics might seem to require. It is rather character, and bodily voice.

## Notes

1. Stephen Cushman in *William Carlos Williams and the Meanings of Measure* (New Haven: Yale University Press, 1985) discusses these questions with superb insight and clarity. I should also recommend this book for its splendid general discussions of the formal operations of free verse.

2. This text appears in William Byrd's 1588 book of madrigals. See the discussion of it in Derek Attridge, *Well-Weighed Syllables* (Cambridge: Cambridge University Press, 1974), 196–98.

3. These passages are from, respectively: Robert Bridges, "Kate's Mother" and "Cheddar Pinks," in *Poetical Works* (London: Oxford University Press, 1953), 514, 507; Elizabeth Daryush, "Still-Life," quoted in Yvor Winters, *In Defense of Reason* (Denver: Swallow Press, 1947), 148–49; Robert Penn Warren, "Part of What Might Have Been a Short Story, Almost Forgotten," in *Being Here: Poetry 1977–1980* (New York: Random House, 1980), 51; and W. H. Auden, "In Memory of Sigmund Freud," in *Collected Shorter Poems: 1927–1957* (New York: Random House, 1966), 166–70.

4. See my *Vision and Resonance* (New York: Oxford University Press, 1975), 272–79.

5. As in the case of line 2 of the second stanza of "Fear Is Hope," discussed below.

6. Oliver Goldsmith, *The Vicar of Wakefield*, ed. Arthur Friedman (London: Oxford University Press, 1974), 133.

7. T. S. Eliot, *The Waste Land*, in *Collected Poems: 1909–1962* (New York: Harcourt, Brace, and World, 1963), 62.

8. Marianne Moore, "Marriage," in *Complete Poems of Marianne Moore* (New York: Macmillan/Viking, 1967), 62–70. Hereafter, poems from this collection will be documented parenthetically within the text with *CP* followed by the pagination of the poem under discussion.

9. Marianne Moore, "Fear Is Hope," in *Observations* (New York: Dial Press, 1925), 15.

10. Marianne Moore, "'Sun,'" in *A Marianne Moore Reader* (New York: Viking, 1961), 88.

11. Horace, "Ode 1.22," in *The Odes and Epodes*, trans. C. E. Bennett (New York: Macmillan, 1924), 64.

12. Moore, "To a Chameleon," in *Observations*, 11.

13. William Carlos Williams, "The Right of Way," *Spring and All* (Dijon: Contact, 1923), 120. See the fine discussion of this poem in Cushman, 48–50. For a more general theoretical consideration of the workings of enjambment, see *Vision and Resonance*, 91–116.

14. Emily Brontë, "Stanzas," in *Oxford Anthology of English Literature*, eds. Frank Kermode and John Hollander, 2 vols. (New York: Oxford University Press, 1973), 2: 1482.

15. Marianne Moore, "People Stare Carefully," in *Complete Prose of Marianne Moore*, ed. Patricia C. Willis (New York: Viking, 1986), 125.

16. Wallace Stevens, "Esthétique du mal," in *Collected Poems* (New York: Knopf, 1954), 315.

17. In her excellent *Language and the Poet* (Chicago: University of Chicago Press, 1979), 125.

18. George Santayana, "At Heaven's Gate," in *Soliloquies in England and Other Soliloquies* (New York: Scribner's, 1922), 116.

19. Daryl Hine, "Epilogue: To Theocritus," in *Theocritus: Idylls and Epigrams*, trans. Daryl Hine (New York: Atheneum, 1982), 139.

Marianne Moore, Winner of the 1968 National Medal for Literature
Photo by George Platt Lynes.

# 7

# Marianne Moore:
# The Art of a Modernist Master

## A Symposium

*Following the presentation of their papers at the Newberry Library, David Bromwich, Sandra Gilbert, John Hollander, Alicia Ostriker, and Robert Pinsky gathered for a panel discussion moderated by Joseph Parisi. The panel entertained questions from the audience during the discussion.*

I

PARISI   I know that Robert [Pinsky] and Sandra [Gilbert] wrote their papers separately and did not confer during the process, so I thought perhaps one of you would like to respond in some manner to the other's remarks.

GILBERT   We just seem to agree with each other.

PINSKY   The most boring possibility. But I did know the title of Sandra's talk and, in a way, based a big element of mine on what I, it turns out, correctly guessed to be what she meant by "female female impersonator." I guessed it because the idea has so much truth in it. One question that occurred to me is what it means in one's own life and in the culture at large to respond to a stereotype or an expectation. Whether you respond to it parodically or try to undermine it or just accept it, there are always costs, personal or social costs. I was trying to think of figures who decline completely to play to expectation. W. E. B. Dubois occurred to me. It is interesting that the stereotype, no matter how subversive or inflammatory it is, or how strongly you reject it, plays a role in your psyche. It's mostly books about race that evoke this. Another thing I think about is *The Invisible Man*, which asks, "How do you respond to other people's failures to see you?" Finally you have to learn to manipulate screens. It's an idea that came to me after hearing the Millay comparison.

GILBERT    For both Millay and Moore, the adoption of roles as costumes was frequently very empowering.

PINSKY    I, frankly, was thinking about it in a practical way as regards one's career. Dressing up the way people want you to and playing the poet in some way that people want at first might seem very profitable and shrewd, but it seems ultimately to be self-defeating or, at the very least, obfuscatory.

GILBERT    I think it might be particularly tiresome in practical terms. If it's aesthetically empowering, it might go on being aesthetically empowering, but you might get really sick of the clothes. You just might want to wear a different dress.

PINSKY    I find Moore to be such a mysterious person. I wrote about her withholding of herself. She does it so successfully that I don't have any sense of what the issue of roles means in her life.

OSTRIKER    The same thing is often said about Dickinson, I think for the same reasons. I thought the comparison of Millay and Moore was brilliant. However, I have one question about it. Though both poets have achieved popularity and both were marginalized, there really is a difference. Millay was much more popular, and then was much more thoroughly and contemptuously dismissed. Moore was never as popular and the dismissals are light, not severe. I connect this difference in degree, and I wonder if you do also, not simply with stylistic matters—one is writing sonnets and one is inventing new prosodies—but also with the obvious fact that Millay was using her sexuality in her poetry and Moore was withdrawing from sexuality in hers. Moore was respected because she was respectable. It happens over and over in the history of the woman artist that to write as a sexual woman is to be immediately popular and then damned by the critics. And as soon as you die, if not a little before.

GILBERT    I think that's true. What Millay was doing was intensely heterosexualized. On the other hand, I would say that Moore was valued because of what I'm calling her "parodically spinsterish asexuality." I'm not sure I would agree that she never achieved the sensational popularity of Millay; think of her correspondence about the Edsel or her throwing out the first ball at the Yankees game.

OSTRIKER    But people did not actually read her as much as they read Millay.

GILBERT    Yes, in a certain sense Moore's kind of popularity was almost worse. Because of the Edsel business and baseball, she became just a public figure. She was a public personality, and what people did read was the Edsel correspondence when it showed up in *The New Yorker*; what they saw was her throwing out the first ball. So the role, which I'm claiming facilitated the art, ultimately, for great masses of the public, got disentangled from the art. But it might have given her great pleasure.

PARISI  Isn't it often the case that when you adopt a pose, you become it eventually? That what might have been a strategy initially becomes reality? One thing that militates against that for me is what I see in the work as a remarkable consistency. The moral portrait that we see in Moore's work, whatever it may be, is remarkably constant all the way through. She revises and revises, but that just makes the work pithier and even more pointed.

GILBERT  I think that's absolutely right. It's consistent from the very beginning.

BROMWICH  I'd like to suggest a distinction between what Moore was doing in her writing and what Millay was doing in hers. The audience for the kind of poetry Moore wrote hardly could be said to have existed before Moore arrived, whereas the audience for the kind of thing Millay was doing was well in place. In fact, I don't think we are well situated even now to say for sure what Marianne Moore was doing. A very different sort of claim to originality is in question for those two persons, although they are both women, both are poets, and both are seeking by some combination of public and private strategies, as you call them, to enter the reader's consciousness. I agree with Robert Pinsky on one point: I also find Moore still quite mysterious in a way that I don't find Millay mysterious, though the vicissitudes of Millay's reputation have a special cultural interest and are, perhaps, themselves a mystery worth unraveling.

GILBERT  As Robert was saying in his paper, in Moore's case, the costume or role became a kind of fortress. Even the apartment in Brooklyn is a kind of fortress. The mother is the guardian of the fortress and the brother is a sort of gatekeeper.

I want to say one thing about the kind of poetry that she was writing. It is true that one can hardly imagine where it comes from, but I was astonished to find that some of her earliest poems—several of which were in *Poetry* in 1915—are surprisingly conventional for Moore. She started out writing rather conventional, epigrammatic, neatly rhymed, and carefully metered verses. It would be interesting to think how her style, which needed to create its own audience, evolved.

PARISI  I was thinking, in regard to what David Bromwich said, that we are certainly meant to see content in Moore's poetry. We are given messages left and right. It's good, old-fashioned religion in many ways, shot through with Judeo-Christian morality of a certain sort—abnegation, humility, all those sturdy virtues—so that it's very reassuring in a way. It is also interesting that, as a rule, the more you conceal, the more you invite people to find out what it is you're hiding.

PINSKY  It's one of the things about a fortress.

PARISI  Yes. So why is she doing this? And, at the same time, it is remarkable how much energy she invested in all of her strategies of controlling.

QUESTION   Was there ever a time in Marianne Moore's life when she went out?

GILBERT   Well, she went out. She was not a reclusive, you know.

QUESTION   But was she ever involved with people or activities in a way that might evince qualities other than the steadfast moral values she constantly talks about?

GILBERT   She belonged to very avant-garde literary circles. I think that's one of the things David [Bromwich] is getting at.

BROMWICH   I'd like to put on record a hunch which I may have gotten from Elizabeth Bishop's memoir or possibly from some biographical sketch of Moore. In the twenties she did have a difficult, important relationship with a man, which she ended. I think "Marriage" is partly about that. It doesn't seem to me, perhaps quite as much as it seems to Sandra Gilbert, a poem written from an extraplanetary perspective. In particular, the phrase about marriage "requiring all one's criminal ingenuity to avoid," which Sandra quoted, seems to carry a strong personal animus and to point to something, though we're not asked to speculate about what that might be.

GILBERT   It could be indeed that she wants and needs to avoid marriage because, having had some sort of relationship with someone, she discovered that she's just not cut out for it at all.

PARISI   If you're not going to get married, you're somehow criminal in conventional society. She was proposed to by one of the editors of the *Dial*—Watson, I believe.

BROMWICH   I have something to throw in for the remark Joe [Parisi] made a minute ago concerning the ease of getting at Moore's subject matter. I was even in doubt in one instance about a passage Robert Pinsky quoted which I thought of quoting in my lecture, but finally did not because I couldn't decide on the tone of it. In "Critics and Connoisseurs," she writes, "I have seen ambition without / understanding in a variety of forms." The whole poem is made to turn on what it would be to have ambition without understanding, and I think Robert, given the drift of his talk, made the decision in the end that it had a satirical undertone. I was going to quote it along the same lines, but I couldn't decide in the end.

QUESTION   Maybe I misunderstood something in Sandra's lecture, but there seems to be a large difference between her paper and Robert's. Toward the end Sandra spoke of Moore as being anti-hierarchical. It's hard for me to square that with all the disdainful poems Robert quoted in which Moore is always discriminating between what gets in and what doesn't, what is superior and what is inferior. I certainly see the anti-hierarchical strain with regard to flowers, the natural world, and subject matter generally. But with regard to people, social classes, and so forth, I'm not so sure.

GILBERT    It seems to me that what she disdains is precisely the arrogance that is the consequence of hierarchy. I had to cut out a passage from "The Jerboa" where she writes

> Africanus meant
> the conqueror sent
>    from Rome. It should mean the
>    untouched: the sand-brown jumping-rat—free-born; and
>       the blacks, that choice race with an elegance
>       ignored by one's ignorance.

That is, "the conqueror sent from Rome" epitomizes exactly what she loathes throughout the "Too Much" section of "The Jerboa." It seems to me that throughout her work she elevates the hero for respect, but that's not exactly a reversal of hierarchies; it's a refusal of hierarchies. I don't think Robert and I disagree.

OSTRIKER    What she satirizes is the desire to dominate, on which hierarchy is based.

QUESTION    How can a poet speaking with her voice be satirical in such a way? She completely dominates in her poems. Her poems are about strategies for dominance.

OSTRIKER    Well, one can disagree with that. I don't think that's so.

GILBERT    I'm also not sure that's true, although it is probably possible to make an argument. But the proliferation of flowers in the passage you mentioned, the way she sometimes doesn't seem to leave things out, and the way she keeps putting in quotations, are refusals to make certain kinds of choices and show a desire to present us with all the evidence and not, as it were, to hierarchize it or choose this rather than that. And the proliferation of footnotes, of course, functions in the same way.

PINSKY    To me it's very complicated because I think she is an autocratic writer. When she was asked about using quotation so much, her standard response was, "Well, if the thing has been better said by someone else, then why say it differently?" I don't buy that for a second. Her use of quotation is highly autocratic, even when compared to that of, say, Ezra Pound—plenty autocratic himself. In a way Pound is the more naïve quoter. Moore is very much in charge in the way she quotes and apostrophizes. The thing that I couldn't quite get at in my piece, because I don't know the terms for it and also because it's somewhat incendiary, is the more explicit dealing with social classes in her writing. There's a Jeffersonian and very democratic strain in the best of nativist American aristocratic life, and I think Moore as a person represents that. Her relation to New York and the Dodgers is like that. But the voice in her poems, insofar as it is asking "Whose property is poetry?" is formal in its constructions; it is sententious in an old-fashioned way. She likes the impersonal *one*. Her style is often quite paraphrastic, even when it's fastidious and precise. All of this is counter to another side of Modernism that we identify with Williams, which is to make language more demotic. She represents in my mind a figure like the very best grade school and high school teachers one had—I identify them with New England—who were extremely aristocratic in a certain way, but democratic in the direction they wanted to go. So you could construct a conflict in Moore's attitude toward hierarchy: one could say that she's against hierarchy and domination from a feminist perspective, but not from a social perspective.

OSTRIKER  It is interesting that the quotations always do two completely opposite things simultaneously. On the one hand, they are a gesture of modesty: they tell us, "These are not my words. This was said by so-and-so." On the other hand, they are a gesture of authority: "I've read so-and-so." So much in her work does conflicting things at the same time, which I think is part of the energy of her poetry. As Robert was saying, she wants to achieve these opposite ends simultaneously and discovers devices and gestures which enable her to do what others can't.

PARISI  Even the word *one* is a good example: *one* the generic *one* and also *one*, meaning *I*.

PINSKY  It is both very modest and very assertive. I was fascinated by the characters that members of the Moore family assign themselves from *The Wind in the Willows*. Rat, who corresponded to Marianne, is the most socially competent of the three animals. In the novel, Rat is the one who is out in the world. Mole, who was the mother, is rather a lovable but befuddled and common character. Then there was the brother who was identified with the solitary and curmudgeonly Badger, but who, in the paradigm of Moore's family, was actually the guy who was out in the world. He had a pad. He was working. So, in a way it's an inversion: the real world is the imaginary world of the family. But in another way, Moore had a very active professional life. She had this other, bohemian life. She was like Rat, in a sense, in that she was a very civic character.

OSTRIKER  She was actually more out-in-the-world than her brother.

PINSKY  If I were to have assigned those three characters from the children's book, I would have assigned them quite differently.

GILBERT  Well, you make me so nervous that I hope I've copied this down right. [*General laughter.*]

AUDIENCE MEMBER  Sandra is correct. Rat is the poet in *The Wind in the Willows*, which is why he was assigned to Marianne.

GILBERT   Why don't we go back to the issue of hierarchy? Obviously there is a tension in Moore, and there is a classic kind of female maneuver. She was passionately against hierarchy, and wrote against it, yet she was also filled with aesthetic desire and creative ambition, and therefore adopted a mode that is simultaneously self-effacing, as we have discussed, and authoritative. Because she was successful, the voice comes through; it is a very powerful voice, but a voice against certain kinds of domination.

QUESTION   That is certainly true, but the poems Robert discussed—"The Steeple-Jack" and the odd poem not reprinted in *The Collected Poems*—are about snubbing.

PINSKY   And her prose models were Dr. Johnson and seventeenth-century ecclesiastical authorities, not the dissenting writers of that period.

GILBERT   But she was going back into history and appropriating strategies so that she could use them to tell the story from her own point of view.

PINSKY   It was not a matter of finding an American popular model. She did not, like Mark Twain, create a prose style that reflects some democratic idea.

OSTRIKER   Right, but her ethos is more the dissenting ethos, even though she used the High Anglican rhetoric.

PINSKY   I think, just as you said before, it's partly these contradictions that make her prose interesting.

BROMWICH   Our sense of the word *democratic* has changed from what it was in Moore's time. Robert Pinsky tried to capture that when he talked about a certain kind of New England school teacher, and a desperate grab at trying to retrieve something we've almost lost. And it does come from the atmosphere of a dissenting household. The heroes of her prose are not just hierarchal Anglicans; there are dissenters, too—Bernard Shaw, for example. It seems to me that that went with an attitude of discrimination and fastidiousness that she could take for granted in her time. That's what's hard for us to feel easily now, because democratic, that is to say left-wing, politics in our time have such a leveling tone. Elizabeth Bishop, to cite one witness, wrote somewhere—maybe in one of her letters—that the two most democratic individuals she ever met were Marianne Moore and John Dewey. It's an interesting pair.

OSTRIKER   Discrimination and fastidiousness evoke the school mistress. I think we forget how much the democratic impulse was wound up with education in the twenties and thirties. Through education, any immigrant group could improve itself and become American.

QUESTION   I think that the idea of dominance is less appropriate to her work than the idea of mastery and Moore's feeling that her task was to master her instincts and to refine them into something acceptable to herself. I think she was striving for that in her work, more than dominance.

GILBERT   I think there is a real impulse toward mastery. The major syllabic verses like "The Jerboa," where the syllables cluster together like chromosomes, as she says, are an example. She seems to suggest that it just *happens*. But then she writes thirty more of those lines where it "just happens" again. It's really quite impressive. Now obviously, this is the pose of humility that Joe Parisi was calling our attention to. It's a pose of quiet arrogance: "Watch what I can do."

QUESTION   But one feels that she is doing it for herself, that it's her task, and that's what counts most of all. If others like it, that's great.

GILBERT   She certainly works with a kind of compulsiveness, yes.

BROMWICH   There's a phrase about Shakespeare that she uses once and then she quotes herself using it. I don't remember any other place where Marianne Moore wants to look like the sort of person who would quote herself. In speaking of Shakespeare, her phrase is "well-nested effects of helpless naturalness," and I think the feel of naturalness for yourself matters, but so does the "well-nested," which comes from building up the syllabics.

QUESTION   Do you have any real information about her formative years? Her father was gone, and we know that there was a triangular family, but it seems to me we have little biographical information about her youth. We have no real information about her years at Bryn Mawr.

GILBERT   It's very hard to find. One can go to the Rosenbach Library and read a lot of stuff, but there is no really good biography. I wish we had more.

QUESTION   There seems to be no masculine figure.

GILBERT   There's her brother, who is older and who begins to take the place of a father, it seems to me. Like her grandfather, with whom the family lived, Moore's brother, Warner, was a minister.

BROMWICH   I've always gotten the feeling, as I read more about her and reread things that she wrote, of someone who lived, as much as possible, inside a certain atmosphere of morality. For example, the way she acquired W. H. Auden as a late preceptor, as somebody she could look up to in the way that she had earlier looked up to Shaw and Milton, is quite unusual. It's especially unusual given the competitiveness of poets, which Moore was not free of. But Auden, as she felt— and I think she's right—had a moral voice that echoed the voices she grew up with, and she liked him for that perhaps more than for anything in his poems. The poem she refers us to again and again is "New Year Letter," the least, convention-ally speaking, poetic of his poems. It would take a critic of enormous tact even to begin to write Moore's moral biography. Laurence Stapleton's book is awfully good in this respect and very suggestive about the kind of morality that her poems inhabit.

GILBERT    Laurence Stapleton's book also gives the most background. It goes through various stages of her life and very carefully traces the composition of a number of poems. It also talks about how she and her mother belonged to the Women's Suffrage Party and is extremely useful in this respect. But there clearly needs to be something much more thorough and wide-ranging.

QUESTION    This week in the United States we had two major news stories. We had Mr. Hart's withdrawal from the presidential race and we had the Iran-Contra affair. What would Marianne Moore have said about all of this?

PARISI    Marianne, can you hear us?

GILBERT    Maybe we should have a séance.

PARISI    Perhaps she has already said it. In the last years of her life there were situations that one might have thought a moralist would have spoken more directly to. But in a way, she has laid down her principles rather clearly, again and again, about power and the abuse of power.

QUESTION    So what would she advise us that we read?

GILBERT    Her *Collected Poems.*

PARISI    Now available in paperback.
[*General laughter.*]

PINSKY    She wrote a topical poem that was extremely popular in its time but now is not very popular with critics, "In Distrust of Merits." The poem relates to a specific issue—her loathing for war. I don't think it particularly applies to either of the topics you mentioned; it wouldn't help Gary Hart, and wouldn't help Secord and company. But if one wanted to read a poem of Moore's as an example of the artist we've described trying to respond to the newspaper, "In Distrust of Merits" is a good place to begin.

OSTRIKER    *What Are Years* and *Nevertheless* are the two volumes that respond to the prewar and the World War II years, and I see all the poems in them as public, political poems.

PINSKY    "In Distrust of Merits" is a poem that was adored in its time.

GILBERT    But then it was violently attacked. . . .

BROMWICH    Randall Jarrell thought she didn't understand how brutal the war was.

GILBERT    She sent "postcards to only the nicer animals" was his phrase. He attacked her violently, and she got, in many ways, lumped together with Edna St. Vincent Millay, whose reputation as a poet, arguably, declined in the ten years or so before her death because of her involvement in the writing of war poetry and propaganda poetry. It's a problematic issue.

## II

PARISI    Although we've been reassured that each of our speakers was working independently, it would seem that there was a conspiracy. But I'm very pleased that the essays turned out to be so complementary in so many ways. In trying to think of a single adjective to apply to this vision or revision of Marianne Moore, I found that the word that kept coming to me was *subversive*. In one way or another, we've seen in these examinations of her work this quality on many levels: in the personality that she presented to the world, in the persona in the poems, in the use of prosody, and so on. Perhaps we could begin on that note.

HOLLANDER    All true poetry is always subversive of vulgarity.

GILBERT    There's a consistent attempt on all our parts to revise the image of Moore as a pious, decorous, ladylike, or precious and recherché figure, and to emphasize the ways in which she's a powerful figure. Don't you think we're all trying to do that in one way or another?

PINSKY    It will be very boring if we keep agreeing with one another. Scientists shoot for this and always find it doesn't work. I disagree entirely. I take back everything I said about her. I will strive for a little disagreement, although I'm mainly in agreement with what Alicia [Ostriker] had to say. I'll return to my theme where I was implicitly opposing gentility and vulgarity. I think there's a reason that critics, especially male critics, have found her off-putting. Often that kind of strong response is a high form of tribute. The article by Susan Schweik that Alicia mentioned proposes that Randall Jarrell, in the violence of his reaction to "In Distrust of Merits," wrote his poem, "Eighth Air Force." His poem is largely about how she *should* have written hers, which indicates that she got under his skin. But I haven't gotten to my disagreement yet. Alicia said something to the effect that Moore never shows allegiance to old, cultural hierarchies or social hierarchies. But there are exceptions that make her not the most sympathetic of poets to me, such as this passage from "The Hero":

> The decorous frock-coated Negro
> by the grotto

> answers the fearless sightseeing hobo
> who asks the man she's with, what's this,
> what's that, where's Martha
> buried, "Gen-ral Washington
> there; his lady, here"; speaking
> as if in a play—not seeing her; with a
> sense of human dignity. . . .

This woman is played by Shelley Winters, in effect. She's a tourist. She says "Martha." She makes that little joke, and asks, "What's this, what's that?" She does violate a set of manners represented by the word *decorous*, by the fact that the Negro is "frock-coated," and by the word *gen-ral*, which is an implied corrective of the familiar "Martha," vulgar "Martha." "Not seeing her" is a classic representation of hierarchical manners dealing with uncouth vulgarity. Part of me thinks, "Isn't it great to have a servant, referred to as a Negro in a frock-coat, decorously put this woman down?" Passages like that are a reason for the stereotyping that makes me join you in thinking there is a trivializing and blind stereotyping in a very powerful writer. That's my disagreement.

HOLLANDER   Since I tabled the notion of vulgarity, let me be very clear what I meant. I didn't mean her snobbery about the tourist lady's vulgarity. I agree that's just a gross, but forgivable, momentary lapse in taste. What I meant by vulgarity is the bringing up of a clichéd instance: "Oh, here's this Black servant who's a classier act than this slob, arriviste tourist woman." That's a vulgar move that was very popular in certain kinds of writing, but is the sort of thing that Moore's poetic intellect usually leaps way above.

GILBERT   Don't you think she has a kind of bemused affection also for the "fearless sightseeing hobo"?

OSTRIKER   Otherwise, she wouldn't call her a hobo.

GILBERT   There's something so affectionate about that phrase. It's as though there's a wonderful interaction going on.

PINSKY   It's an interesting word.

GILBERT   But the phrase "fearless sightseeing hobo" is not one that strikes me a real put-down of a slob tourist. She doesn't say the "obnoxious tourist." She would never say that, but one can imagine some phrase more acerbic than "fearless sightseeing."

HOLLANDER   "Fearless" is very ironic, as when Henry James says of a character in *The Awkward Age*: "In short, she was with unconscious heroism thoroughly herself."

QUESTION    Which readings of Moore should be taken seriously and not ironically?

OSTRIKER    As to which critical statements to take seriously, I would say read them and decide for yourself whether you want to agree or disagree with them. I think it is certainly the case that the older readings which we're all disagreeing with are readings that Moore set up for herself. She was asking for them. As Sandra said, she played those roles, wore those costumes, and behaved in public and at the surface level of the poems as a lady. It's a screen and a veil, but there it is, beautifully, at the surface of the poems. The fact that a millimeter below that surface is someone who is not very ladylike, who is subversive, does not cancel the fact that the surface is what it is. The surface is the first thing to be seen and is indeed the first thing that *was* seen.

QUESTION    Would it be news to Jarrell that Moore was subversive?

GILBERT    There is a way in which a person gets trapped in a role, and as Moore became increasingly a kind of public poet, with the weight of public responsibility on her, some feel her poetry deteriorated. The same thing was true of Wordsworth, too, and I don't think we need to worry too much about it. But I find the Jarrell remarks on "In Distrust of Merits" so amazing, because a poem like "Virginia Britannia" was available to him, with its actual, explicit, and ferocious statement about colonial rapacity. What in the world was he thinking of when he made that remark about how she sent "postcards only to the nicer animals"? That poem is directly on the subject of exploitation, enslavement, and colonialism. When Jarrell made his statement, it seems to me that it was totally off-the-wall and based entirely on Moore's self-presentation.

OSTRIKER    Once she had been enshrined as the perfect virgin, she couldn't do anything unvirginal. She had to stand there on the pedestal and shut up.

GILBERT    In the face of the explicit political statements made by Moore, how could Jarrell, who was usually such a fine reader of her work, who read so scrupulously, who extracted lines, who showed us how to understand her wonderful rigor as an artist and as a perceiver of the world—how could he have made such a remark?

BROMWICH    May I answer that question? First of all, just as a clarification, Jarrell's articles on Moore in his book *Poetry and the Age* include a short review he wrote on "In Distrust of Merits," and that review contains a paragraph of denunciation about her. It's a paragraph we've been talking about for the last five minutes. Bear in mind that Jarrell at this time was stationed in Texas. He was a member of the Army, but not seeing any fighting. He made his poems largely out of newspaper accounts of the war by Ernie Pyle and other reporters, although people who read his poems without knowing much about him have often had the impression that Jarrell was a fighting soldier. I think what struck him in reading

"In Distrust of Merits" was something allegorical and old-fashioned about it which his, at that time, very New Critical taste led him to suspect. I think he was wrong. As a declaration of the sort which tries to mate solidarity with a more common sentiment, I think Moore's poem is much better than the war sections of Pound's *Mauberley*, with which it may be competing in its talk about frankness and self-inquest. But I suspect that Jarrell had some competitive instincts about writing a kind of poetry that made plain some of the material harshnesses of war. That might seem now, in retrospect, quite as parochial a prejudice as the almost archaic conventionality of Moore's exclusion in her poem. But I think that's what's at stake, and it didn't really color a great deal of Jarrell's judgments of Moore over the years.

To get back to an earlier question about criticism of Moore, I like Jarrell's essay and I like Burke's in the appendix of *The Grammar of Motives*. I think Eliot's preface [to *Selected Poems*] has some remarkable sentences in it. In one he speaks of Moore's use, and he implies conscious use, of the curious, demotic jargon which has been produced in America by "universal university education," as Eliot says. And I think Bishop's memoir contains implicitly critical observations that are fine and useful, too. So those are the commentaries that I have felt drawn to in thinking about Moore's work.

But I'd like to go back to something about her tone, and even about "Gen-ral Washington" and the "fearless hobo." If you wanted to pick out Moore's affinities and characterize her somehow against a background of social history where she may be more at home than she was in America, at least toward the end of her career, you might want to think of the Duke of Queensbury's circle, to which John Gay belonged. It is close enough to the style of irony she was at work on. There is that moment in *The Beggar's Opera* where one of the beggars says, "She might as well marry a lord, if she's going to be treated like that." A similar kind of irony gets into the fearless hobo: you might as well be a hobo if you're going to be as fearlessly vulgar as that.

Another analogy might be helpful. Think of the kind of class irony you get in the movies of Preston Sturges in the 1930s. We are aware that there is a degree of affection in a scene like the one in which the fox-hunting club of gentlemen go amok on the train in *The Palm Beach Story*, and you see the whole twenty-minute extravaganza, which begins with the tally-ho and the trumpet flourish. We know there's a degree of satire on the whole New Deal situation, on the attempts at rapprochement, and on what the rich are doing anyway. We can still feel the funny combination of motives that was at work. I think that kind of scene may be as hard to get a grip on in twenty years as Moore is for us now. But it's not for that reason less interesting in helping us think about our culture.

QUESTION   How much of a sense do you see in Moore's work of the psychoanalytic theories that were pretty current at the time? I tend to think that she was very resistant to them.

GILBERT   That's a fascinating question that I haven't really thought about. But I think I agree that she did resist them.

QUESTION   Patricia Willis's exhibition currently at the University of Chicago shows a particular chameleon photograph which is clearly a major basis for one of the poems discussed by the panel. The exhibit shows the extent to which Marianne Moore was dealing with particular artifacts that she herself saved. I wonder to what extent we can analyze the poems without having those artifacts in mind.

BROMWICH   Not only with Moore but with any writer one is interested in to the degree that you want to learn all sorts of minutiae about him or her, I think that knowing the archeological layers or marginal materials both helps and hinders, but mostly it just gives a different view, although not necessarily a better one than you get from reading. I think, for example, of a lot of things I know now about the composition of, say, "The Steeple-Jack." Stapleton and other critics have covered the materials underlying composition. But I don't think that knowing these things has given me a deeper insight into what makes that poem beautiful and altogether distinctive. You can have a different perspective, but I don't think knowing intentions takes you deeper. It just take you elsewhere.

HOLLANDER   There is one instance where a glance at the artifact invoked would be of some interest and that is in the case of the very late poem, "Charity Overcoming Envy," about a tapestry. She gives the tapestry, which she had probably seen in a loan exhibition from Glasgow, a tendentious reading. In a strategy dating from the Renaissance, all poems addressing images designed by someone with one intention claim to have the truer intention. In this case, I think it does help to look at the artifact if you want to talk about the poem in any detail.

PINSKY   I find it illuminating without seeing it. I'm quite curious, though, in the spirit of what David Bromwich said, to look at particular pictures. Seeing the artifact can be illuminating about the spirit of a poem such as "The Jerboa." The drama in Moore's poems is not the drama of seeing an animal in a zoo or in the wild, but rather the drama of examining a photograph. Likewise, "The Steeple-Jack" takes place in a town that is, to some extent, in suspended animation. Her poems suggest the tact and authority of a scholar in a room rather than in the field. The rhythm of autocracy, reticence, and asseveration in the poems confirms the sense that Moore is studying a static representation.

OSTRIKER   She doesn't write like Thoreau. But while we're on artifacts, I have a question for John [Hollander]. In "What Are Years?" whenever I read "The very bird, / grown taller as he sings, steels / his form straight up," I see Brancusi's bird and think that Moore is causing him to sing, to vibrate. We don't hear that he is captive until after we see him being steel and singing. And it's not necessarily the case that he is captive in a cage. He may be captive as any body or artifact is.

HOLLANDER   That's possible, but Brancusi's bird does not exist in steel form—only in brass and bronze, as far as I'm aware. That wonderful verb—"*steels* / his form straight up"—brings to mind, and I wonder whether or not it should, structural steel and a building steeling itself up. It is, of course, possible, but I think that usually when she does have something like that in mind, she will let you know very emphatically.

Another kind of artifact is, of course, the texts she quotes from. There is a much wider range of strategies in her quotation than has been suggested. Some of it is of that very evasive, complex, echoic sort that depends on your going to the source of the quotation and seeing what is left out. David Bromwich once taught me a wonderful lesson about that, pointing out that sometimes all of the lines preceding a quotation are absolutely relevant to a poem, while the part quoted actually deflects the attention. "Marriage," which is a sensational poem, ends up with that figure of Daniel Webster and a quotation that every school child knew: "'Liberty and union / now and forever.'" But every school child knows that there are three elements to that quotation, and the one that is suppressed is the one that glosses the middle and last stages of that poem most interestingly. She says, "'Liberty and union / now and forever'" as if she were celebrating, near the end of the poem, the marriage of the abstractions liberty and union. But no. The suppressed line is "Liberty and union now and forever *one and inseparable*" [italics added]. The omission constitutes the kind of imaginative power of "Marriage" in its substitution for usual stories about what marriage is.

So, I think if you want to possess yourself of the artifact, you must return to the text quoted. I checked out a passage the other day where she simply refers you, with an incorrect notation, by the way, to the Loeb Library *Greek Anthology* for something you would think would be a centipede emerging, but it isn't; it's a fight against a very fierce dragon. It's important that you know that's what she's domesticating in a very complicated way.

Just today I remarked to David [Bromwich] that the title of "The Paper Nautilus" is, I am certain, a turn against the most famous nautilus in American poetry, "The Chambered Nautilus" of Oliver Wendell Holmes. Holmes's poem ends with a complicated proto–Moore-like prayer: "Build thee more stately mansions, O my soul." This is precisely what Moore is doing with her poetry in a different mode of stateliness—you might say subversive stateliness, revisionary stateliness. So I think that her quotations are artifacts that you do have to look at.

AUDIENCE MEMBER    I'd like to pick up on what John [Hollander] said. I think there has been resistance on all our parts to tracking through Moore's footnotes and the things that we can live without, as her contemporary critics did. On the other hand, she left us an elaborate trail, not only through her footnotes, but also through the enormous collection of her stuff. And one purpose in putting it together in an exhibition is to suggest that she left it for a reason. She could have thrown it all out—the clippings, the little notes scratched everywhere, and the magazines from her library. Moore was somebody very much of her time and place, and that doesn't always show up on the surface of the poems. In a poem like "An Octopus," of the 231 lines, she suggests that she has quoted or interpolated 50 or 60 lines. But I'm up to 131 and still counting! Some lines are in quotation marks, some aren't, but they're all from elsewhere. And the speculation is that maybe all 231 lines came from someplace outside her imagination. If that's the kind of poet she is, maybe we ought to move toward another view of her. The quotations seem to break down between what the poet wants to claim in her own voice and what she wants to distance herself from.

HOLLANDER    That's a fascinating question, Pat [Willis]. We don't have a good conceptual apparatus for dealing with the devices of quotational mosaic. Cento is a medieval practice where you make up a whole poem out of half-lines of Virgil, variously arranged. There are capricci, in which you occasionally put in something borrowed. There is the whole Modernist notion of collage. A remarkable early essay, from 1939 perhaps, by Clement Greenberg discusses the theory of collage in painting, and the question of whether or not it is applicable to language is brought up. In collage, does a bit used in a new assemblage yield its source or hide it, and how can this be tuned in and out of somebody's consciousness? I think that's a fascinating idea. Contrary to what we tend to think, a poem made of quotations from other poems is not like, in its method of doing this, any other poem.

BROMWICH    One contrast you could make to help define Moore's position about tracking sources and how they are perhaps meant to help readers, is the contrast between her and Pound. She felt indebted to him as a catalyst of the literary movements to which she felt an allegiance. She calls the *Cantos*, in the first sentence she writes about it, an "epic of the farings of the literary mind," and she says with a degree of irony that I think is still audible to us that Pound tells you not only that he read the book, but also "Where you may see it"—namely, in his notes to certain libraries and so on. One way of connecting Pound's fascist and hierarchical politics with what he was doing in literature—I wouldn't take these connections too far by the way, but there is something to them—is to see that he is playing a game of hide-and-seek with the reader. He doesn't want the reader to know everything he knows. There is a distinctly authoritative relationship between him and the knowledge which he connects superstitiously with the sources that he's citing. Moore's leaving her tracks so out in the open suggests a more democratic attitude in that old-fashioned, early-Dewey spirit of democracy we were talking about earlier. There is a strong contrast between her and Pound that could be traced in lots of ways. Think about *Mauberley* and its procedure of quotation. Pound is not the master there, I think, but the servant of a kind of optional irony. When he quotes things, he's not always sure what he thinks of them, or he thinks on both sides of those raised-eyebrow kinds of quotation marks. Moore is very different. She always knows what she thinks of the source she's using and even has a reason why she's using it. I think Moore's quotation is finally much harder to talk about, much less a matter of source hunting and more a matter of imagination, and that's one reason why literary scholarship is far behind in talking about her use of allusion as compared with Pound's.

QUESTION    Could the panel speculate about Moore's place in literary history? She seems to be an anomalous figure in that her allegiance was to the Modernists, but after World War II she is admired by, and perhaps even an influence on, James Merrill, Richard Wilbur, and other poets who often write as though Pound and Williams had never written. Literary taste is often shallow, but it is odd that she could seem so experimental early in the century and after World War II become a model for the kind of poem based on the feature article, as Marie Boroff calls it.

OSTRIKER    Something similar has happened in the literary histories of H. D. and Gertrude Stein. They were marginal and appreciated by only a very few compeers at first, but have more recently become tremendously influential.

HOLLANDER    In the interest of jazzing it up a little, I would disagree strongly. I think that Moore is as one with a lot of poets who are neglected at first. Look at the critical reputation of Stevens up to about 1953 or 1954. Look at Hart Crane's reputation. Stephen Vincent Benét, William Rose Benét, Archibald MacLeish, etc.—these were the top poets when the great poetry was being written and not recognized. I think Moore, despite attempts to claim her for all sorts of sectarianisms, is simply like a number of other major poets in not being understood or appreciated except by other major poets, and being gotten systematically wrong by literary journalism in all sorts of ways for a long time, until finally the point begins to emerge.

QUESTION    Merrill has expressed great admiration for her and no admiration really for Pound or Williams.

HOLLANDER    That simply means that Pound, Williams, and Moore are all very original poets and that there is no necessary linkage among them. There is a way of talking about a great deal of Williams which is not contra-Pound, but is just of a totally different realm. For example, the large element of working against Keats and Shelley in early Williams is not at all an element in Pound, for whom Keats and Shelley were not important.

What has emerged is the recognition of Moore's striking originality, which is not an originality of mere quirkiness. In time the clouds of fashionable discourse blow away and leave what was there to be seen. It's just harder to see at the beginning.

QUESTION  There's a sense in which Marianne Moore was very influential after World War II when poems about objects and art objects were very popular. That's not the kind of poem that one would have seen emerging from Modernism.

GILBERT  What was originally experienced as radical stylistic experimentation, cleansing words of their old contaminating qualities, as Williams said, was later identified with a kind of formal conservatism. That is, her use of syllabics and her presentation of stanzas that look alike got associated with a kind of poem that people were increasingly writing after World War II. She had a very heavy influence, for example, on Sylvia Plath, a number of whose early poems in the fifties are in Moore-like syllabics. Plath was influenced by other sources, too, but she said very explicitly how much she admired Moore.

HOLLANDER  There may be a difference between deep response and superficial or stylistic response. The more kitschy thing influenced a lot of uninteresting poetry because it was stylistic and had to do with subject matter. The kinds of things that Merrill and Wilbur would respond to are far deeper matters than style. This is paradigmatic: if you look at a lot of very good poets, you'll find that certain other poets have very deep business with them and others have shallower business which is much more visible and widespread.

BROMWICH  Poets of my generation are now writing a good deal in Marianne Moore's vein. An obvious affinity with Moore in choice of subject matter—it's almost a salute—is visible in a lot of volumes by both men and women which have come out in the last few years. But it doesn't seem to me to be at the level of Wilbur's poem, "A Baroque Wall-Fountain in the Villa Sciarra."

HOLLANDER  One major poet whose relation to Moore remains to be investigated, because I'm sure that it is not stylistic but very deep, is May Swenson. Her relation to Moore is quite complicated and I would like to see somebody study it.

QUESTION  Were there any poets other than Elizabeth Bishop on whom Marianne Moore had a direct and deep influence of the sort you are discussing?

BROMWICH  I think Jarrell is one, oddly enough. He understood very well the psychology of parody, which is closely related to homage. The only two poets that he wrote parodic imitations of are Corbière and Moore. Some of Jarrell's work starting in the late forties has her kind of emotional pitch and movement more than her diction or form. However, I don't notice much influence through Jarrell on poetry of recent years. Moore's influence may have come to fruition much less through Jarrell than through Bishop, who has immediately influenced many recent poets.

# 8

# "Determination with Resistance": On the Prose of Marianne Moore

*Joseph Parisi*

*I have a mania for straight writing—however circuitous I may be in what I myself say. . . .*
"Idiosyncrasy and Technique"

As a critic, Marianne Moore was an excellent poet, in the opinion of most commentators on her reviews and other prose. An ambivalent compliment, to be sure, and noted over thirty years ago by Randall Jarrell, who rephrased it in his usual acute fashion: "One critic has said that Miss Moore's poetry is not poetry at all, but criticism—actually even her criticism is not criticism but an inferior sort of poetry."[1] In any case, or rather in both cases, poetry and prose, Moore applied principles that would come to be called Modernist: precise observation and shifting perspective, odd dissociation and abrupt juxtaposition, concision and ellipsis. Moore's distinctive use of exact description, of sharp fragmentation, and unexpected realignment, most famously in quotation (mainly from prose sources), produced, in her experimental poetry, assemblages whose artful combinations of assertiveness and ambiguity continually intrigue, delight, and prompt further interpretation.

Beyond the licensed precincts of verse, however, Moore's application of similar methods in prose has provided somewhat less satisfaction, at least for many critics of her criticism. While quick to praise Moore's astute individual perceptions, shrewd citations, and gift for aphorism, they also point to her apparent lack of analytical depth. The liberties permitted the poems, the elements of style which give what she called her "exercises in composition" their peculiar strengths, now become liabilities in the essays: centones substituting for logically developed paragraphs, apophthegms for arguments. Brilliant in detail, Moore the essayist is found to be deficient in Basic Rhetoric and remiss in her duty as critic. Her deviations from conventional prose technique, particularly her lack of smooth transitions, have led critics to call these other exercises in composition "impressionistic"—itself an adjective neither precise nor immediately persuasive when one considers Moore's admiration for Dürer, the incisiveness, the bite of whose woodcuts she emulates in her verbal art.

Writing in 1928, when Moore had already published a substantial number of reviews and other prose pieces—most of them in the *Dial*, where she had then served as Editor for three years—Gorham Munson first put the case for the opposition succinctly:

> She attempts to make no more than a sensitive impressionistic sketch of her reading, a sketch that is always liberally studded with quotations from the author under review, and carries a valuable sentence or two of acute technical understanding for good measure. The quotations are ably selected for the object she has in mind, which is to give the "flavour" of the author. . . . The critic must do more than that. At any rate, he should not be backward about handling ideas.[2]

Few today would suggest that Moore was "backward about handling ideas"; but in approaching them, she often followed (as she admitted) a circuitous route. Or routes: Moore took several tacks toward the diverse authors and texts under her purview, adapting her own style to accommodate them. Moore's early critical writings, the majority reviews or short articles, including her many items in the "Comment" and "Briefer Mention" sections of the *Dial*, are her most idiosyncratic and adventurous. Printed between 1916 and 1929 and addressed to the select readers of little magazines—including of course her fellow "emerging" authors who also made their earliest appearances there—these pioneering essays offered important contributions to the dialogue of the incipient Modernist movement. In giving discerning notices to the variety of authors she championed and in emphasizing the particular aesthetic values she so sharply delineated, they also helped establish the canon during that formative, often confusing period.

Viewing these essays and the body of prose that followed, one is struck by Moore's shift in emphasis, from severity to increasing sympathy, between the early reviews and commentaries and the later, better known articles. Early and late, Moore is preoccupied with the matter of criticism itself—its uses and misuses, its proper relation to the products of imagination—so much so that it becomes the dominant motif. Therefore, I want to begin with a short survey of this extensive enterprise, focusing on the distinction Moore draws between criticism, which she defines primarily as an offensive, even destructive, activity, and appreciation, which, in the early work especially, becomes a strict process of "subjection" as a wide variety of art comes under the diffident scrutiny of her demanding mind.

One way to understand Moore's negative definition of criticism and her distinctive approach to appreciation is to consider how she arrived at them; and so the second section of this essay briefly examines Moore's early experiences as a student and a young writer. To an extraordinary degree, Moore was able to turn restrictions into means of self-fulfillment; "when obstacles happened to bar / the path," she rose courageously to the occasion. The disappointments which greeted her in college and in her first ventures into publishing suggest the origins of her determination and creative "resistance," as well as her animus against conventional criticism. At the same time, we see positive factors which contributed to the formation of Moore's fiercely independent attitude toward art and her catholicity of taste. Notable among them are certain ideas of Ford Madox Ford, which may have been more influential for Moore's practice than is usually acknowledged. Particularly as they advocate pluralism in modern art and constructive criticism which encourages the new, Ford's positions inform Moore's critical attitudes as expressed in both her poems and her essays, and they are embodied in her work at the *Dial*. With this context in mind, I will turn in the final section to the early prose, to examine Moore's central themes and the range of approaches she takes toward a diversity of subjects. Important as primary documents in literary history, Moore's strict appraisals are among the first to identify the most significant writers of the Modernist movement and to define its terms. They also form a remarkable record of the poet-critic's continuing resistance and determination, a story of hard-won poise that carried her through a distinguished life as a writer spanning half a century.

I

Until the recent appearance of Patricia Willis's long-awaited, splendid edition of *The Complete Prose*,[3] the entirety of Moore's numerous prose publications was difficult to survey. The hundreds of reviews, articles, and shorter pieces remained scattered in the issues of little magazines, journals of opinion, and newspapers, as well as general-interest and popular monthlies. In *Predilections*, published in 1955, the author chose to reprint just twenty-two pieces, the majority from the thirties and forties, leading with "Feeling and Precision," "Humility, Concentration, and Gusto," and "Henry James as a Characteristic American," followed by nineteen short reviews and critical sketches. She represented her nearly two hundred contributions to the *Dial*—twenty-five review articles, 121 "Briefer Mention"s and scores of "Comment"s—with only four pieces. A decade later, *A Marianne Moore Reader* retained "Humility," "Henry James," and the Pound and Eliot reviews from the thirties, but replaced the more demanding essays of the first collection with the 1956 lectures on "Idiosyncrasy and Technique" and the more discursive reviews and the pleasant feature articles of Moore's last years. Thus, substituting for Wallace Stevens, Sir Francis Bacon, "Besitz und Bemeingut,"

"Ichor of Imagination," and "'Literature the Noblest of the Arts,'" the new compilation offered Robert Andrew Parker, Abraham Lincoln, "Brooklyn from Clinton Hill," George Plimpton's brief career in baseball, and the Ford Correspondence on the Edsel. The partial *Reader*'s updated, popular assortment seemed designed to present a handy print version of the adorably wise elderly eccentric one "knew," thanks to *Life*, from her visits to the Bronx Zoo and Yankee Stadium.

By the time of her death, in 1972, both *Predilections* and the *Reader* were out of print, like all the individual poetry volumes. In the Rosenbach Museum and Library, the constant writer's reading, conversation, and working notebooks, as well as her voluminous correspondence, still await publication. Until these materials, the complete *Dial* correspondence in particular, become readily available, a full account of Moore's influence in shaping the Modernist movement cannot be made. But, meanwhile, *The Complete Prose* offers invaluable aid in recovering, if not the whole of Marianne Moore, then a significant part, particularly the young author-editor—a figure rather more formidable and complex as a critic than the post-1929 prose publications, and public image, suggested.

In his brief but comprehensive review of *Predilections* (first published in *Poetry* in 1956), Kenneth Burke offers a variation on the "impressionistic" theme: "[S]he can infuse an almost pedantic literalness with the moodiness of impressionistic criticism." He adds, "[T]he page becomes wholly an act of collaboration, a good thing that seems to transcend any one person's ownership, though only someone as expert at this art as she could bring such effects into being."[4] These "fine acts of identification" (in Burke's phrase) display, in fact, a double talent. The critical acumen which enables the poet to point unerringly to another author's most characteristic utterances arises from Moore's capacity for empathy. Particularly with writers she admires, she evaluates while subordinating her own style, "presenting the essential picture," as she said of Marchette Chute, "with self-effacement that becomes an intensive" (477).

Burke notes that "*Predilections* treats of no bad books, the selections dealing with the best in the best of our contemporaries."[5] It is often remarked that Marianne Moore reviewed only those books of which she approved, a notion reinforced by the fact she chose to reprint only her favorable commentaries. But this is not accurate. Her policy (paraphrasing Leo Stein in a "Comment" piece of 1928) states, more precisely: "never to review a book unless essentially in sympathy with it and never to proffer [a] critical verdict without at the last again consulting the book to be sure that what [one] has written is apt and dependable." She adds, "we agree with Mr. Stein in choosing, *when we can*, to analyze what we instinctively like" [emphasis added] (201). As an editor she could not restrict her choices only to what she personally liked; and as a critic, before and during the *Dial* years, she did not send postcards (to paraphrase Jarrell) only to the nicer authors.

Moore's sympathies were wide, but not boundless, as attested by the decidedly cautious receptions given several in the large assortment of authors she surveys early in her career. It is true that, when she finds herself in the company of such as Eliot, Stevens, Edith Sitwell, or Gertrude Stein, her verdicts can be singularly affirmative, combining affectionate concentration with gusto. But, with the notable exceptions of Eliot and W. H. Auden, even paragons are found wanting. Especially in her reviews of early volumes by the Modernist masters, she is as careful to reveal flaws as to highlight beauties.

As editor, Moore's tastes were catholic, but strict. In her selections for issues of the *Dial*, she recognized and promoted a variety of individual talents in literature and the arts. But in her commentaries, she also defines acceptable limits according to her aesthetic standards. To be sure, Moore was never a theorist; but her repeated statements about precision and truth, imagination and individuality, do make clear her basic criteria. In her reviews, she finds much she instinctively likes, and praises what she can; but her close consultations reveal much that is less than "apt and dependable" in her contemporaries. Those who know Moore from her post-1929, mostly laudatory reviews and the more leisurely nonliterary essays, encounter a sterner analyst in the pages of the young professional.

From her first review in 1916, Moore sets a tone of remarkable authority; and within a decade, she announces virtually all the central predilections and delineates most of the major artistic criteria she reiterates and exemplifies in her later, more well-known essays. Moore is always an interesting writer; but besides presenting the unusual pleasures of the new, her first articles are especially intriguing because of the puzzling undertone they carry. Observing the operations of this keen intelligence in development—or, rather, in process of exposition—one discerns the mind of a critic questioning her own procedures. The discourse of the essays seems not only directed outward to the audience but back toward the conscientious author. This reflexive quality—evidenced in the frequent constriction, abruptness, and odd strain of the early prose—does not betoken Moore's "impressionism"; it betrays her unease. This apprehensiveness, born not of fear but of a scrupulous nature, is reflected in the strategies of criticism Moore devised.

Toward the end of a long career, she writes: "Criticism should stimulate understanding of the subject discussed—'with a truce to politeness,' as Montaigne says; unmannered and 'without the pestilent filth of ambition'" (593). As in many of the first poems—notably, "Critics and Connoisseurs," "To a Steam Roller," "Pedantic Literalist," "Picking and Choosing," "To Be Liked by You Would Be a Calamity"—throughout the first prose Moore displays distaste for or ambivalence about the enterprise of criticism. This duality—the conflict between the duty to render truthful judgment and a desire to respect the sensibilities of others—produces the tension evident in the writings. It is this stress, delicate as the deliberating mind it mirrors, that heightens the effect of Moore's lines.

"[W]e must be as clear as our natural reticence allows us to be," Moore famously advises in "Feeling and Precision" [1944] (396). But her preoccupation with balancing candor with tact is also registered more specifically in scores of comments on critics and criticism which stud the other essays. In the sizeable anthology one could assemble of such Sayings of Marianne Moore, the author expresses attitudes ranging from irritated tolerance to deep antipathy, with the concentration heavily weighted toward the latter. For inclusion in our compendium, we have this late item—the lead paragraph of "Subject, Predicate, Object," first published in *The Christian Science Monitor* on Christmas Eve 1958—which best summarizes Moore's final position: "Of poetry, I once said, 'I, too, dislike it'; and I say it again of anything mannered, dictatorial, disparaging, or calculated to reduce to the ranks what offends one. I have been accused of substituting appreciation for criticism, and justly, since there is nothing I dislike more than the exposé or any kind of revenge" (504). In Moore's lexicon, *criticism* is almost always a pejorative term connoting attack. For example, we have this passage from "Idiosyncrasy and Technique," printed immediately after the *Monitor* piece: "We are suffering from too much sarcasm, I feel. Any touch of unfeigned gusto in our smart press is accompanied by an arch word implying, 'Now to me, of course, this is a bit asinine.' Denigration, indeed, is to me so disaffecting. . . ." (511–13). Thirty years before, we find this opinion, in a brief review of *Notorious Literary Attacks*: "We perceive that there has since the time of Byron and Shelley, been a change in literary manner and are forcibly persuaded by it, of the tediously ineffective dullness of published personal invective" (252).

In "The Knife," a discourse on cutting implements which wends its way from the kitchen to the cathedral to the quarry to the killing fields, Moore concludes with a "moral" on the uses of tools and, by extension, the misuses of the critic's trade: "In valor, there is small room for egotism. As Confucius says, 'If there be a knife of resentment in the heart, the mind fails to act with precision'" (568). Moore herself had had cause for resentment, especially early in her career, when editors rejected her manuscripts and critics dismissed her unconventional verse as prose. In advising against indignation or retaliation, Moore emphasizes where the artist's and the critic's energies should be directed. "As we are aware," she says recalling Whistler's annoyance at "Ruskin's 'teachings,'" "it is determination with resistance, not determination with resentment, which results in poise" (177). In a 1934 review of *A Draft of XXX Cantos*, she chastises Pound, the lifelong student of Confucius, "when he dwells on worthlessness as in the imprecatory cantos, forsaking his own counsel which is good! One may vanquish a detractor by ignoring him ('or could have found the correction where he assumed the fault'); or may 'turn and build'" (324).

At the *Dial*, "building" art, not tearing down reputations, was Moore's objective. Her attitude to the work presented in the magazine and to her own book reviewing is most comprehensively set forth in a "Comment" essay of 1927, midway in her editorship. With its implications for both her essays and her poetry, it is worth quoting at length:

> Common sense is not innately favorable to Dick Minim, "the great investigator of hidden beauties," and has no particular need of the writer who is so obsessed with his own identity that he cannot refrain from deploring what is merely deplorable. *The Dial* may be abecedarian on occasion, despite its liking for naturalness, substance, and simplicity; but it would rather exposit the treasurable than advertise mediocrity. It agrees with the editor of Copleston's warning to reviewers that "the unbearable repartee" is silence. . . . A business-like rancor may exist in the heart of one who has learned from Erasmus "the smoothest form for each suggestion of politeness," but ill-nature on the part of those who have not learned politeness from Erasmus results usually in a collapse of unequestrianism. If criticism is "the effect of the subjection of the product of one mind to the processes of another," is not the reviewer's own mind disparaged by him in resorting to an inconsequent and disrespectful *ruade?* (192)

In closing the piece, Moore commends "a zeal for enjoyment and for not keeping that enjoyment to one's self" (193).

As principles, admirably put, and in the main adhered to over a long career. From the thirties on, Moore's essays are consistently positive in tone and notably warm when she assesses the genius of Henry James, the mature achievements of Eliot, Auden, and Stevens, and the more limited but genuine accomplishments of Cummings and Louise Bogan. During her last two decades, Moore wrote on many of the nonliterary subjects that interested her, and published where she pleased. Genially fluid, flecked with humor, and generous with facts, her feature articles do indeed demonstrate Moore's "endless curiosity, observation, research, and a great amount of joy in the thing" (592).

In contrast to these late pieces, Moore's pre-1930 prose, with its exclusively high-cultural content and cerebral tone, makes far greater demands on the reader's attention. In this hyperserious endeavor, Moore's curiosity is more inquisitive, if not inquisitorial, her observations even more meticulous, and fault-finding. Within its literary and artistic purlieus, the research ranges further and in greater depth, while the presentations of the findings are not always obvious on first reading. The prose is not so much "impressionistic" as incisive and intensely concentrated. And as the writer travels toward truth, she tries to keep her pact with "politeness"—a tortuous course to pursue, reflected in the dense syntax and studied diction. Further, even assuming the "professional" audience of little magazines, Moore's references and allusions can be unusually recondite. Though the essays are often witty, the humor can approach archness. By more recent standards, at any rate, the style of the early reviews seems artificial or sophisticated in the worst sense, a type of lofty ambition thwarted by all-too-literary overreaching. The long passage on book-reviewing quoted above is not untypical of Moore's early prose style (to use the tactful double-negative she often used in hedging).

During her four years as Editor and chief critic of the *Dial*, her "joy in the thing" was not unalloyed (*pace*, "*The Dial*: A Retrospect"). If criticism became a bad word for Moore (and increasingly so as she aged), in the early years appreciation was not synonymous with encomium. She does say, in reviewing a novel, that "the writing is so good that it is not necessary that it should be flawless"—once, in the *Herald Tribune*, in 1931 (277). In the *Dial* era, as always, she accords the books and artworks she reviews the greatest respect a critic can offer: close attention. But now her scrutiny is especially intense. Her minute observations usually discover defects—from illogic and sloppy diction to misplaced commas and ugly book bindings—and she evinces little pleasure in listing them. Her own idealism and meticulous attention to detail make her assume (or at least hope for) similar standards in others. Of course, she is disappointed. After a particularly trying time with Vachel Lindsay's *Collected Poems* in 1923, she concludes, more in sadness than in anger: "If a reader felt no responsibility for a writer, and were merely culling felicities, certain of Mr. Lindsay's poems would undoubtedly give complete pleasure" (90); she then lists such of them as she can find.

Although "'the unbearable repartee' is silence," in the case of Lindsay, she cannot refrain from deploring the deplorable; he indeed has it coming to him. In this and other instances, she lets authors condemn themselves out of their own mouths, through lengthy recitations. In addition, Moore frequently finds it useful later to quote others who have rendered judgment on a text she has under review, thus offering her opinions by proxy. Moore finds this distancing device convenient when the conflicts between "refusing to be false" (437) and trying to be kind are especially troublesome, as, for example, when she calls in Williams and Eliot to issue dissenting opinions on Pound's *Draft of XXX Cantos* (272–73).

In lesser cases of malpractice, her "responsibility for the writer" demands at least a partial accounting of failures. But in the spirit of the advice offered Pound, Moore does this by way of "'correction'" in order to "'turn and build.'" In "'Literature the Noblest of the Arts,'" she commends George Saintsbury's "statement, 'It will be only in a way for [a man's] greater glory if you find out where and wherefore he is sometimes wrong'" (115). After noting her reservations about certain phrases in a 1928 novel by Mary Butts, she hastens to add: "But to doubt is merely a part of liking, and of feeling" (147). Usually Moore is gentle in her remonstrances; the exceptions are cases of extreme ignorance, inaccuracy, prejudice, and what Moore perceives as destructive pride. Late in life she offers a general counsel with specific import to the artist and critic: "'Superiority' is at the opposite pole from insight" (503).

For the most part, Moore prefers to dwell on artistic successes. In her policy statement citing Leo Stein, Moore agrees, "in search of pure art we tend to feel betrayed when experts tell us merely where it is not" (201). In 1937, reviewing a not very exemplary text called *How Writers Write*, she notes dryly: "Writing is like living, better taught by example than by precept" (356). Hence the quotations. In the final, best-known defense of her approach by "mosaic of quotations," Moore asks: "why paraphrase what for maximum import should be quoted verbatim?" (512). Generally, Moore limits her excerpts to phrases or passages that point up an author's central themes or most characteristic strengths (or faults) of style. After submitting her evidence, she doesn't provide the usual kind of summary judgment; in most cases, "[a] suggestion, however, is as strong as an assertion" (286–87). In "Humility, Concentration and Gusto," she remarks, "I myself, however, would rather be told too little than too much" (422). In considering poetry, she usually follows this preference. As she explains in a review of José Garcia Villa, "only the purblind would dissect a rose to determine its fragrance, or a poem to discover its secret; for a poem deprived of its mystery would no longer be a poem. And mystery is different from obscurity" (370). What she says of William Carlos Williams's poetry might well be applied to Moore's prose: "Disliking the tawdriness of unnecessary explanation, the detracting compulsory connective, stock speech of any kind, he sets the words down, 'each note secure in its own posture, singularly woven'" (325).

In the same review, titled "Things Others Never Notice," Moore writes that "Williams objects to urbanity—to sleek and natty effects—and that is a good sign if not always a good thing" (326). In the essays, as in the poems, Moore's avoidance of "unnecessary explanation" and the "compulsory connective" gives her texts a jumpy, momentarily disconcerting quality. In their succinctness, her remarks can impart a note of "mystery" that approaches obscurity. But the authoritative tone, so "secure in its own posture," helps the reader keep faith when Moore's compression turns cryptic. This credibility is reinforced by Moore's penchant for aphorism. "Aphorism is one of the kindlier phases of poetic autocracy," she writes regarding Cocteau's occasional usage (351). "But beyond mere incisiveness, M. Cocteau sometimes imparts to a word a lovable neatness," she continues; and in her own case, aphorism tends to finish off her several strands of thought ("singularly woven," after her fashion) in a neat verbal knot.

In his review of *Predilections*, Burke remarks that "the cult of the succinct (in either image or idea) can lead, through the love of aphorism, to a particular concern with the maxims of morality, and so to an interest in strategies and tactics generally."[6] Although her aphorisms or "maxims of morality" inevitably carry an old-fashioned, comforting resonance, Moore does not moralize, in a narrow religious sense; her dicta pertain to technical mastery, the rigorous craftsmanship of the artist, which for her implies integrity of personality. To give but one example, in "Humility, Concentration, and Gusto" she asserts: "Originality is in any case a by-product of sincerity; that is to say, of feeling that is honest and accordingly rejects anything that might cloud the impression, such as unnecessary commas, modifying clauses, or delayed predicates" (421). Burke concludes his analysis of

"Feeling and Precision" by noting: "the term 'moral' in her scheme ambiguously belongs on both sides of the feeling-precision alignment. . . . One can never be quite sure whether her judgments are ethical or esthetic. . . . Whereas people generally tend to think of 'humility' as a moral virtue, Miss Moore often thinks of it as an intellectual or technical one—or, rather, as the point at which personal character and poetic aptitude meet."[7]

Eight years following Burke's review, Moore addresses the question more directly and concretely in a short *Writer's Digest* article, "Education of a Poet": "As will have been inferred, the most important influence on my writing technically has been ethical—as my brother once said of a florid piece of description, 'Starve it down and make it run'" (572). In shrinking her arguments down to aphorisms, Moore follows Bacon's lead, as well, when he advocates use of aphorism and epigram as aids for the advancement of learning: because their compression does not reveal all, it stimulates interest and prods the scholar to further exploration. Ultimately, Moore's aim in reviewing is not to digest the matter of a book for potential readers; rather, she wishes to entice them to pick it up and explore on their own. In a rare direct address to the audience, in the review of Pound noted above, she advises: "You must read it yourself; it has a power that is mind and is music" (272).

Locating the specific "power" of an individual work is the primary motive in the reviews; and since they are *individual* creations, Moore's approach to each differs. The leitmotif running with several variations throughout all of Moore's criticism is the paramount importance of personality and integrity of individual character in the making of works of art. To take but two examples: just before assuming the editorship of the *Dial* she asks, "is not style invariably a concomitant of content—the prototype of personality?" (105); and shortly after the magazine's demise, she says: "There is no easy way if you are to be a great artist; and the nature of one, in achieving his art, is different from the nature of another" (276), a statement from the *XXX Cantos* review which she liked well enough to reprint twice. The usual forms of critical argument, much less the journeyman reviewer's shortcuts or the hack writer's clichés, are inadequate to Moore's purpose.

"If," as she says, "criticism is 'the effect of the subjection of the product of one mind to the processes of another'" (192), in Moore's practice, the process is through a kind of empathy that is rare. In one of her earliest *Dial* reviews, a 1922 piece on George Moore, she writes: "Mr. Moore succeeds in seeming 'unaware of conventional appreciations'; undependable as a critic—inspired as an appreciator of those writers with whom he is in sympathy" (78). As evidenced by the extremely diverse and large number of works she is receptive to and carefully approves of over her career, Moore's sympathy was remarkably great. And because she has such empathy with creative individualists, a capacity both of thought and "of feeling," she can be extremely acute in "reading" their works (not only texts, but sculpture, painting, dance) and in recognizing the artists' designs.

At the same time, of course, the critic has to make aesthetic judgments which may be and quite often are negative. And it is here that, for one such as Moore, the matter of criticism becomes especially problematical: the reviews truly become *"efforts* of affection." For Moore, value and style in art are inextricably related to and expressed by the individual personality. This theme recurs throughout the essays, as noted; but to take a final summary example, in "Idiosyncrasy and Technique," she quotes F. O. Matthiessen: "'style means that the author has fused his material and his technique with the distinctive quality of his personality.'" She continues with her own reflections: "In saying there is no substitute for content, one is partly saying there is no substitute for individuality—that which is peculiar to the person (the Greek *idioma*)" (514). Since this is so, there arises a delicate question: how to allow for individuality of personality (and by extension, of style), as dictated by her own belief and sensibility, while rendering "fair judgment," which necessarily implies some set of criteria that transcend the merely particular and personal.

That such standards exist for Moore is everywhere apparent. Since conventional methods of analysis and argument can only accentuate the conflicts between the subjective and objective here, Moore's methods of resolving these difficulties require strategies of compromise which vary from work to work. These allow her to be or seem authoritative without appearing authoritarian, while she keeps her "truce with politeness." On the one hand, her invocations to Truth and Beauty and Self-Discipline are so lofty as to be unassailable, while sufficiently vague as to allow for any number of interpretations. On the other hand, she is firmly concrete in matters of technique, applying quite specific criteria of logic, accuracy, and precision to the individual case in point with punctilious rigor. As she invokes and applies her standards, with utmost seriousness and infinite care, whether the mood is one of gusto or dismay, it is extremely difficult to fault her. "And, indeed," she says in naming what is probably the fundamental justification of her approach by specifics, "if technique is of no interest to the writer, I doubt that the writer is an artist" (510). The meticulous quotations are the essence of her strategy, and the best proof of her concern for the author. Only through the particular can one "exposit the treasurable"—the unique instance where the power of the individual talent manifests itself. Even in the negative illustrations, Moore seems not so much interested in advertising failure as intent upon finding where and why talent has been betrayed, and perhaps how the artist might again touch or find his way back to the authentic self. Ultimately, it is the search for this authentic "individual genius" in each specific creative work—an almost mystical quality—which is the mission of Moore's prose.

"One also recalls the remark by Henry James: 'a thing's being one's own will double the use of it.' Discoveries in art, certainly, are personal before they are general," the critic remarks in "Idiosyncrasy and Technique" (514). And with those words in mind it may be useful to examine some of the factors which contributed in the self-creation of the distinctive personality of Moore the poet-critic and of the unconventional style she forged in both verse and prose. The early experiences at college and shortly thereafter as Moore began her career as a writer give some index to the acerbic tone of many of the early poems, and to the wary seriousness of her approach in the early essays.

"The aesthetic malcontent is out of court, for wherever there is art there is equilibrium," Moore wrote in 1926 (176–77). She herself arrived at this "equilibrium" through "determination with resistance," but not without some "resentment." When she was 62, the author could assert: "Moreover, any writer overwhelmingly honest about pleasing himself is almost sure to please others" (426). In her youth, the aspiring writer found, like many another iconoclastic Modernist, that pleasing was not easily accomplished. Like M. Carey Thomas of Bryn Mawr, she was "sobered by obstruction" (417); and with Joyce, she could attest: "'without suffering we do not advance'"(419). Like Moore's other aphorisms—from Confucius, Longinus, the Bible, and the quasi-biblical paradoxes of her own devising—these maxims are not mere sayings, but truths confirmed by personal experience.

## II

*. . . yet we must have the courage of our peculiarities.*
                                    "Feeling and Precision"

In "Pym," a short story printed in 1908, Moore has her young hero caught at a critical moment when he must choose between continuing as an unsuccessful writer or following his Uncle Stanford's advice that he return to law. He recalls their discussions:

> I bring up . . . the subject of writing, touch . . . upon the possibilities of the art. Also say there are times when I should give anything on earth to have writing a matter of indifference to me. Then add . . . that it is undeniably convenient, in time of expressionary need to be able to say things to the point. And, irrelevantly, that I like the thing for the element of personal adventure in it. (14)

Ten days later, about to give up his aspirations and with pen poised to inform his uncle, he jots these final notes: "In the effort to compass things in an original manner, however, anything can be made to come failure-end up. The effort of individual isolation, above all others. Nothing done for effect, is worth the cost" (15–16).

As in "Pym," other protagonists in Moore's adolescent fiction face the classic dilemma of deciding between the romantic ideal of a life as an artist and the mundane reality of making a living; and it is tempting to find in "Pym" and "A Pilgrim" and "The Discouraged Poet" portraits only slightly veiled of the college student and her sense of crisis, with its alternating moods of optimism and despondency. At least, Pym's sentiments about writing are echoed in Moore's later nonfiction, and the young man's troubling situation seems not unlike the nineteen-year-old author's own during her years at college and shortly thereafter. Unlike Pym, but like Carey Thomas, Moore "was not afraid of failure" (417). Sticking to it, she found "that to be hindered is to succeed" (502).

Moore's academic career was less than stellar, and in the six years following her graduation, she faced several disappointments, as Donald Hall, Laurence Stapleton, Grace Schulman, and others have related.[8] Despite her great desire, poor grades prevented her from majoring in English, but the courses in histology and biology and the hours in the lab proved "exhilarating" and invaluable. In his biography, Hall notes that at first Moore "had some trouble" even in biology, and that she took a "class in torts because the professor of law from Columbia who taught the course seemed humane. He was a relief, she felt, from some of her more frightening instructors."[9]

When she was finally allowed to take English electives, in her junior year, the only course open was Seventeenth-Century Imitative Writing. Again, restriction proved good fortune; here were authors she instinctively liked. In Jeremy Hooker, Launcelot Andrewes, and the other worthies, doctrine and diction are meetly conjoined, providing models Moore would continue to imitate, as she adopted both their *sententiae* and their syntax in her own distinctive prose. Sir Francis Bacon and Sir Thomas Browne must have been particularly appealing, as both iconoclasts happily combine modern "scientific" attitudes with idiosyncratic English prose styles: Bacon striving to reform learning by turning from the outmoded abstractions and unproductive syllogisms of scholastic philosophy to a new methodology based on observation and experiment; Browne indefatigably gathering all manner of arcane knowledge and curious lore as he attempts to dispel Vulgar and Common Errors in his monumental *Pseudodoxia Epidemica*; both employing epigram, aphorism, and marvelous concrete examples to do so. In the eighteenth century she found congenial stylists, as well, especially in Addison and Doctor Johnson.

Stylistically, Moore follows all these past masters, in their words and manner of expression, and in the habit of precision they encouraged, a scientific attitude reinforced by her nonliterary school studies. In the essays, Moore focuses on texts as on other specimens, preferring close observation of particulars to theoretical abstractions. Smooth arguments and neat logical structures were never her fortes, and these lacks account for her difficulties in pleasing her English instructors. "Having entered Bryn Mawr with intensive zeal to write, I examined, for comment, the margin of a paper with which I had taken a great deal of trouble and found, 'I presume you had an idea if one could find out what it is,'" Moore writes in "A

Burning Desire to Be Explicit" (606). That Moore can recall the remark verbatim, sixty years after the fact, suggests the deep impact of the criticism, the lingering hurt such disapproval caused the conscientious student.[10]

Despite her initial difficulties, Moore succeeded in having eight short stories, a review, and eight poems published in the student literary magazine, *Tipyn O'Bob*, of which she was elected a board member, her first editorial appointment. One of the poems, "Progress," was retitled and reprinted in *O to Be a Dragon* in 1959 as "I May, I Might, I Must"—not exactly *Veni, vidi, vici*, but a fair and admirably succinct statement of Moore's persistence in college and her endurance as she ventured into the world. Hall relates that in college she briefly considered medicine, an interest that is reflected in Moore's metaphors of surgery, scalpels, and the like in both the poetry and the prose, where other examinations and dissections take place. Besides her gifts for verbal description, Moore had a talent for drawing, as the more-than-competent sketches in her notebooks indicate. But in choosing the means of a livelihood, she had to be practical.

"With every reason to feel confident—except that we were in straitened circumstances financially (my mother, brother, and I)—I felt insecure, and took a day at a time, not because I knew it was the best but because I had to," Moore writes in "If I Were Sixteen Today" (502), recalling the situation during her adolescence. By 1909 the family's fortunes had not improved (indeed, they were always marginal), and after graduation in that year, she returned home to Carlisle, took a course at a commercial college, and for the next three and a half years taught, not literature, but "commercial English," typing, bookkeeping, stenography, and commercial law. She also served as an outdoor sports coach, and had under her charge the future Olympian Jim Thorpe (or James, as she properly insisted).[11]

The realities of Moore's life at this time were less than bright; yet again from limitations she achieved improbable success. What Pound said of Eliot was equally and more remarkably true of Moore: she "modernized" herself "on her own";[12] though, in her case, the author did not have much choice. In relative "individual isolation" during the crucial years 1908–15, when Eliot and Pound were pursuing advanced studies, formally or informally, and travelling abroad to absorb new theories and to refine their technique, Moore stayed home and maintained her aesthetic independence. From "the fabric of existence" (552)—the immediate facts of her experience and her eclectic reading—she discovered the substance from which she could weave the particular textures of her art. In contrast to Eliot and Pound, who draw primarily upon literary and high-artistic sources in quotation, Moore gathers from letters, newspapers, government pamphlets, old prints, "business documents and // school-books" too, to fashion her collage-poems: "Marriage" and "An Octopus" are her answers to *The Waste Land* and the *Cantos*.

In her prose, as well, she offers strong contrast. In comparison with the broad historical, literary, philosophical, and other cultural bases Eliot and Pound use as references in their criticism, Moore's resources appear all the more restricted and mundane, her focus narrow. Unlike Eliot, however, she was eager to comment on her contemporaries, and with Pound she had a striking ability to recognize the different original talents of others. In her efforts to acknowledge them in her reviews, she proved to be, like Pound, an indispensable champion of the new, though Moore was blessedly free from the contentiousness and tendency to dogmatize that characterized that irascible impresario. Eventually, of course, as Editor of the *Dial*, she assumed the preeminence of place in America which Eliot held in England at the *Criterion*. For the young industrial school teacher, such prospects would have seemed impossible in 1910.

Moore herself first travelled to England, with her mother, in the summer of 1911. Like Harriet Monroe on her trip the year before, Moore "discovered" Pound at Elkin Mathews's London book shop—not in person, but in photographs "which we were much pleased to see," she wrote in her first letter to him, in 1919.[13] They did not meet until 1939, nor did she meet Eliot until 1933; and, improbable as it seems, she did not personally encounter Wallace Stevens until 1943.[14] As she relates, the young poet met no other writers until 1915, when she first visited New York City and was introduced through Alfred Stieglitz and Alfred Kreymborg. Like her other peers, Pound discovered Moore through her first appearances in the little magazines, which prompted him to write inquiring about her origins. Impressed by her work, Pound assumed Moore had been influenced by European models, and he inquired whether she was "working on Greek quantitative measures or on René Ghil or simply by ear (if so a very good ear). . . . I wish I knew how far I am right in my conjecture of French influence. . . ."[15] She replied:

> I have no Greek, unless a love for it may be taken as a knowledge of it and I have not read very voraciously in French; I do not know Ghil or La Forgue, and know of no tangible French influence on my work. Gordon Craig, Henry James, Blake, the minor prophets and Hardy, are so far as I know, the direct influences bearing on my work.[16]

In "Education of a Poet," written in 1963, Moore recalls: "After leaving Bryn Mawr, I came under the spell of the *English Review* edited by F. M. Ford (F. M. Hueffer) who wrote many of the book reviews—some of which I transcribed, having borrowed the copies" (572). Though this remark is often cited, Ford's importance for the young Moore has not been adequately credited. Stylistically, his influence is not particularly discernible, as his fluent prose has a leisurely spaciousness that is absent even in Moore's later articles; and the ironic manner of urbane superiority which characterizes Ford's criticism is incompatible with Moore's general attitude and practice, though she can approach him in wit and tartness in her early reviews. Ford's more fundamental significance for Moore lies, rather, in his philosophical stance toward criticism and his particular assessment of the state of contemporary literature.

While Pound received Ford's theories at the master's feet in London shortly after his arrival in 1908, Moore almost certainly discovered them in a series of articles Ford presented in the *English Review* at the time she says she was transcribing his reviews. These essays were collected as *The Critical Attitude*, and published in 1911.[17] Whether in Elkin Mathews's shop, or back home, it is unlikely that Moore would have missed this work. Almost eighty years after it appeared, *The Critical Attitude* still gives good value; indeed, it often sounds like a prophetic book. The key ideas in the volume must have been a revelation to Moore; as evidenced by her own criticism, she certainly was in sympathy with Ford's position and appears to have taken most of his major tenets to heart. Not only does his expansive attitude toward contemporary life and literature coincide with Moore's own practice in poetry; many of his obiter dicta eventually are echoed in her reviews and essays.

In his opening chapter, Ford asserts the importance of criticism in a fragmented, chaotic modern world surfeited with information impossible for any one person to comprehend, let alone a single Great Writer or Poet to epitomize. After lamenting the technical deficiencies of current English writers and the debilitating effects of "existing in the backwash of the Romantic Movement," in his second chapter, "On the Functions of the Arts in the Republic," Ford arrives at his central theme:

> that the life we live to-day renders us dependent on the arts for our knowledge of life in a degree that probably never before obtained. We have so many more small contacts with our fellow-men; we have so much less knowledge of how men really live. So that almost every man of normal life to-day has the greater part of his view of the world from vicarious experience. . . . The painter who neglects to see beauty in the things which surround him, the poet who cries that happiness was only to be found in remote fields of distant ages, sin, in their degree, as much against youth as the novelist who, forcing always happy endings to his tales, draws a picture of life too easy and too slack. For, if the arts have any functions at all, that function is truly educational—nay, it is truly scientific.[18]

Of even greater import for Moore, in her own poetry as in her practical criticism, are Ford's prescriptions for the contemporary author and his emphasis upon individuality as paramount in the artist: "The province of the imaginative writer is by exaggeration due to his particular character—by characteristic exaggeration, in fact—precisely to awaken thought." At this point Ford restricts his argument to a practical apology: the modern artist's function, "his actual and first desire must be always the expression of himself—the expression of himself exactly as he is, not as he would like other people to think him, the expression of his view of life as it is, not as he would like it to be."[19]

In his final chapter, Ford considers the matter of "Modern Poetry," and both his general thesis and the specific terms of his argument are affirmed throughout Moore's prose; and next to her preoccupation with what constitutes proper criticism, the ideas concerning individuality, sincerity, originality, and "the real self" which Ford expresses here are Moore's most frequently recurring motifs in her reviews and essays. Ford begins by indicating why the traditional role of the poet is no longer tenable, and why today's poet "has altogether lost the ear of the public." Today, "With the flood of new knowledges let loose upon the world by the Renaissance . . . the task of mastering all that could be known grew appreciably more difficult." Since the time of *Paradise Lost*, "until just yesterday," Ford notes, "poetry and prophecy went hand in hand." And that's the problem: the public still "looks to its poets to be prophets."[20] Except for Kipling, no poet now "attempts successfully to sing of patriotism or any of the other eternal verities." And so we have the situation "with all the poetry of to-day":

> We are producing, not generalisations from facts more or less sparse, but the renderings of the moods of many individuals. . . . Literature is hardly so much a matter of books as of the personalities that the books reveal to us. . . . Instead, that is to say, of making the acquaintance of two or three enormous poets like Tennyson or Rossetti . . . we have made the acquaintance of a number—of a whole circle—of smaller, more delicate, and more exquisite beings.[21]

Ford is not disparaging the new poets; he is merely describing their current position: "until all the sciences have been so crystallised by specialists that one poet may be able to take them all in, and until we have that one poet, we cannot have any more poetry of the great manner." Meanwhile (and that would seem to be quite a long while), "the great figure has been replaced by groups."[22]

In concluding the book, Ford ventures several opinions: "We have not got any great poet, but we have an extraordinary amount of lyrical ability"; "with the extension of technical ability, and above all with the extension of desire for expression, we are enormously widening the net."[23] Unfortunately, Ford finds, the poets "seem to shut themselves up in quiet book-cabinets, to read for ever, and to gain their ideas of life for ever from some very small, very specialised group of books. . . . To do nothing else implies a want of courage." Ford's final remarks must have had a special resonance for Marianne Moore: "If the poet is timid in his life, he will be shrinking in his thoughts and over-delicate in his words. He will express, not himself, but himself as he would like to appear to other gentlemen."[24] In his peroration, Ford asserts that we go to the poet for his real self. And unless he speaks to us sincerely, without affectation, and in such language as he ordinarily uses, his poems will ring false, and we shall find little pleasure in him. . . . Originality of handling or courage of conviction have hardly as yet had time to gather themselves together. But that one day a stirring of the pool will come we need have no doubt. And it will come when some young poets get it into their heads to come out of their book-closets and take, as it were, a walk down Fleet Street.[25]

When Moore first ventured forth into Fleet Street, as it were, the reception she received was disheartening, both when she sought regular freelance work and when she tried to get her early poems into print. Shortly before the family moved from Carlisle to New Jersey in 1916, she set out, with her mother, for Philadelphia, hoping to get a job writing reviews or articles for the *Evening Ledger*, but was disappointed. She wrote her brother Warner, playing upon the family nicknames: "Rats need room to experiment and grow that is the main thing and *they need pay.*"[26] She had already been sending out poems while she was teaching at the Industrial Indian School in Carlisle, but all of her submissions—to the *Atlantic Monthly*, *Smart Set*, the *New Republic*, the *Century*, the *Masses*, *Yale Review*—were sent back. In March 1915, she wrote Warner complaining of the editors' "pigheaded and churlish prejudice against anything new."[27] Moore was now twenty-seven years old.[28]

Undaunted by the numerous rejections, Moore tried to improve her work. She also searched for other outlets, and in the *Editor* she located the new little magazines.[29] But even with these presumably more enlightened editors, Moore's relations were not always happy. As early as July 1914 she sent work to *Poetry* in Chicago, edited by Harriet Monroe, and a group was accepted. She also submitted to the *Egoist*, edited in London by Richard Aldington, husband of her Bryn Mawr classmate H. D. Aldington managed to get his Moore poems to press before Miss Monroe, and the *Egoist* gave Moore her first professional publications in April 1915. (One of the poems, "To the Soul of Progress," was later retitled "To Military Progress.") The following month, *Poetry* offered Moore's first appearances in America.[30] Soon after this welcome change of fortune—*Poetry* had the added attraction that, alone among little magazines, it paid contributors—Moore found herself at odds with both publications. In her letter to Pound in 1919, Moore recounts her unstately progress:

I do not appear. Originally, my work was refused by the *Atlantic Monthly* and other magazines and recently I have not offered it. My first work to appear outside of college was a poem, which one of three, I do not recall—published by the *Egoist* in 1915 and shortly afterward, four or five poems of mine were published by *Poetry*, a fact which pleased me at the time, but one's feeling changes and not long ago when Miss Monroe invited me to contribute, I was not willing to.[31]

Moore had felt *Poetry*'s reception was not wholehearted and became irritated when Miss Monroe offered criticism and suggested changes—practices she herself would indulge in as editor of the *Dial* (notoriously with Hart Crane, with whom *Poetry* also had difficulties). When Miss Monroe returned another submission in 1915 with an impersonal notice, Moore responded: "Printed slips are enigmatic things and I thank you for your criticism of my poems. I shall try to profit by it." She did not submit another poem to *Poetry* until 1932.[32]

With the *Egoist*, author-editor relations were more cordial; but old school ties did not prevent H. D. from rejecting some poems as well. Like Monroe, Doolittle also accepted Moore's prose; but when "The Accented Syllable" appeared in October 1916, Moore's copy had been slightly edited, as Taffy Martin has shown.[33] In this instance at least, the choppiness of Moore's prose appears to be the product of editorial tampering rather than authorial intent. In any case, the piece was the first and last essay Moore contributed to the *Egoist*. When H. D. and Harriet Shaw Weaver took it upon themselves to gather Moore's early work and print *Poems* at the Egoist Press in 1921, without her knowledge, the author expressed gratitude, but held mixed feelings.[34] Relations with the *Little Review* were more strained, especially after the editor, Margaret Anderson, appended a note to a Moore contribution ("You Say You Said") expressing the opinion that her work was "intellectual" and thus not poetry.[35] Continuing in her letter to Pound, Moore alludes to the incident, and her general feelings after a rocky four years in the literary world:

> I grow less and less desirous of being published, produce less and have a strong feeling for letting alone what little I do produce. My work jerks and rears and I cannot get up enthusiasm for embalming what I myself, accept conditionally.
>
> Anything that is a stumbling block to my reader, is a matter of regret to me and punctuation ought to be exact. Under ordinary circumstances, it is as great a hardship to me to be obliged to alter punctuation as to alter words, though I will admit that at times I am heady and irresponsible.[36]

Moore's disillusionment and pique are registered in several acerbic poems from this period; in some cases, their titles telegraph Moore's contempt for her satiric objects. Rather than confronting the offending critics and unappreciative readers or informing editors of her displeasure directly, Moore has transferred her anger by addressing various "you"s in the poems, as in "Pedantic Literalist": "You invite destruction. / You are like the meditative man / With the perfunctory heart"; lacking spontaneity or imagination himself, this dullard looks upon that of others, "[p]resenting obstruction" (*Observations*).[37] A more complicated variation on this theme occurs in "Novices," which mocks the young men who are "blind to the right word, deaf to satire," and "write the sort of thing that would in their judgment interest a lady"; in short, these inept critics and competing writers are "supertadpoles of expression." "To a Stream Roller" (another 1915 *Egoist* presentation) expresses resentment more plainly, in language even a bulldozer of a conventional critic can understand: "You lack half wit. You crush all the particles down / into close conformity, and then walk back and forth on them" (*Observations*, 21). In "My Apish Cousins" (1917, later retitled "The Monkeys"), Moore's scorn produces this image of the critics:

> trembling about
> in inarticulate frenzy, saying
>   it is not for all of us to understand art; finding it
>   all so difficult, examining the thing
>
> as if it were something inconceivably arcanic [*sic*]. . . .
>
> (*Observations*, 40)

Through the animal figures of "Critics and Connoisseurs" (*Others*, 1916), Moore presents a longer and more subtle examination of the deficiencies of her judges. Both the swan and the ant share attributes of their prototypes in the literary world, and in their varying degrees of ineffectualness neither is attractive.

In "To Be Liked by You Would Be a Calamity," Moore proposes the response that will largely characterize her method of dealing with detractors in future:

> but when
> You tell me frankly that you would like to feel
>   My flesh beneath your feet,
>     I'm all abroad; I can but put my weapon up, and
>     Bow you out.
>
> (*Observations*, 37)

Rather than descend to their level, she chooses the superior course of ignoring them; for, as she again advises in 1928: "'the unbearable repartee' is silence" (192). But as Moore also observed, silence signifies restraint of emotion, not its absence. The feelings of disappointment and hurt during her early struggles were not forgotten; and the memories may have helped to temper Moore's own critical responses to the writers she treats in her reviews.

As she informed Pound, Moore did find one truly receptive editor in Alfred Kreymborg at *Others*, which he founded in part as an alternative to *Poetry*. Though its circulation was small,[38] the magazine offered Moore something probably more important at this time than professional advancement: the friendship of other serious artists. Kreymborg proved "hospitable" indeed; for, as Stapleton has written, besides taking some poems (a "real breakthrough"), he "almost demanded that she come to New York."[39] When Moore arrived in the winter of 1915, she went first to 291, the famous gallery of the photographer Alfred Stieglitz, whom she had learned about from her art history teacher at Bryn Mawr. The same evening, Kreymborg invited her home to dinner with his wife. By their second meeting, Stieglitz and Moore were also friends, and through the two men the young poet was introduced to the New York avant-garde and the Bohemian environment of Greenwich Village. Moore was now determined to move there, and in 1918 she and her mother took an apartment at St. Luke's Place.

Though the story of this exciting period for Moore is well known, two examples of the impression Moore made on her peers at the time bear recalling, for the light they shed on Moore's approach in her essays. In his autobiography, Kreymborg remembers that Moore "talked as she wrote and wrote as she talked, and the consummate ease of the performance either way reminded one of the rapids of an intelligent stream."[40] Concerning her "felicitous speech," Hall adds, paraphrasing Kreymborg, that the style of Maxwell Bodenheim (also a member of the *Others* "circle") was "equally erudite and convoluted. They spoke in elaborate periodic sentences, subtly allusive and coming always to graceful conclusions just when Kreymborg felt surely the syntax would buckle."[41] From this it would seem that the artifice displayed in Moore's essays was not so much studied as practiced to the point it came naturally to her. Equally informative is Williams's recollection in his *Autobiography* that in conversation "She would laugh with a gesture of withdrawal after making some able assertion as if you yourself had said it and she were agreeing with you."[42] This gentle habit of putting others before oneself, with its ambiguous combination of self-effacement and assertiveness, is of course characteristic of the prose, as well. Recalling this crucial period herself in the 1961 *Paris Review* interview, Moore remarks that the first experiences in New York, "seeing what others wrote, liking this or that," encouraged her. She then adds: "With me it's always some fortuity that traps me."[43]

Few events then could have been more fortuitous than her first encounter with Scofield Thayer in 1919, when he and J. Sibley Watson, Jr., were restructuring the *Dial*. Ironically, considering her future long association, Moore's initial approach to the magazine was rebuffed. As she relates the famous story, Moore had "sent the editors a couple of things and they sent them back." At a party given by Lola Ridge, she was "induced" to read some of her work. "And Scofield Thayer said of my piece, 'Would you send that to us at *The Dial*?' 'I did send it,' I said. And he said, 'Well, send it again.'"[44] The poem in question, curiously enough, was "Picking and Choosing," the first of twelve poems to appear between 1920 and 1925. During the same period, Moore contributed eleven reviews and shorter pieces.

By 1925, the *Dial* was the foremost journal of literature and the arts in America. But the effort of maintaining the highest standards in the magazine drove the perfectionist Thayer to a nervous breakdown. Moore was appointed editor in July of 1925. (She was actually a second choice.)[45] At this time, the distinguished staff included Burke, as editorial assistant and later as music critic, and Gilbert Seldes, as theater critic. Foreign correspondents included Thomas Mann, Maxim Gorki, Ortega y Gasset, Eliot, and Pound. Three-quarters of the magazine was devoted to criticism, and the leading schools at the time were represented by I. A. Richards, Yvor Winters, Burke, Valéry, and Eliot, with Williams also contributing to the diversity in point of view.

While she espoused no specific theory herself, Moore did demand perfection in technical matters in the works she accepted for publication (in consultation with Dr. Watson), as she did in the books she reviewed. When Hall asked her whether she asked for revisions, she replied, "No. We had an inflexible rule: do not ask changes of so much as a comma. Accept it or reject it."[46] But the facts indicate otherwise. Like Miss Monroe, Miss Moore often demanded rewrites, to the chagrin of authors. Moore herself related, in her usual circumspect manner, some of the problems in "*The Dial*, A Retrospect," and Hall and others have filled in the details.[47]

Among Moore's famous rejections were poems by Yeats, sketches by Hemingway, and a section from *Finnegans Wake*, which she first accepted then reconsidered and finally, with great awkwardness, "unaccepted."[48] Moore later remarked, in a 1936 piece for the *Nation* called "Courage, Right and Wrong": "Is publication always better for one's talent than temporarily thwarted ambition?" (344). (Obviously, this is a question only an editor, and never a writer, would answer in the negative.) Writing to her in 1929, when Moore had accepted some poems and rejected others, D. H. Lawrence said: "I knew some of the poems would offend you. But then some part of life must offend you too" (360). In Moore's reviews and essays, certain matters do provoke negative responses of a peculiarly personal sort; specifically, the more vulgar expressions of sex, perceived or real insults to religion (particularly disrespect for the Bible), and misogynistic comments or portrayals.

Although the general opinion has it that, as it neared its demise in July 1929, the *Dial* had lost its edge (or the once-startling works it published and promoted had now become respectable), the magazine still stands as a remarkable achievement. Virtually all the important writers of the time contributed to its pages; likewise, the artists represented in the issues include almost every significant figure of the twenties. In a late piece for the *Herald Tribune* in 1960, Moore offers an apology both for herself and for the editorial profession by rehearsing the tiresome objection: "'What does an editor know of life and art? the algebra of existence?—that is why they are editors in the first place.'" Her answer is short and will suffice: "*Some* epitomize the genius they attract, do they not?" (549).

From her "debut" in New York, Moore attracted the admiration and affection of a wide gathering of extraordinary talents, and within a year she began taking their measure, as well. In the years to follow, her critiques and other commentaries came to epitomize the genius of that age of experimentalists. These assessments also became another measure of her own genius, as well as evidence of a generous personality endowed with a gift for genuine friendship. That friendship was often tested as Moore tried to balance truth with tact in her early prose. "In connection with personality," she remarks in "Idiosyncrasy and Technique," "it is a curiosity of literature how often what one says of another seems descriptive of one's self" (514). The truth of this statement is confirmed in Moore's many appraisals (and self-appraisals) in those remarkably productive years 1916–29, the high season of High Modernism.

### III

*If he must give an opinion it is permissible*
       *that the*
*critic should know what he likes.*

"Picking and Choosing"

In "Reticent Candor," Moore repeats Eliot's opinion that Pound's critical writing "forms a corpus of poetic doctrine. . . . It is on his total work for literature that he must be judged: on his poetry, *and* his criticism, *and* his influence at a turning point in literature. In any case, his criticism takes its significance from the fact that it is the writing of a poet about poetry; it must be read in the light of his own poetry, as well as of poetry by other men whom he championed" (456). Except that she would not have considered her prose as constituting "a corpus of poetic doctrine," the same might of course be said of Moore and her "total work for literature." The late general statements in "Idiosyncrasy and Technique," "Feeling and Precision," and "Humility, Concentration, and Gusto" are not so much codifications of dogma as distillations of many years' reading and practical experience writing. The primary materials for these grand summations, the bold reviews Moore gave the Modernists and others during the fertile period 1916–29—pungent practical critiques written near the moment of creation, often under pressure of deadlines, and bearing the scent of "expressionary need"—convey a sharpness, a sense of confident adventure that makes these early articles rather fresher, and more challenging, than the more measured reiterations in those late set pieces. Moore's essays of the teens and twenties, culminating with her prodigious contributions to the *Dial*, provide, if not a formal literary chronicle and classification of principles, then certainly a sharp outline of Moore's poetics, along with a revealing index to the art of her time.

As a young commentator, Moore found her "responsibility for the writer" presented piquant opportunities to affirm the new while refining the "propensities of the age," in Burke's phrase.[49] Her freedom from rigid theory allowed her to be much more inclusive, and far less acrimonious, in her appraisals than her often contentious colleagues. Indeed, amid the professional rivalry and disagreement of the Modernist poet-theorists, Moore was virtually alone in gaining the acceptance and then the affection of almost all in this diverse group.[50] Although relations with some became strained, particularly during the *Dial* years when Moore wielded considerable power (and a number of authors came to feel it), she still was held in respect by most of her peers. And it is to her peers that the first essays are primarily addressed.

In her critiques, as in her editorial decisions for the *Dial*, Moore's discerning catholicity of taste reflects her ideal of finding artistic "equilibrium." Restating her cardinal principle in a 1928 "Comment" piece, Moore notes that "many sagacities seem in Dürer not to starve one another," and affirms the *Dial*'s "capacity for newness inclusive of oldness" (203–4). One of the pleasures of surveying Moore's complete prose is seeing this inquisitive mind as it subtly sifts recent work and returns to the classics in a continuing interplay between new and old corroborating works of art.

Moore's authoritative tone, as noted earlier, combines with the idiosyncrasies of style which allow her to accommodate her prose to the variety of texts she treats. The strong effect and high finish of the essays is all the more remarkable when one considers the circumstances under which most were composed. Almost all of Moore's essays, it is useful to remember, were written on specific occasions for particular periodicals, requested by editors of literary journals and, in later years, commissioned by more popular magazines. The freelance writer, even a critic holding the highest standards, discovers that practical considerations can impinge on philosophical imperatives. "One writes because one has a burning desire to objectify what it is indispensable to one's happiness to express," Moore writes in "Idiosyncrasy and Technique"—in a paragraph which concludes with this advice about revising: "for most defects, to delete is the instantaneous cure" (507). In "The Past Is the Present" she notes: "'Ecstasy affords / the occasion and expediency determines the form.'" And one suspects that, especially during her four-year editorship when she was producing six or more prose pieces per monthly issue, constraints of time (and tight space) increased Moore's usual impatience with dull connectives and transitions. (As at the *Egoist*, the author's copy may also have been tampered with on occasion at other journals.) But limitations of time or space may have happily prompted more frequent use of aphorism, which becomes a type of critical shorthand.

Other constrictions of the prose might also be taken as the author's compliment to her readers' intelligence. In "Poetry and Criticism" (1965), she says, "I find that we become more and more concise—take for granted more and more as not needing to be explained"; in the same passage she adds: "Dr. Johnson's critical observations and didacticisms throw light, or stimulate resistance" (592–93). As she likes to say of works she likes: "We delay over" her remarks; her odd constructions are meant "to detain" us. In "Perspicuous Opacity" (1936), Moore observes with regard to Gertrude Stein's style, "the mind resists a language it is not used to" (338); and similarly in her own prose, Moore uses concision and various stylistic devices, particularly of earlier periods, to provide resistance and thus provoke the reader into further thought. In the early reviews and articles, the compression doubtless reflects the assumption that her audience is made up largely of other well-versed professionals. Turning now to the early prose in detail, we can follow her side of this conversation among equals and witness how criticism, in Moore's distinctive practice, "is the effect of the subjection of the product of one mind to the processes of another."

In her very first articles, Moore announces the major themes which will dominate all her future prose, and with a confidence that seems prescient. In "Samuel Butler" (*Chimaera*, July 1916), she quotes the novelist: "Surely we may do whatever we like, and the better we like it, the better we shall do it. The great thing is to make sure that we like the style we choose better than we like any other; that we engraft on it whatever we hear that we think will be a good addition, and depart from it wherever we dislike it" (30). In her second essay, "The Accented Syllable" (*Egoist*, October 1916), Moore addresses the central question for the artist, the modern writer particularly: how does one assert individuality and establish a unique "tone of voice"? By tone of voice she means "that intonation in which the accents which are responsible for it are so unequivocal as to persist, no matter under what circumstances the syllables are read or by whom they are read." Through several disparate examples of prose she suggests that "the meaning has very little to do with the pleasure the words give us" (31). She illustrates with Poe, whose "narrative tone of voice is flavoured with artifice," not of the "detective-story expert," however, but of the "drawing-room"; thus, she shrewdly observes, "the slightly repellant flavor of the writing is to be attributed to the tone of voice rather than to the trend of the ideas."

Turning to poetry, she notes "a distinctive tone of voice is dependent on naturalistic effects, and naturalistic effects are so rare in rhyme as almost not to exist." She then focuses on free verse, and identifies the inherent limitation of its freedom: "it is the easiest thing in the world to create one intonation in the image of another until finally one has assembled a bouquet of vocal exclamation points." Her illustration (aptly to hand for one who liked to sketch) is from an advertisement for Venus pencils, and is as amusing as it is to the point. In saying that she can read the ad "with a great deal of pleasure" but that she is not sure she would like to read it "every day in the week," Moore offers sardonic commentary of the monotony and predictably of much free verse. She also suggests the deficiencies of imagistic technique. Moore herself objected to being grouped with the "Imagists" (or any others, for that matter), for the restriction thus implied. And it will be recalled that Pound, who haphazardly named the "movement," quickly abandoned it and temporarily embraced Vorticism, not only because of "Amygism," but because of the static quality of purely imagistic approaches: "exclamation points" are not the same as poetic progression and development.

Moore's next publication, "A Note on T. S. Eliot's Book" (*Poetry*, April 1918), is most curious, as it does not mention the title poem, "The Love Song of J. Alfred Prufrock." Even though the poem first appeared in *Poetry* and she could assume subscribers had read it, it seems odd that she offers no discussion at all of a work that had already aroused considerable controversy. But it soon becomes apparent (the piece is only two paragraphs long) that Moore is well aware of the controversy, and that she has in fact reversed direction in her commentary to reflect the opposition's presumed point of view. She begins sarcastically: "It might be advisable for Mr. Eliot to publish a fangless edition of *Prufrock and Other Observations* for the gentle reader who likes his literature, like breakfast coffee or grapefruit, sweetened" (35). She then suggests a "mere change of arrangement of the poems" would make the volume more palatable. Even Moore (who already calls herself "this hardened reviewer") admits to unease with Mr. Eliot: (s)he "cursed the poet in his [her] mind for this cruelty" while reading "Portrait of a Lady." But then came "that ending. It is hard to get over this ending with a few moments of thought; it wrenches a piece of life at the roots." Returning to her rearrangement "for the gentle reader," Moore suggests the poem "could be followed by the lighter ironies of 'Aunt Nancy,' or the 'Boston Evening Transcript,' etc." Her concluding remarks imply a strong rebuke to Eliot's critics and "gentle readers" who prefer more genteel verse: "But Eliot deals with life, with beings and things who live and move. . . . Whatever one may feel about sweetness in literature, there is also the word honesty, and this man is a faithful friend of the objects he portrays; altogether unlike the sentimentalist who really stabs them treacherously in the back while pretending affection" (35). This combination of astute praise for the honesty which gives innovative forms their validity and wary tolerance of those elements which personally offend her will characterize Moore's commentaries henceforth.

Her next review, "Jean de Bosschere's Poems," also appeared in *Poetry* (April 1918), and commends this author who, "like certain modern poets of our own language, sees the characteristics, as of individual life, which lurk in inanimate objects and even in situations, as well as in living beings" (36). She locates in his vision a kind of mysticism, in that with his "developed sensitiveness" "individuality is a thing as real—in this world of illusions—as material appearances are."

In her brief review of *The Wild Swans at Coole, Other Verses and a Play in Verse* (*Poetry*, October 1918), Moore seems more perfunctory in her praise ("the critical care evidently spent on this thin volume, saves the reviewer most of his labor"). The longer poems seem "somewhat old-fashioned"; yet they "can still be read with the same critical alertness that one would give to the best of the younger poets" (39–40). She commends Yeats's verse play *At the Hawk's Well*, but doesn't hesitate to add that, to her, it is not really a Noh play. More interesting is a somewhat digressive passage midway in the review, in which Moore takes exception to an idea of Yeats's, where "the poet would have us believe that great poems are the result of the poet's 'opposite' image—an expression of what the poet is not." Her reasoning indicates the distinctions and correspondences Moore finds between the ethical and the aesthetic:

> I think this opposite, and not his little everyday thoughts and actions, *is* the poet; Dowson's drunkenness, and Dante's lecherous life, are somewhat beside the mark, as their effects on the poet's soul are mainly those of health and sickness. They are ethical and civil sins, but hardly poetic *sins.* . . . But even these, when present, are hardly more than masks of the poet's soul—perhaps hardly more than masks of any soul; it is in his poems that the real soul can be seen. (40)

Unfortunately, she does not develop these ideas, though she touches on the topic in later essays. One wishes she had elaborated here, as in the brief review of *Old and New Masters in Literature*, which rounds out the decade. The piece (originally in the *New York Times Book Review*, October 1919) picks out various summary remarks by the author (Robert Lynd) with which Moore is in accord—on Meredith, Shaw, James, Conrad, Rossetti—but her own treatment of the writers will wait until after the *Dial* years.

Moore's first poem in the *Dial*, "Picking and Choosing," appeared in April 1920, as noted earlier, and was one of the first contributions to the reorganized magazine, as well as the first representation of the New York experimentalists. Not long after, Pound wrote Thayer and Watson urging them to "get some of her prose."[51] In January 1921, her first such contribution to the *Dial* appeared, an essay on Jacopone da Todi. It is a lengthy review of a "spiritual biography" of the poet and mystic which traces his successive stages of subjugation to the divine will. Moore's main interest is of course the poetry, and the effect of "mystical development" on his art. Here Moore presents the first of many remarks concerning the necessity of discipline and inner resources: "Only life can speak of life, and his words are testimony to the fact of an unprecedented vital force within. He speaks of personal oppositions having at last been transcended" (50). Returning to the topic announced in the Yeats review, she agrees with his biographer that it is "Jacopone's poems upon which we base our knowledge of his inner life."

In March, Moore's review of *The Sacred Wood* offers an occasion for a key general statement: "The connection between criticism and creation is close; criticism naturally deals with creation but it is equally true that criticism inspires creation. A genuine achievement in criticism is an achievement in creation" (52). Following Eliot, she finds Aristotle "an example of the perfect critic—perfect by reason of his having a scientific mind. Too much cannot be said for the necessity in the artist, of exact science." Following a number of extracts from the essays, Moore returns to the subjects of honesty, mysticism, and craftsmanship, citing Eliot's example of Blake, whose strangeness is "'merely a peculiar honesty, which

in a world too frightened to be honest, is peculiarly terrifying'" (54). Eliot continues with thoughts Moore echoes in poems and prose:

> And this honesty never exists without great technical accomplishment. Being a humble
> engraver, he had no journalistic-social career open to him, nothing to distract him from
> his interest, and he knew what interested him and presents only the essential—only
> what can be presented and need not be explained. . . . There was nothing of the
> superior person about him. This makes him terrifying. (55)

In her next printed piece, Moore identifies a "right man" of another sort,
William Carlos Williams, with an incisive review of *Kora in Hell: Improvisations*.
It would seem inappropriate that the essay appear in Williams's own magazine,
*Contact* (4, January–March 1921); but this does not prevent Moore from carefully
evaluating both the shortcomings and the strengths of her friend. She begins with
an example—"The unready would deny tough cords to the wind because they
cannot split a storm endwise and wrap it upon spools"—which indicates "a part
of what gives" Williams's work "'a character by itself.' It is a concise, energetic
disgust, a kind of intellectual hauteur which one usually associates with the
French." She notes the poet's "power over the actual." Williams himself explains
this power in his statement: "By the brokenness of his composition, the poet makes
himself master of a certain weapon which he could possess himself of in no other
way"; but Moore more precisely identifies it with a traditional definition of *wit*,
and compares her contemporary's methods with those of Sir Francis Bacon, in his
"ability to see resemblances in things which are dissimilar." Without transition,
she then almost casually notes the discrepancy between Williams's favorite pose
as *naïf* and the actuality: "Despite his passion for being himself and his determination not to be at the mercy of 'schoolmasters,' it is only one who is academically
sophisticated who could write: 'Fatigued as you are, watch how the mirror sieves
out the extraneous'" (56–57). Following other examples, Moore develops this
insight into Williams: "It is not after all, the naïve but the authentic upon which
he places value. To the bona fide artist, affectation is degradation and in his effort
to 'annihilate half truths,' Dr. Williams is hard, discerning, implacable and deft.
If he rates audacity too high as an aesthetic asset, there can be no doubt that he
has courage of the kind which is a necessity and not merely an admired accessory"
(57). For the remainder of the review Moore calmly exposes the discrepancies
between Williams's rasher assertions and the example of his own writing. Williams's petulance, she finds, sometimes pushes him into overstatement: "'Nowadays poets spit upon rhyme and rhetoric,' he says. His work provides examples
of every rhetorical principle insisted on by rhetoricians and one wonders upon
what ground he has been able to persuade himself that poets spit upon rhyme?
Possibly by rhetoric, he means balderdash; in this case then, we are merely poorer
by one, of proofs for his accuracy" (59). She also gently alludes to the poet's

touchiness: "But one who sets out to criticize him, has temerity since he speaks derisively of the wish of certain of his best friends to improve his work [doubtless a reference to Pound in particular] and after all, the conflict between the tendency to aesthetic anarchy and the necessity for self-imposed discipline must take care of itself." Further mild admonitions conclude with a sympathetic understanding of the poet's irritation: "So disdainful, so complex a poet as Dr. Williams, receives at best, half treatment from the average critic or from the ambitious critic. . . . There is in Dr. Williams, an appetite for the essential and in how many people may one find it?" (59).

Moore's next contribution to the *Dial* (May 1921) is a review of Bryher's novel *Development*. Though generally laudatory, Moore does discover a slight flaw, in the author's having her "little heroine . . . protest against woman's *role* as a wearer of skirts—in her envying a boy his freedom and his clothes," a view Moore finds "somewhat curtailed." Her explanation is not without implications for herself:

> One's dress is more a matter of one's choice than appears; if there be any advantage, it is on the side of woman; woman is more nearly at liberty to assume man's dress than man is able to avail himself of the opportunities for self-expression afforded by the variations in color and fabric which a woman may use. Moreover, women are no longer debarred from professions that are open to men, and if one cares to be femininely lazy, traditions of the past still afford shelter. (61)

If the highly personal tone of this critique seems unduly pronounced, especially for Moore, one should recall that not long before she and her mother were active as suffragettes.[52] Here too, besides Moore's own famous liberated garb, one cannot help thinking of her later article on Charles Frederick Worth (*Harper's Bazaar*, April 1962), in which she offers the great couturier the high accolade: "He worked his seams well—a craftsman of genius, Mr. Worth" (559–60). In any case, having noted a slight imperfection in Bryher's construction, Moore congratulates her on the basic design of her book.

In the following month, a short review of Stewart Mitchell's *Poems* elicits these observations to be echoed later in "Humility, Concentration, and Gusto": "in so far as a poem is a work of art, one does not wish to know and must not know too definitely, the facts which underlie the expression" (62), and concludes: "One's taste in verse forms varies as one's taste in gems varies. It may vary with the occasion but it is essentially a matter of temperament"—a motif which will recur often. In fact the topic receives fuller treatment in Moore's next published article, an extended study of "George Moore, Aesthete" (*Broom*, May 1922). While she praises the novelist, she also finds: "Aesthetic feeling sometimes plays Mr. Moore false"; and these lapses—"passages in which crudeness, mawkishness, indecision and lame unnatural cadences spring out at one"—are all the more lamentable in one of such exquisite sensibility. Moore's censure extends to the production of the book itself (though this may not be the author's fault): "One expects the taste of an aesthete to be impeccable; then why the pale print and clamorous bourgeois binding of the American edition?" (65). More substantively, she rejects Moore's reasoning when he asserts: "'If we are to have genius we must put up with the consequences of genius, a thing the world will never do; it wants geniuses but it would like them to be just like other people.'" Moore's acerbic response again betrays personal animus: "The average person has seen genius walking erect too many times to accept the implication that genius progresses best when it crawls; innate sensuality is a mildew and in defense of an author who is aesthete pure and simple, one recalls Abelard's observation respecting Madelon: 'We owe her a good deal . . . and we are paying with our patience all that we owe her'" (65). But as indicated by her lengthy citations (and her return to him in "A Portrait of George Moore" [December 1922], 75–79), Moore is fascinated by this temperament, "the romantic warpedness of his imagination," and its form of expression, which is so unlike her own; and she particularly admires her name-sake's ability to give "a facsimile of the mental process in which the mind picks up and drops an idea and picks it up again" (68).

Moore herself gives an illustration of this mental process in her detailed critique of the sculpture of Alfeo Faggi, reproductions of which appeared in the *Dial* several months before her commentary there. In "Is the Real Actual?" (December 1922), she is particularly taken with the artist's bronze of Dante, and in minutely describing the piece Moore traces the poet's intellectual and spiritual qualities in the physical presence recreated through Faggi's work. Her interpretation of the piece becomes an analysis both of Dante's essential character and of the sculptor's methods; at the same time it portrays her own way "into" a work of art. Moore's treatment is extremely subtle and unparaphrasable.[53] One may only note here the continuing preoccupation with the spiritual dimensions of art, and the difficulty Moore perceives in trying to criticize or render a just account of the ineffable.

Moore's first essay on H. D., a short review of *Hymen*, appeared in *Broom* the next month (January 1923). "One recognizes here," she writes, "the artist—the mind which creates what it needs from its own subsistence and propitiates nothing, willing—indeed wishing to seem to find its only counterpart in the elements; yet in this case as in the case of any true artist, reserve is a concomitant of intense feeling, not the cause of it," a thought Moore rephrases in other reviews and famously in "Silence": "The deepest feeling always shows itself in silence; / not in silence, but restraint." Moore admires the "wiry diction, accurate observation and a homogeneous color sense," and the last quality elicits a veritable aria from the critic, who concludes with this reflection:

> Talk of weapons and the tendency to match one's intellectual and emotional vigor
> with the violence of nature, give a martial, an apparently masculine tone to such

writing as H. D.'s, the more so that women are regarded as belonging necessarily to either of two classes—that of the intellectual free-lance or that of the eternally sleeping beauty, effortless yet effective in the indestructible limestone keep of domesticity. Woman tends unconsciously to be the aesthetic norm of intellectual home life and preeminently in the case of H. D., we have the intellectual, social woman, non-public and "feminine." There is, however, a connection between weapons and beauty. Cowardice and beauty are at swords' point and in H. D.'s work suggested by the absence of subterfuge, cowardice and the ambition to dominate by brute force, we have heroics which do not confuse transcendence with domination and which in their indestructibleness, are the core of tranquillity and of intellectual equilibrium. (82)

This thought of course underlies Moore's attitude toward criticism, as well; and it is rephrased, in another context (a "Comment" from April 1929): "We need 'the feminine ideal . . . (not the female)'; that is to say, 'the compassional' not 'the forceful,' and willingness to work for 'the establishment of a world-polity not founded upon fear and hate'" (218).[54] She also returns to it in her next essay (September 1923), a review of books of fairy tales: "one need not avenge oneself; in improving the morals of the world, one should begin by improving one's own; these are the mordant preoccupations about which Mr. Housman's fancy plays" (84).

Reading her next review, one is reminded of a sentence in Moore's tribute to the Sitwells' father: "Poetic implacability was never seen to better advantage than in the style of Sir George Sitwell, in which nicety is barbed with a kind of decorous ferocity, as when he says, 'Forgery in art is not a crime unless it fails to deceive'" (431). In "An Eagle in the Ring" (*Dial*, November 1923), Moore's "decorous ferocity" is loosed upon Vachel Lindsay. She starts by acknowledging the poet's "instinctive charity" and benevolent intentions. Mere sentiment, however, is not enough in an artist: "It is impossible not to respect Mr. Lindsay's preoccupation with humanitarianism, but at the same time to deplore his lack of aesthetic rigor" (85). Moore then proceeds to instance the poet's ineptitude on every level, a detailed listing tantamount to a bill of indictment for art fraud. "In a lover of chant," she begins, "one expects a metronomelike exactness of ear; it is the exception, however, when the concluding lines of Mr. Lindsay's stanzas are not like a top which totters, or a hoop which rolls crazily before it finally stops." Besides "metrical barbarism" and wrenching rhyme, "we have that popular weak misuse of the present tense"—surface defects which betray more basic inadequacies—a "lack of neat thinking in such phrases as 'Lining his shelves with books from everywhere,'" a "copybook concept of Dante," and other inexactness. Moore is particularly irritated when the poet speaks of "Christ, the beggar," and she smartly corrects him: "it has never been said of Christ that he begged; he did without" (86). Lindsay's illogic is also scored: "he says in alluding to the San Francisco earthquake, 'Here where her God has scourged her.' Not that San Francisco was or is a godly city, but many another city has gone unscourged."

Perhaps more damnable are Lindsay's corruption of the populist tradition he purports to champion and his habitual mishandling of materials he appropriates, as in his "conscious altering of great familiar expressions," his "startlingly" inept adaptations of "Negro dialect," and his "suicidal" (if perhaps unconscious) imitations of his poetic betters, Cummings, Poe, Blake, Swinburne. Though she continues relentlessly for five more pages, Moore summarizes the matter early in the review: "As a visionary, an interpreter of America, and as a modern primitive—in what are regarded as the three provinces of his power, Mr. Lindsay is hampered to the point of self-destruction by his imperviousness to the need for aesthetic self-discipline" (86). In short, Lindsay's insincerity, to paraphrase both Pound and Moore, may be measured by his weaknesses in technique.

In counterpoint to this extended *exemplum in obliquo*, Moore begins the new year with "Well Moused, Lion," her first assessment of Wallace Stevens. As usual, her examination quickly locates the major merits of her subject; but the essay is extraordinary in that, stylistically, Moore's identification results in near imitation. She notes "the love of magnificence and the effect of it in these sharp, solemn, rhapsodic elegant pieces of eloquence"—and, as even this sentence hints, she is off uncharacteristically on a rhapsody herself: "The riot of gorgeousness in which Mr. Stevens's imagination takes refuge, recalls Balzac's reputed attitude to money, to which he was indifferent unless he could have it 'in heaps or by the ton.'" Continuing with a lushness approaching Stevens's, inspired by a passage cited from "The Comedian as the Letter C," she volunteers her own baroque profusion: "One is excited by the sense of proximity to Java peacocks, golden pheasants, South American macaw feather capes, Chilcat blankets, hair seal needle-work, Singalese [*sic*] masks, and Rousseau's paintings of banana leaves and alligators. We have the hydrangeas and dogwood, the 'blue, gold, pink, and green' of the temperate zone, the hibiscus, 'red as red' of the tropics" (92) As the essay progresses, the mix of quotation and Moore's interpretive mimicry is no less pronounced; her "reading" of the text has resulted in an assimilation that transforms her own style, so that here imitation is indeed the highest form of praise.

Nevertheless, Moore finds that even Stevens is not without flaw. "One resents the temper of certain of these poems," Moore writes. "Mr. Stevens is never inadvertently crude; one is conscious, however, of a deliberate bearishness—a shadow of acrimonious, unprovoked contumely." And she continues: "Despite the sweet-Clementine-will-you-be-mine nonchalance of the 'Apostrophe to Vincentine,' one feels oneself to be in danger of unearthing the ogre and in 'Last Looks at the Lilacs,' a pride in unserviceableness is suggested which makes it a microcosm of cannibalism" (93). (To which one responds, citing Auden: "O dear, o dear, o dear.")[55]

"Sunday Morning," she shrewdly observes, "gives ultimately the effect of the mind disturbed by the intangible; of a mind oppressed by the properties of the world which it is expert in manipulating." "One's humor is based upon the most serious part of one's nature," she continues. "'Le Monocle de Mon Oncle'; 'A Nice Shady Home'; 'Daughters with Curls': the capacity for self-mockery in these titles illustrates the author's disgust with mere vocativeness" (93–94). "Instinct for words is well determined by the nature of the liberties taken with them," she asserts, not hesitating to compare Stevens with Shakespeare in this regard. Following several examples, she finds Stevens adheres to a criterion enunciated in her earliest reviews: "The better the artist . . . the more determined he will be to set down words in such a way as to admit of no interpretation of the accent but the one intended" (96). In a final gesture of her familiar care for this artist, Moore lists poems regrettably absent from the volume. Despite Moore's glowing review, *Harmonium* was little attended and the book sold poorly. But surely the tribute and its style must have encouraged an author who, like Williams and Crane, had the misfortune of publishing a major book in the wake of *The Waste Land.*

Perhaps as an interlude amid so many reviews, Moore next presents an elective essay on a favorite writer, "Sir Francis Bacon" (*Dial*, April 1924). This article is followed by an appreciative but unexceptional review of Edwin Arlington Robinson's *The Man Who Died Twice* (*Dial*, August 1924). The next month the aforementioned Maxwell Bodenheim, who had already achieved considerable personal disrepute, has the dubious distinction of receiving the harshest review Moore ever wrote, "Thistles Dipped in Frost."

By way of prelude to this exceptional performance, Moore notes the condition which Eliot mentions as presenting an "obligation to denounce": "Maxwell Bodenhim's work has been honored in almost every notable type of current publication" (103). Unfortunately, in his several offices as "social philosopher, literary critic, novelist, and poet" Bodenheim has proven to be a pernicious influence: "as a critic of modern life, he goes but part of the way, sparing himself accurate exposition of the things he advocates, impetuously dogmatizing so that one is forced in certain instances to conclude that he is self-deceived or willingly a charlatan." She continues: "Our anger is stirred by his epitome of Christ's 'mistakes' in emancipating humanity. He says Christ approved the repressing of instinct and that he 'told people to believe with their feelings and let their minds go on a vacation.'" Moore's ire is further aroused when the author "offers definitions which detain without enriching," and further still when he misuses aphorism. To these violations Bodenheim adds another affront: "this author's concept of woman puzzles one." Moore then catalogues Bodenheim's misogyny: "analysis which results always in the exhibiting of woman's 'enticing inferiority'; which finds her an embarrassing adjunct, 'cooing and crawling for your money,' a creature of perfumed effeteness, of 'interminable evasions,' 'waving surrender in the foreground,' never other than a receiver of 'men's ornaments and poverties'" (104). For its ferociously logical neatness of reproof, the rest of the review is unequaled in Moore's prose.

Yet, despite this syllabus of errors, Moore is able to find redeeming features, as in Bodenheim's "crystal statement that 'simplicity demands one gesture and men give it endless thousands.'" She also commends his fiction, which is "somewhat stark and emphatic, showing dispatch and quick firm action, with that condensed finality of implication which is an attribute of the genuine narrator." Soon, however, Moore is back on the attack:

> But again we disagree with him when he says, "The novel should be far more interested in style than in message." It is Mr. Bodenheim's misfortune that he has attained this ideal, since in his work, there is much to arrest one yet not enough to detain; his work lacks substance—his unscientifically careless pronouncement for the bettering of fiction, explaining the lack on his own part of a genuine triumph; for is not style invariably a concomitant of content—the prototype of personality? (105)

While she allows that in both poetry and prose "there is the elected right to be superficial," Moore remains firm in her insistence upon honest craftsmanship; and she finds, "Waiving the matter of content, Mr. Bodenheim's technique varies in soundness." (Yet it is a wonder to her that in the midst of "a very bad poem such strokes of excellence" can occur.) After noting a number of other annoying defects, Moore closes by turning the table on the would-be satirist: "Dissatisfied with the irony and unrest of Mr. Bodenheim's spirit, we await an exposition of that which to him would make life satisfactory. . . . [I]s not the best corrective, an exemplifying at white heat of the accuser's indigenous, individual genius?" (107).[56]

Having exposed mediocrity, Moore returned to her preference of advertising the treasurable. Before assuming the editor's chair, she published her third notice of George Moore and a review of a biography of Goethe (*Dial*, March and June 1925), the latter titled "Besitz und Gemeingut" and reprinted in *Predilections*. In the baker's dozen of titled reviews and full-length articles that she contributed to the magazine during her tenure, there is a noticeable increase in verve, playfulness, and, especially in the reviews of H. D., E. E. Cummings, George Saintsbury, and Gertrude Stein, a degree of affection which suggests that not only these works but Moore's own tasks at the editor's desk were highly agreeable.

In "'The Bright Immortal Olive,'" Moore offers the *Collected Poems of H. D.* highest praise: "We have in these poems, an external world of commanding beauty. . . . Also, we have that inner world of interacting reason and unreason in which are comprehended, the rigor, the succinctness of hazardous emotion" (112). Also we have, from Moore, extensive quotation but rather less depth of analysis. The final paragraph of the review isn't so much a postcard as a fan letter to the author. "'Literature the Noblest of the Arts'" follows in October, and is an equally warm tribute to George Saintsbury, in the form of a review of his *Collected Essays and Papers*, which concludes with a marvelously constructed sentence of praise sharpened with a witty reservation: "One does not correct the speech of those who make our speech correct, but Mr. Saintsbury's 'Heaven knows' seems a needless superlative on completeness" (116).

In "'An Illustrious Doctor Admirable for Everything,'" Moore turns to Peter Abelard, with a lengthy review of his newly translated autobiography, indicating her fascination with this romantic figure in which intelligence, passion, great craftsmanship (she particularly notes his gift for "good story-telling"), "sensibility and understanding" were brilliantly and tragically combined (November 1925, 117–19). One need only note here, in her reflections on *The Story of My Misfortunes*, Moore's continuing interest in the mystical, especially trials of the spirit, and their relation to creativity.

Of more immediate interest is Moore's extremely compact critical history of "'New' Poetry Since 1912," written for Stanley Braithwaite's *Anthology of Magazine Verse for 1926* (120–24). Within five pages she compresses the principle ideas and critical doctrines, beginning with Imagism; credits the little magazines which promoted innovative work; lists major figures and their distinctive contributions to the New Poetry; notes contemporary critical responses, mostly negative, to the new verse forms, with her own appraisals; and provides what amounts to a table of contents for her own ideal anthology (with several samples) from work of the period. The piece remains a superb introduction to the early Modernists. As a record and an assessment of their work as perceived by one of the movement's most active participants, the article is also important since it clearly indicates how Moore has already begun to define the canon.

Moore's stock-taking of the *anni mirabiles* identifies the leading figures with capsule critiques: Ezra Pound heads the list as chief theorist ("A Few Don'ts by an Imagiste" is cited), "best apologist," and gatherer of the Imagistes presented in *Poetry* in 1914, including Williams. Frost is given separate notice for the appearance of *North of Boston* in 1914. Williams is more properly located next with Kreymborg's *Others*, and his "emphatic work" in *The Tempers* (1913) is noted. Mina Loy is given a glance, while Walter Arensberg is complimented with the quotation of his poem "Ing." "Wallace Stevens' sensory and technical virtuosity was perhaps the 'new' poetry's greatest ornament and the almost imperceptibly modern." Next: Mr. Eliot, who "'has not confined himself to genre nor to society portraiture,' says Ezra Pound." After noting, "Writers of free verse were, for the most part, regarded as having been influenced by Laforgue, Rimbaud, and other French poets," Moore lists several (Kreymborg, Bodenheim, Sandburg, Marsden Hartley, Man Ray, Muna Lee, Conrad Aiken, and others), saying only that they "contributed to making respectable as poetry, verse which was not rhymed" (123). She mentions the "Spectrist" hoax immediately before the sentence: "Vachel Lindsay's declamatory and in some respects unaesthetic pictorialism (1915–16), pleased, displeased, and pleased the public." Finally, "Resisted and advertised, Edgar Lee Masters's *Spoon River Anthology* (1915) seemed a technical pronunciamento."

From the early twenties, she singles out Cummings: "A great deal has been made of the small 'i' . . . and of certain subsidiary characteristically intentional typographic revivals and innovations on his part. While 'extreme,' he is, however, 'only superficially modern.' . . . The truly major aspects of his work are 'feeling for American speech,' 'rapid unfailing lyrical invention,' ability to convey the sense of speed, 'of change of position,' 'the sensations of effective effort'" (123). In closing, Moore gives passing notice to "various child poets," "American Indian poetry," and "the Negro spiritual"; then mentions Glenway Wescott, Yvor Winters, the Sitwells, Peter Quennell, Archibald MacLeish, and George Dillon, as well as a few others now forgotten. Her last paragraph bears remembering:

> It is perhaps beside the point to examine novel aspects of successive phases of poetic expression, inherited poetry having been at one time new, and new poetry even in its eccentricities seeming to have its counterpart in the poetry of the past—in Hebrew poetry, Greek poetry, Chinese poetry. That which is weak is soon gone; that which has value does, by some strange perpetuity, live as part of the serious continuation of literature. (124)

In "People Stare Carefully" (*Dial*, January 1926), Moore enlarges upon her remarks in the preceding essay with a discriminating review of Cummings's *XLI Poems*. She focuses particularly upon the technical aspects of Cummings's "verbal topiary-work," noting that here, however, we do not have the "too literal typographic wine-glasses, columns, keys, and roses" of the Elizabethans, "not a replica of the title, but a more potent thing, a replica of the rhythm—a kind of second tempo, uninterfering like shadow" (125). For all her enthusiasm, Moore does hit upon a central shortcoming, a problem more perhaps of the poet's personality than of his technique. "Love is terrible," she declares, but finds Cummings has trivialized love into something which lacks the capacity for (or nobility of) terror. Then she adds: "If there is not much love in these pages, however, there is glamour" (126).

Moore's next long review is devoted to another American original, Gertrude Stein. "The Spare American Emotion" finds *The Making of Americans, Being the History of a Family's Progress* a major achievement both for its "enticing simplicity of construction" and its "truly psychological exposition of American living" (128). While the essay includes, as usual, extracts from the work in question, here Moore also adapts her own prose style to the repetitive patterns and cadences of Stein's, a compliment previously reserved for Wallace Stevens. While it is obvious that Moore is drawn to the content of the book and admires Stein's technique, one also feels that through the article Moore is offering something else, as well, a more personal tribute from one author (who at one time tried to write fiction and a memoir)[57] to another who was a fierce individualist and who was also frequently misunderstood and underappreciated.

In "Memory's Immortal Gear" (May 1926), Moore offers a tribute as well, in an extended essay which defends Thomas Hardy from the charges that he is "a pessimist," pointing out Hardy's gifts of perception and description, and his "justly dramatic interest in the significance of what seems insignificant." She is not quite taken with the "apparently unpermissible plots" in some of his ballads (though a bit of curious lore, on an old village custom concerning the burial of spinsters, does pique her interest). The next reviews, of three now little-known poets and of Glenway Wescott, are written in a similarly graceful fashion but do not detain one.

Among the last four titled *Dial* reviews, there is another short piece on Cummings (approving *Is Five*) and a detailed appreciation of a novel by Mary Butts (cited earlier). "The Way We Live Now," a pseudonymous review of Sacheverell Sitwell's "Autobiographical Fantasy" *All Summer in a Day* (January 1927), presents an occasion for several perspicacious comments on biography in general. Moore also establishes, with some amusement, various categories of autobiography: "the devoir"—"conceived by the writer out of respect for his past and in solicitude for the rights of posterity"; "the personal cyclorama—a thing of expletives, italics, and untriumphant puns"; "photographs"; and the "spiritual" reminiscence (such as those by Yeats, Henry James, and the Venerable Bede). Then there is the sort that Sacheverell Sitwell has written. Moore's usual characterizing extracts make it clear that Sitwell has the eye and tongue of a poet; his human beings, she observes, "are truer even perhaps than his inanimate ones" (142).

As if to mark the end of an era, "A Poet of the Quattrocento," printed four months before the *Dial* ceased publication, offers a fine assessment of William Carlos Williams and by extension the indigenous American branch of Modernism; and many of the things Moore says of her friend apply to her, as well. "It was Ezra Pound's conviction some years ago," she begins, "that there could be 'an age of awakening in America' which would 'overshadow the quattrocento.'" Though his tone is somewhat patronizing, Pound found in Williams character fit to create a poetic renaissance, in the "'absolute conviction of a man with his feet on the soil, on a soil personally and peculiarly his own'" (144). Noting examples of Williams's transformation of "American topics" into poetry, Moore repeats: "Essentially not a 'repeater of things second hand,' Doctor Williams is in his manner of contemplating with new eyes, old things, shabby things, and other things, a poet." Following this bow to Walt Whitman and his descendant, she presents one of her favorite Williams quotations: "Where does this downhill turn up again? Driven to the wall you'd put claws to your toes and make a ladder of smooth bricks." Though she finds, "One sees nothing terrifying in what Doctor Williams calls a 'modern traditionalism,'" in the preceding remarks and in her final words there is more than a little personal resonance: "Incuriousness, emptiness, a sleep of the faculties, are an end of beauty; and Doctor Williams is vivid. Perhaps he is modern. He addresses himself to the imagination. He is 'keen' and 'compact.' 'At the ship's prow' as he says the poet should be, he is glad to have his 'imaginary' fellow-creatures with him. Unless we are very literal, this should be enough" (146).

Besides the twenty-five full-length articles, Moore contributed over forty essays to the "Comment" section of the *Dial*, and over 120 "Briefer Mention" items. In the latter category, she provided incisive one-paragraph reviews of books, many of them on nonliterary topics that interested her: history, biography, travel, philosophy, art. Here her habitual frugality is displayed to great advantage, as she packs information and opinions into very tight spaces with harmonious concision that is virtually fugal. In that regard, the "Briefer Mention" pieces provided the ideal format for the author who admitted that in larger formats her ideas could not be "regularized." In the many "Comment" articles, one may browse happily, discovering the enormous variety of Moore's interests and the many current events, particularly museum and art exhibits, that prompted her pen to incisive and often witty reflections. Many of her most trenchant general observations are recorded here, including, as we have seen, several key statements on criticism. The "Comment" essays also contain several variations on another major theme for Moore, that modern culture should encourage individuality and that it should be inclusive. It may be most fitting, then, to offer as a coda to this third movement a few of her more amusing notes welcoming a diversity of talents in life and letters.

Perhaps Moore's cleverest objection to official lists appears in a "Comment" from November 1925, which questions the restricted canon of "foremost educators" selected by the illustrious Dr. Eliot, President Emeritus of Harvard. His faculty includes, predictably, Aristotle, Galen, Leonardo, Bacon, Milton, Shakespeare, Locke, Kant, Newton, and Emerson. "Advantaged by his fearlessness to choose," says Moore, "one acknowledges that one might choose similarly." And yet, and yet . . . Is Aristotle's "compactness" "more alluringly succinct than Roger Ascham's"? "Emerson's attitude of friendship has seemed to one surely, not less a platitude than the devout firmness of Maria Edgeworth in *The Parent's Assistant*." "Has one consciously been more in debt to Galen's subtlety than to Doctor Goldsmith's therapy of man and dog, or less in debt to Luther Burbank whose witchcraft we are told is merely the suncraft of an observer, than to Sir Isaac Newton?" She dares to add: "Even within the range of our vision, yet distant—a kind of poetic Mt. Everest—Milton's greatness has in certain instances, been less to us than the great simplicity of Isaac Watts" (154–55). But the constant reader has to close her case with a realistic acknowledgment of local conditions: "Unmenaced as is the greatness of Dr. Eliot's decemvirs, the unbookish are intimidated by greatness so inclusive. Indeed it is perhaps an imaginary America which pores over either a preeminent or a miniature greatness" (155).

From the early months of 1926, we find these obiter dicta: "Contemporary audacity of dissimilarity recalls the assertion that opposition is wise, since to be in agreement with everyone is as bad as being alone" (157). "It is a luxury to have large truths in modest form and gratitude should perhaps hinder the beneficiary from being entirely sure that he knows the difference between large truths and little ones" (159). And against trendy *or* conservative imitation, and following a dictum from Quintilian—"Whatever we say, and wherever, let it be perfect, according to its own kind"—these remarks: "To exclude the speciously attractive, is difficult. . . . The writer, however, seems in certain respects, either more pridelessly or more recklessly than others, susceptible to current cleverness. Much as the victim of the fashionable *couturier* participates in successive epidemics of cut and color—of shutter green, serpent blue, or Venetian fuchsia—or the wet seal *coiffure* or the powdered wig, the sciolist subscribes to the tyranny of timelessness, of delightful dubiety, of what is acute or effective" (161–62). And a final bit of *sagesse* from Moore's friend George Saintsbury:

> *The religion of literature is a sort of Pantheism. You never know where the presence of the Divine may show itself, though you should know where it has shown. And you must never forbid it to show itself, anyhow or anywhere.* (189)

Having followed a rather circuitous route ourselves through Marianne Moore's prose, let us end, then, almost where we began, with the great critic-poet of whom our poet-critic writes in one of her very last review articles: "Randall Jarrell's evaluation of others is descriptive of himself. He says, '. . . the poems of Miss Bishop or Mr. Williams or Mr. Graves are a lonely triumph of integrity, knowledge, and affection'" (612)—just evaluation of Miss Moore in both her guises.

### Notes

1. Randall Jarrell, "The Humble Animal," in *Poetry and the Age* (New York: Alfred A. Knopf, 1953), 179.

2. Cited in Charles Tomlinson, ed., *Marianne Moore: A Collection of Critical Essays* (Englewood Cliffs, N.J.: Prentice-Hall, 1969), "Introduction: Marianne Moore, Her Poetry and Her Critics," 15. See, for example, Bernard Engel, *Marianne Moore* (New York: Twayne, 1961), 129; even so correct a judge as Donald Hall finds the essays "impressionistic and unaimed" in *Marianne Moore: The Cage and the Animal* (New York: Pegasus, 1970), 136.

3. *The Complete Prose of Marianne Moore*, ed. Patricia C. Willis (New York: Viking, 1986). Page numbers for quotations from this edition are indicated in the text in parentheses.

4. Kenneth Burke, "Likings of an Observationist," in Tomlinson, 127.

5. Burke, 126.

6. Ibid.

7. Ibid., 130–31.

8. Donald Hall, *Cage and the Animal*; Laurence Stapleton, *The Poet's Advance* (Princeton: Princeton University Press, 1978); Grace Schulman, *Marianne Moore: The Poetry of Engagement* (Urbana:

University of Illinois Press, 1986). For biographical facts this section is much indebted to these authors.

9.  Hall, 19.

10. In a 1951 Harvard Summer School conference publication, she puts the matter of her uneasy relations with the professoriate in amusing terms: "The chairman of English at Brooklyn College, when I gave a talk there, said that their lectures were highly schematized, but that I afforded an interesting contrast. I trembled to realize that I had, and I tremble again. My observations cannot be regularized" (436).

11. Hall, 20. Moore's interest in baseball long predated her throwing out the first ball at Yankee Stadium in 1967; she was able to amaze Alfred Kreymborg with her knowledge of the sport gleaned from Christy Matthewson's book; Hall, 26.

12. *The Letters of Ezra Pound*, ed. D. D. Paige (New York: Harcourt, Brace, 1950), 40. The letter was to Harriet Monroe.

13. "A Letter to Ezra Pound," in Tomlinson, 17.

14. Stapleton, 234–35; *Complete Prose*, 582.

15. Pound, *Letters*, 142–43.

16. "A Letter," in Tomlinson, 17. It is interesting to note, immediately before this passage, that Moore is not afraid to tell Pound: "I like a fight but I admit that I have at times objected to your promptness with the cudgels."

17. Ford Madox Ford [Hueffer], *The Critical Attitude* (London: Duckworth & Co., 1911). In "Poetry and Criticism," Moore again gives specific credit: "Ford Madox Ford's book reviews in the *English Review* (1908–12) were of inestimable value to me, as method" (593).

18. Ford, 26–27.

19. Ibid., 32–33.

20. Ibid., passim, 174.

21. Ibid., 178–79.

22. Ibid., 179–81.

23. Ibid., 182–83. Ford himself willingly includes ballads and folksongs, for "what exquisite pleasure they can give us, and what a light they can throw upon the human heart! And that, in essence, must be the province of Modern Poetry for some time to come—to give pleasure and to throw light upon the human heart." Moore comes very close to these sentiments in "'Teach, Stir the Mind, Afford Enjoyment'" (447–50); see also Burke's discussion, in Tomlinson, 131.

24. Ford, 188.

25. Ibid., 189–90.

26. Undated letter [January 1916], cited in Stapleton, 52; 241, n. l.

27. Cited in Stapleton, 5; 233, n. 8.

28. Moore's feelings at this time can be surmised from a comment she makes (in her review of *How Writers Write*) regarding Virginia Woolf's "Letter to a Young Poet": the piece could come "under the head of humor," but, she finds, "as words of advice, 'And for heaven's sake, publish nothing before you are 30' is frightening" (356).

29. Stapleton, 5.

30. It is evident from H. D.'s first letter to Moore, written in September of 1915 (and now in the Rosenbach), that only after the poems appeared in the *Egoist* in April did H. D. connect the author's name with the woman she had known but slightly at Bryn Mawr. It is interesting to note one of the four poems printed in *Poetry*, "To an Intramural Rat," closely echoes Ford's description of modern life in the last chapter of *The Critical Attitude*, 185–86.

31. "Letter," in Tomlinson, 17.

32. Ellen Williams, *Harriet Monroe and the Poetry Renaissance: The First Ten Years of* Poetry *1912–22* (Chicago: University of Chicago Press, 1977), 154–55. Moore returned with "No Swan So Fine," her first poetry publication after the long hiatus while editing the *Dial*; it was sent to *Poetry* during a financially difficult period for the magazine.

33. Taffy Martin, *Marianne Moore: Subversive Modernist* (Austin: University of Texas Press, 1986), 34–35; 144, n. 9. Martin notes that Moore's typescript in the Rosenbach Museum and Library does not indicate the deletion; presumably Harriet Shaw Weaver made the cut.

34. Hall, 32–33. Cf. Stapleton, 28.

35. Cited in Schulman, 2; 123, n. l; the statement was reprinted in *The Little Review Anthology* (New York: Hermitage House, 1953), 187–88.

36. "Letter," in Tomlinson, 17.

37. Marianne Moore, *Observations* (New York: The Dial Press, 1925), 33.

38. Stapleton says *Others* "never obtained a circulation of more than 300"; 6.

39. Ibid.

40. Alfred Kreymborg, *Troubadour: An Autobiography* (New York: Boni & Liveright, 1925), 236; cited in Hall, 24.

41. Hall, 25.

42. William Carlos Williams, *Autobiography* (New York: Random House, 1951), 147; cited in Hall, 25.

43. *A Marianne Moore Reader* (New York: Viking, 1965), 256. Moore adds: "I certainly never intended to write poetry. That never came into my head. And now, too, I think each time I write that it may be the last time; then I'm charmed by something and seem to have to say something. Everything I have written is the result of reading or of interest in people, I'm sure of that. I had no ambition to be a writer." Here, as with other facts about her early life, Moore seems to misremember in the 1961 interview.

44. *Reader*, 265.

45. Hall, 61. Cf. n. 47 below.

46. *Reader*, 267.

47. Hall, 66–67. See William Wasserstrom, *The Time of the* Dial (Syracuse: Syracuse University Press, 1963), 110–14. In an angry letter to Allen Tate, Crane asked, "How much longer [will] our market . . . be in the grip of two such hysterical virgins as the *Dial* and *Poetry!*" (Hall, 66). For her part, Moore observed that "*The Bridge* is a grand theme. Here and there I think he could have firmed it up. A writer is unfair to himself when he is unable to be hard on himself" (Hall, 67)—her usual attitude, whether the writer was "minor" or world-renowned. But Moore's annoy-

ance is expressed in the *Reader*, 267: "Hart Crane complains of me? Well, I complain of *him*. He liked *The Dial* and we liked him—friends, and with certain tastes in common. He was in dire need of money. It seemed careless not to so much as ask if he might like to make some changes ('like' in quotations). His gratitude was ardent and later his repudiation of it commensurate—he perhaps being in both instances under a disability with which I was not familiar. (Penalizing us for compassion?) I say 'us,' and should say 'me.' Really I am not used to having people in that bemused state. He was so *anxious* to have us take that thing, and so *delighted*. 'Well, if you would modify it a little,' I said, 'we would like it better.' I never attended 'their' wild parties, as Lachaise once said. It was lawless of me to suggest changes; I disobeyed."

48.   Hall, 70–71; Stapleton, 65.

49.   Moore cites Burke on presenting him with the Dial Award in 1929 (214).

50.   Recalling the early years, Williams writes in his *Autobiography* (146): "Marianne was our saint— if we had one—in whom we all instinctively felt our purpose come together to form a stream. Everyone loved her."

51.   Stapleton, 53, 241, n. 3, citing Moore's letters to her brother, 19 September 1920.

52.   Stapleton, 4.

53.   For an extended analysis of the essay, see Martin, 38–40. In her discussions of the first Stevens review and the article on Gertrude Stein, Martin also notes Moore's imitations of their styles.

54.   Moore cites Claude Bragdon, *The New Image* (219).

55.   W. H. Auden, "Papa Was a Wise Old Sly-Boots," *Forewords and Afterwords* (New York: Random House, 1973), 453.

56.   Alas, this was not to be; in her final notice of him, a "Briefer Mention" in the *Dial* for January 1926, she leaves a short, damning, hilarious paragraph of plot summary of Bodenheim's novel *Replenishing Jessica* (241).

57.   Stapleton, 52; *Reader*, 254.

# Bibliography

Atkins, Elizabeth. *Edna St. Vincent Millay and Her Times*. New York: Russell & Russell, 1964.

Attridge, Derek. *Well-Weighed Syllables*. Cambridge: Cambridge University Press, 1974.

Auden, W. H. *Collected Shorter Poems: 1927–1957*. New York: Random House, 1966.

————. *Forewords and Afterwords*. New York: Random House, 1973.

————. "Marianne Moore." In *The Dyer's Hand and Other Essays*. New York: Random House, 1962.

Bishop, Elizabeth. *The Complete Poems*. New York: Farrar, Straus & Giroux, 1969.

————. *Complete Poems: 1927–1979*. New York: Farrar, Straus & Giroux, 1983.

————. Correspondence. The Rosenbach Museum and Library, Philadelphia.

————. "Efforts of Affection: A Memoir of Marianne Moore." In *The Collected Prose of Elizabeth Bishop*. New York: Farrar, Straus & Giroux, 1984.

————. *Geography III*. New York: Farrar, Straus & Giroux, 1976.

Bogan, Louise. Review of *Huntsman, What Quarry?*, by Edna St. Vincent Millay. *The New Yorker* (20 May 1939): 80–82.

Borroff, Marie. *Language and the Poet*. Chicago: University of Chicago Press, 1979.

Brazeau, Peter. *Parts of a World: Wallace Stevens Remembered*. New York: Random House, 1983.

Bridges, Robert. *Poetical Works*. London: Oxford University Press, 1953.

Brittin, Norman. *Edna St. Vincent Millay*. rev. ed. Boston: Twayne, 1982.

Brontë, Emily. "Stanzas." In *Oxford Anthology of English Literature*, edited by Frank Kermode and John Hollander. New York: Oxford University Press, 1973. Vol. 2, 1482.

Brophy, James D. *Edith Sitwell: The Symbolist Order*. Carbondale: Southern Illinois University Press, 1968.

Burke, Kenneth. "Likings of an Observationist." In *Marianne Moore: A Collection of Critical Essays*, edited by Charles Tomlinson. Englewood Cliffs, N.J.: Prentice-Hall, 1969.

Byron, George Gordon, Lord. *Complete Poetical Works*. Oxford: Clarendon Press, 1986.

Costello, Bonnie. "The Feminine Language of Marianne Moore." In *Women and Language in Literature and Society*, edited by Sally McConnell-Ginet, Ruth Borker, and Nelly Furman. New York: Praeger, 1980.

————. "Marianne Moore and Elizabeth Bishop: Friendship and Influence." *Twentieth Century Literature* 30 (1984): 130–49.

————. *Marianne Moore: Imaginary Possessions*. Cambridge: Harvard University Press, 1981.

Cushman, Stephen. *William Carlos Williams and the Meanings of Measure*. New Haven: Yale University Press, 1985.

Daryush, Elizabeth. "Still-Life." In *In Defense of Reason*, by Yvor Winters. Denver: Swallow Press, 1947.

D[oolittle], H[ilda]. "Marianne Moore." *Egoist* 3 (1916): 118.

Eliot, T. S. *Collected Poems: 1909–1962*. New York: Harcourt, Brace, and World, 1963.

————. *The Complete Poems and Plays.* New York: Harcourt Brace, 1950.

————. "Marianne Moore." In *Marianne Moore: A Collection of Critical Essays,* edited by Charles Tomlinson. Englewood Cliffs, N.J.: Prentice-Hall, 1969.

————. "Tradition and the Individual Talent." In *Selected Essays: 1917–1932.* New York: Harcourt, Brace, 1932.

————. *The Waste Land: A Facsimile and Transcript of the Original Drafts Including the Annotations of Ezra Pound.* Edited by Valerie Eliot. New York: Harcourt Brace Jovanovich, 1971.

Ellmann, Richard, and Robert O'Clair, eds. *Norton Anthology of Modern Poetry.* New York: Norton, 1973.

Engel, Bernard. *Marianne Moore.* New York: Twayne, 1961.

Farr, Judith. *The Life and Art of Elinor Wylie.* Baton Rouge: Louisiana State University Press, 1983.

Ford, Ford Madox [Hueffer]. *The Critical Attitude.* London: Duckworth & Co., 1911.

Friedman, Susan. "Who Buried H. D.? A Poet, Her Critics, and Her Place in 'The Literary Tradition.'" *College English* 36 (1975): 801–14.

Garrigue, Jean. *Marianne Moore.* Minneapolis: University of Minnesota, 1965.

Gilbert, Sandra M., and Susan Gubar. *Shakespeare's Sisters: Feminist Essays on Women Poets.* Bloomington: Indiana University Press, 1979.

Goldsmith, Oliver. *The Vicar of Wakefield.* Edited by Arthur Friedman. London: Oxford University Press, 1974.

Graham, Jorie. *The End of Beauty.* New York: Ecco, 1987.

Hacker, Marilyn. *Love, Death, and the Changing of the Seasons.* New York: Arbor House, 1986.

Hall, Donald. "The Art of Poetry: Marianne Moore." In *Marianne Moore: A Collection of Critical Essays,* edited by Charles Tomlinson. Englewood Cliffs, N.J.: Prentice-Hall, 1969.

————. *Marianne Moore: The Cage and the Animal.* New York: Pegasus, 1970.

Hartmann, Geoffrey. "Six Women Poets." In *Easy Pieces.* New York: Columbia University Press, 1985.

Heymann, C. David. *American Aristocracy: The Lives and Times of James Russell, Amy, and Robert Lowell.* New York: Dodd, Mead, 1980.

Hine, Daryl. "Epilogue: To Theocritus." In *Theocritus: Idylls and Epigrams,* translated by Daryl Hine. New York: Atheneum, 1982.

Hollander, John. *Vision and Resonance.* New York: Oxford University Press, 1975.

Horace. *The Odes and Epodes.* Translated by C. E. Bennett. New York: Macmillan, 1924.

Irigaray, Luce. *This Sex Which Is Not One.* Translated by Catherine Porter. Ithaca: Cornell University Press, 1985.

James, William. "The Dilemma of Determinism." In *The Will to Believe.* New York: Longmans, Green, 1897.

Jarrell, Randall. *Kipling, Auden & Co.: Essays and Reviews, 1935–1964.* New York, Farrar, Straus & Giroux, 1980.

————. *Poetry and the Age.* New York: Vintage, 1953.

Kalstone, David. "Trial Balances: Elizabeth Bishop and Marianne Moore." *Grand Street* 3 (1983): 115–35.

Keller, Lynn. "Words Worth a Thousand Postcards: The Bishop-Moore Correspondence." *American Literature* 55 (1983): 405–29.

Kennedy, X. J. "Marianne Moore." *The Minnesota Review* 2 (Spring 1962): 369–76.

Kenner, Hugh. *The Invisible Poet: T. S. Eliot.* New York: McDowell Obolensky, 1959.

Kreymborg, Alfred. *Troubadour: An Autobiography.* New York: Boni & Liveright, 1925.

Kristeva, Julia. "Women's Time." Translated by Alice Jardine. *Signs: A Journal of Women in Culture and Society* 7 (1981): 17.

Lauter, Estella. *Women as Mythmakers: Poetry and Visual Art by Twentieth-Century Women.* Bloomington: Indiana University Press, 1984.

Levertov, Denise. *The Freeing of the Dust.* New York: New Directions, 1975.

Little, Judy. *Comedy and the Woman Writer.* Lincoln: University of Nebraska Press, 1983.

Litz, A. Walton. "Introduction to *Bowl, Cat and Broomstick.*" *Quarterly Review of Literature* 16 (1969): 230–35.

Martin, Taffy. *Marianne Moore: Subversive Modernist.* Austin: University of Texas Press, 1986.

Millay, Edna St. Vincent. *Collected Poems.* Edited by Norma Millay. New York: Harper and Row, 1956.

———. *Letters of Edna St. Vincent Millay.* Edited by Allan Ross Macdougall. New York: Harper & Brothers, 1942.

M[onroe], H[arriet]. "A Symposium on Marianne Moore." *Poetry* 19 (January 1922): 208–16.

Moore, Marianne. *Collected Poems.* New York: Macmillan, 1951.

———. *Complete Poems of Marianne Moore.* Edited by Clive E. Driver. New York: Macmillan/Viking, 1981.

———. *Complete Poems of Marianne Moore.* New York: Macmillan/Viking, 1967.

———. *Complete Prose of Marianne Moore.* Edited by Patricia C. Willis. New York: Viking, 1986.

———. Correspondence. The Rosenbach Museum and Library, Philadelphia.

———. *A Marianne Moore Reader.* New York: Viking, 1961.

———. *Observations.* New York: Dial Press, 1925.

———. *Predilections.* New York: Viking, 1955.

"Moore, Marianne Craig." In *Twentieth Century Authors: A Biographical Dictionary of Modern Literature,* edited by Stanley J. Kunitz and Howard Haycraft. New York: Wilson, 1942.

Nitchie, George W. *Marianne Moore: An Introduction to Her Poetry.* New York: Columbia University Press, 1969.

Olds, Sharon. *Satan Says.* Pittsburgh: University of Pittsburgh Press, 1980.

Ostriker, Alicia. *Stealing the Language: The Emergence of Women's Poetry in America.* Boston: Beacon Press, 1986.

Pearce, Roy Harvey. "Marianne Moore." In *Marianne Moore: A Collection of Critical Essays,* edited by Charles Tomlinson. Englewood Cliffs, N.J.: Prentice-Hall, 1969.

Phillips, Elizabeth. "Marianne Moore." In *Dictionary of Literary Biography.* Vol. 45, *American Poets, 1880–1945,* edited by Peter Quartermain. Detroit: Gale Research, 1986.

Plimpton, George. "The World Series with Marianne Moore." *Harper's Magazine* 229 (October 1964): 50–58.

*Poesis* 6, nos. 3–4 (1985).

Pound, Ezra. *The Letters of Ezra Pound,* edited by D. D. Paige. New York: Harcourt, Brace, 1950.

———. "Marianne Moore and Mina Loy." In *Marianne Moore: A Collection of Critical Essays,* edited by Charles Tomlinson. Englewood Cliffs, N.J.: Prentice-Hall, 1969.

———. *Personae: The Collected Shorter Poems of Ezra Pound.* New York: New Directions, 1926.

*Quarterly Review of Literature* 4, no. 2 (1948).

Rich, Adrienne. "Compulsory Heterosexuality and Lesbian Existence." In *Blood, Bread, and Poetry.* New York: Norton, 1986.

———. "Disloyal to Civilization: Feminism, Racism, Gynephobia" and "When We Dead Awaken." In *On Lies, Secrets, and Silence: Selected Prose, 1966–1978.* New York: Norton, 1979.

———. *The Fact of a Doorframe: Poems Selected and New, 1950–1984.* New York: Norton, 1984.

Rivière, Joan. "Womanliness as a Masquerade." *International Journal of Psychoanalysis* 10 (1929): 303–13.

Rosenthal, M. L. *The Modern Poets: A Critical Introduction.* New York: Oxford University Press, 1960.

Rossetti, Christina. *The Complete Poems of Christina Rossetti: A Variorum Edition,* edited by R. W. Crump. Baton Rouge: Louisiana State University Press, 1986.

Santayana, George. *Soliloquies in England and Other Soliloquies.* New York: Scribner's, 1922.

Sargeant, Winthrop. "Humility, Concentration, and Gusto." *New Yorker* 32 (16 February 1957): 38–40, 42, 44, 47–49, 52, 54, 56, 58–60, 63–64, 67–68, 70, 75–77.

Schulman, Grace. "Conversation with Marianne Moore." *Quarterly Review of Literature* 16, nos. 1–2 (1969): 154–71.

————. *Marianne Moore: The Poetry of Engagement.* Urbana: University of Illinois Press, 1986.

Schweik, Susan. "Writing War Poetry like a Woman." *Critical Inquiry* 13 (1987): 532–56.

Sexton, Anne. *Complete Poems.* New York: Houghton Mifflin, 1981.

Sorrentino, Gilbert. "An Octopus / of ice." In *Something Said: Essays.* San Francisco: North Point Press, 1984.

Stapleton, Laurence. *Marianne Moore: The Poet's Advance.* Princeton: Princeton University Press, 1978.

Stein, Gertrude. *Letters of Gertrude Stein and Carl Van Vechten 1913–1946.* Edited by Edward Burns. New York: Columbia University Press, 1986.

Stevens, Wallace. *Bowl, Cat and Broomstick.* In *The Palm at the End of the Mind: Selected Poems and a Play,* edited by Holly Stevens. New York: Vintage, 1972.

————. *Collected Poems.* New York: Knopf, 1954.

————. *The Letters of Wallace Stevens.* Edited by Holly Stevens. New York: Knopf, 1966.

Tambimuttu, T., ed. *Festschrift for Marianne Moore's Seventy-Seventh Birthday.* New York: Tambimuttu & Mass, 1964.

Tomlinson, Charles, ed. *Marianne Moore: A Collection of Critical Essays.* Englewood Cliffs, N.J.: Prentice-Hall, 1969.

*Twentieth Century Literature* 30 (Summer-Fall 1984).

Vendler, Helen. *Part of Nature, Part of Us: Modern American Poets.* Cambridge: Harvard University Press, 1980.

Wakoski, Diane. *The Motorcycle Betrayal Poems.* New York: Simon and Schuster, 1971.

Warren, Robert Penn. *Being Here: Poetry 1977–1980.* New York: Random House, 1980.

Wasserstrom, William. *The Time of the Dial.* Syracuse: Syracuse University Press, 1963.

West, Nathanael. *Miss Lonelyhearts and The Day of the Locust.* New York: New Directions, 1969.

Westkott, Marcia. *The Feminist Legacy of Karen Horney.* New Haven: Yale University Press, 1986.

Williams, Ellen. *Harriet Monroe and the Poetry Renaissance: The First Ten Years of Poetry 1912–22.* Chicago: University of Chicago Press, 1977.

Williams, William Carlos. *Autobiography.* New York: Random House, 1951.

————. "The Great American Novel." In *Imaginations,* edited by Webster Schott. London: Macgibbon & Kee, 1970.

————. *Selected Essays of William Carlos Williams.* New York: Random House, 1954.

————. *Spring and All.* Dijon: Contact, 1923.

Wilson, Edmund. *I Thought of Daisy.* New York: Farrar, Straus & Giroux, 1953.

Wolfe, Thomas. *The Web and the Rock.* New York: Harper and Brothers, 1939.

# Contributors

**MAXINE KUMIN** is the author of nine volumes of poetry, including *Up Country*, which won the Pulitzer Prize in 1973, and *Nurture*, which came out in 1989. She has also published four novels, a collection of short stories, two volumes of essays, and several children's books. She served as Consultant in Poetry to the Library of Congress in 1981–82 and has taught at Princeton, Columbia, and MIT, among other universities.

**RICHARD HOWARD** is the Nathaniel Ropes Professor of Comparative Literature at the University of Cincinnati and also teaches at the University of Houston. He has published over 150 translations of Gide, Baudelaire, Barthes, and other French authors. His critical study, *Alone with America: Essays on the Art of Poetry in the United States Since 1950*, came out in 1969 and was reissued in an expanded edition in 1980. His nine volumes of verse include *Untitled Subjects*, winner of the Pulitzer Prize in 1970, and *No Traveller* (1989).

**ROBERT PINSKY**'s scholarly and critical books are *Landor's Poetry* (1968), *The Situation of Poetry* (1977), and *Poetry and the World* (1988). His second collection of poems, *An Explanation of America* (1980), won the Saxifrage Prize, and his third, *History of My Heart* (1984), won the William Carlos Williams Prize in 1985. He has received fellowships from the NEA, the NEH, and the Guggenheim Foundation. He has taught English at the University of Chicago, Wellesley, Harvard, and the University of California (Berkeley), and is now at Boston University.

**SANDRA M. GILBERT** earned her Ph.D. at Columbia and taught at Indiana, Princeton, Stanford, and Johns Hopkins. She is currently Professor of English at the University of California at Davis. She is the co-author (with Susan Gubar) of *The Madwoman in the Attic: The Woman Writer and the Nineteenth-Century Literary Imagination* and *No Man's Land: The Place of the Woman Writer in the Twentieth Century*, and the co-editor of *The Norton Anthology of Literature by Women*. Her four collections of poetry include *Emily's Bread* (1984) and *Blood Pressure* (1988).

**ALICIA OSTRIKER** has published four scholarly works, including *Writing like a Woman* (1983) and *Stealing the Language: The Emergence of Women's Poetry in America* (1986). Her poems are collected in six volumes, the most recent of which are *A Woman Under the Surface* (1982); *The Imaginary Lover* (1986), which won the William Carlos Williams Prize; and *Green Age* (1989). A recipient of fellowships from the Guggenheim and Rockefeller Foundations, she is Professor of English at Rutgers.

**DAVID BROMWICH** holds a Ph.D. from Yale, where he is now Professor of English after a decade at Princeton. He is the author of *Hazlitt: The Mind of a Critic* (1984) and co-editor (with Irving Howe and John Hollander) of *Literature as Experience*. His poetry and criticism have appeared in the [London] *Times Literary Supplement*, *Poetry*, *The New Republic*, and other journals. He was nominated for a National Book Critics Circle Award for Criticism and has held NEH and Ingram Merrill Foundation Fellowships.

**JOHN HOLLANDER** is the A. Bartlett Giamatti Professor of English at Yale University. The latest of his many collections of poetry are *Powers of Thirteen* (1983), *In Time and Place* (1986), and *Harp Lake* (1988). He has also published six critical studies, including *Melodious Guile: Fictive Pattern in Poetic Language* (1988), and edited numerous anthologies. He won the Bollingen Prize in 1983.

**JOSEPH PARISI** holds a Ph.D. from the University of Chicago and taught for several years, most recently at the University of Illinois, Chicago. He joined the staff of *Poetry* in 1976 and has been editor since 1983. He contributes criticism regularly to a number of literary journals, and wrote the *Viewer's Guide* to "Voices and Visions," a companion to the PBS television series. He is co-editor of *The* Poetry *Anthology, 1912–1977*.

# Index